DEEP IN THE INDIAN HIMALAYA

By
Vicki Pomeroy

Copyright © 2007
All rights reserved

Garhwal Publishing
www.deepintheindianhimalaya.com

Published in USA
ISBN 978-0-6151-5697-2

My heartfelt thanks to the people of Pauri Garhwal, for showing me a whole new way to experience the world~

Preface

The stories herein are true. Names of people and places and a few details have been changed to protect people's identity and a couple of anecdotes have been combined for ease of reading.

The first time I meet Kalam Singh, he's wandering aimlessly in Chandpur bazaar and babbling incoherently. He's been drinking whiskey made from Hinsar roots, Kafal bark, raw sugar, one flashlight battery and a store-bought bun. The concoction intoxicates people after two shots and makes them crazy after three. He most likely started drinking at the brewer's place or some other backroom in the bazaar late in the afternoon and by nightfall, when I pass by, he's arguing unintelligibly with his companions and yelling obscenities into the dark. This is his daily routine and has been for years. His excuse is the fingers of his right hand were cut off in a machine fifteen years earlier.

Kalam Singh's family bears the brunt of his drunkenness. A father and husband who's a drunk is embarrassing and further compounded by the family's almost nightly obligation to carry Kalam Singh home from the bazaar, trail or field where he's passed out. And because he drinks up what little money his wife earns selling water buffalo milk to schoolteachers boarding in town, Kalam Singh's family is dirt poor. They not only don't own basic necessities like beds, blankets and warm clothes, they're hungry.

To help them out financially, I hire his wife, Jankari Devi, to wash my laundry. A short time later our foundation (Jwalpa Devi Foundation, JDF) helps her secure a bank loan to buy goats to raise and sell for a profit. Around this same time Kalam Singh starts to feel sick. Besides fevers, a chronic cough and no appetite, he becomes shorter and shorter of breath while walking around the village, requiring him to stop three or four times along a trail to rest before continuing on to his destination. He's not that sick though! He still manages to drink up the remaining loan money set aside to repay the bank.

As the year rolls by, Kalam Singh becomes weaker and weaker until he can't walk to the bazaar anymore. It's at this point he decides to go with JDF on one of our monthly trips to the hospital. There he's diagnosed with TB. It's no surprise to anyone. TB is a common illness here, but it's dreaded like cancer, causing people like Kalam Singh to deny they have the illness and to seek treatment only after they've become incapacitated or when it's too late.

One of our most poignant cases involved an old widower. A JDF worker had gone to his village about another matter and by chance discovered the widower, a man named Sobat Singh Rana, living in a cow shed with the family's cows. He had a fight with his son, who had then kicked him out of the house. Sobat Singh had neither the money to buy nor the facilities to cook food, forcing him to beg door to door from his neighbors. Begging was no easy task. Sobat Singh's TB was so pervasive he couldn't walk ten feet without being obliged to sit down to catch his breath. That evening JDF discussed Sobat Singh's situation and decided to take him to the hospital the next day. Four strong men hiked two kilometers straight up hill to Sobat Singh's village, Bhagard, and seating him in a plastic chair, took turns carrying him all the way back down the mountain.

When they arrived at the hospital, the doctor was reluctant to check Sobat Singh into the TB inpatient program because his TB status couldn't be verified. The electricity wasn't working so the technician couldn't take his x-ray and the results from his phlegm test wouldn't be ready until the following day. JDF employees pleaded with the doctor to let Sobat Singh spend the night, explaining that they'd have to carry him back up the long hill to Bhagard this afternoon and then back down again tomorrow morning, not to mention the two-hour bus ride each way. The doctor acquiesced and let Sobat Singh stay.

That evening we celebrated at JDF, knowing Sobat Singh had a bed to sleep in, food to eat and, starting tomorrow, he'd be taking a regimen of TB medication to make him well. Our jubilation, however, was premature. The x-ray and phlegm test revealed Sobat Singh's TB had advanced too far to be helped by treatment. He was forcibly released from the hospital and the same four guys carried him back to his village. He died the very next day.

Kalam Singh is admitted into the TB inpatient program. From that day forth, he never has another drink of whiskey. He stays in the hospital for the requisite three days and religiously goes with JDF or by himself to the hospital for his monthly check-ups and to get his next month's supply of medication. His health improves dramatically, although he still becomes short of breath now and again.

After eight months of sobriety, JDF gives Kalam Singh a job in the village library. He tends to it like one would a newborn baby, turning out not only to be a responsible guy when he's sober, but a likeable one too. His entire appearance changes. His once raspy voice softens. His beady eyes become thoughtful. Even his perpetually scraggly, five o'clock shadow loses its derelict appearance.

Another year comes and goes. Then one day Kalam Singh mentions he feels sick. He knows JDF is taking patients to the hospital, so he comes along. The doctor simply tells Kalam Singh phlegm is gummed-up in his chest and advises him to drink hot water and to keep his chest warm.

Returning late in the afternoon to Chandpur, Kalam Singh and the other patients are waylaid on the far side of the bazaar by a roadblock. A dump truck full of rocks has just run over an 18-year-old boy named Neru who, along with children from 32 other villages, had just been let out from Chandpur's intercollege (a school for grades 6 through 12).

Because there are no school buses, every day at this time the one lane road and numerous trails leading into the surrounding hillsides are crowded with young people, some walking as far as seven kilometers to get home. Those who travel at least part of the way home by road try to hitch rides with passing trucks and commercial jeeps. Since only one or two jeeps pass by, it's not unusual to see twenty or more kids packed into one vehicle; squished together, sitting six or seven to a seat, forcing late comers onto the luggage rack over head or to hang precariously off the bumper behind. Trucks, once rare, now frequently pass through Chandpur, hauling rocks and other materials to a construction project further up the road. Their loads usually preclude kids from climbing into the back compartment, so drivers allow them to pile into the cab up front.

That's what happened to Neru. His friends had already climbed into a truck cab and were heading home. As they passed by Neru walking along the shoulder, they called to him to join them. He ran after the moving truck and jumped onto the running board, but before he could grab ahold of the open window frame, Neru slipped and fell to the ground. The driver couldn't see him because he was on the passenger side but he felt Neru go under one of the tires, causing him to slam on his breaks and then, fearing Neru might still be under the tire, the driver backed the truck up, running over Neru a second time.

According to everyone who surveys the scene, the insides of Neru's body, including his brains, are lying starkly in the road. Kalam Singh passes by the gruesome sight in order to get home. Disturbed by images and feeling like he's suffocating, he lies awake in his bed until midnight. His wife is worried so she goes to the house next door to ask Birendar, Kalam Singh's cousin, what to do. It takes only a few minutes but, by the time the two of them return to the house, Kalam Singh is dead.

News of his death spreads quickly. Thakur clan men, women and a few children, uncharacteristically still awake, upset by the tragedy earlier in the day, climb out of their beds and gather at Kalam Singh's house to comfort his wife and children. Wails erupt from the courtyard.

Two young men, Surendar and Vinod, immediately head out into the dark, walking to the nearest phone four kilometers away to call Kalam Singh's brother, Pratab. Pratab does not have a phone of his own but he lives in a city where one of his neighbors down the lane has a phone, so the neighbor climbs out of bed, walks to Pratab's house and informs him of his brother's death. Pratab rouses his family and begins searching for a way to get to Chandpur, a three- hour car drive away. It's two-thirty in the morning and all public transportation is closed until sun up.

After the sun rises, a couple of elder Thakur clan women remove Kalam Singh's clothes, wipe his body clean with a wet rag and then wrap him in a red cloth (white is for females). Several young men from the Thakur and Rana clans begin pulling logs from their woodpiles to haul down to the cremation ground located below the village, along the river. The remaining Thakur men construct a stretcher, lashing oak poles together long ways and oak sticks sideways. They scatter long, dry grass on top and then lay Kalam Singh's body on the stretcher.

Pratab and his family arrive in Chandpur around nine o'clock in the morning, prompting Thakur and Rana clan members to re-gather in the courtyard. The story of how Kalam Singh lived his last day and particularly his last moments is recounted over and over again. Finally someone decides it's time to go and four men, including Kalam Singh's oldest son and his brother, lift the stretcher onto their shoulders and silently lead a procession of men and boys, each carrying a log on their shoulder, down to the burning ghat.

Women, girls and small children stay behind. While some of the women hold Jankari Devi in their arms, stroke her back and try to comfort her with words, she howls and moans, crying so hard she can barely keep herself sitting upright on the courtyard wall. At 39 years old and the mother of four, Jankari Devi will not remarry. To symbolize her widowhood she removes her jewelry: Rips the brass stud out of her nose that had been placed there on her wedding day, Smashes the odd assortment of glass bangles around her wrist against the courtyard wall, leaving pieces strewn around her bare feet, and removes her hoop earrings and mangal-sutra, a beaded necklace with a pendant that Garhwali women invariably describe as wearing "out of respect for my husband."

Jankari Devi's two youngest children stand nearby. They look more dazed than sad. The fourth child, the oldest, is married and lives in another village. She was not needed for the funeral procession nor the cremation like Pratab, so there was no middle-of-the-night rushed message sent to hurry her back to Chandpur, but a message has already been dispatched and she will come home to mourn with her family and the village. Throughout today and tomorrow, every single able-bodied person from Chandpur will come and give their condolences to Jankari Devi and her children, some staying with them for hours at a time. Thakur clan women will take turns cooking Jankari Devi and her children's meals and at least one woman will spend the night with them every night for the next couple of weeks. They may even help take care of their animals if the children are too upset to do so. In addition, women from nearby villages will show up in groups of two or more during the next few days to pay their respect. They're not necessarily close friends of the family, but as Chandpur's neighbors, they will come and because Jankari Devi is a woman and her family poor, they will bring rice, lentils or a few rupees to give her.

I tag along behind the men, carrying a thick tree branch as long as I am. It is unusual for me to go to the burning ghat and not unusual. I've been there before. During the first cremation I went to, the elder men talked openly about my presence and how strange it was. A woman had never come to the burning of a body. After some discussion an elder from the Rana clan made a declaration, which proved to be the final word on the subject, "She wants to learn about our culture. This is a good thing!"

We wind our way down through the village, along terraced fields, and then wade across the river. The burning ghat is an inconspicuous sandy patch, no bigger than ten square feet, with sparse sprigs of grass growing on it. What makes this place special is it's located at the confluence of two rivers, which is auspicious. In Pauri Garhwal if a confluence is not demarcated as a pilgrimage spot where people pray and bathe in the water to cleanse their sins away, it inevitably houses a burning ghat that one or more villages share. The Chandpur Thakur clan shares this burning ghat with a few neighboring villages. The only exception is their children under the age of ten are buried underground in unmarked graves in an abandoned field along the river, several bends upstream from here.

Once across the river, we toss our large branches and small tree trunks onto a woodpile started by the young men who had brought logs earlier in the morning. Elder Thakur men immediately grab logs from the pile and begin to arrange them on the ghat in a rectangular-shaped pile a little longer and wider than Kalam Singh's body, carefully crisscrossing the logs to allow for airflow. A few younger men join in, handing the older men logs and, only when told, placing them exactly where they are instructed.

Three generations of Thakurs work diligently together to build the funeral pyre. From a distance, elder Rana clansmen offer technical advice on its construction. The rest of us spread out along the rocky bank: Some stand, others perch on their haunches, still others make a fire and gather around it. The only organizing aspect to our loosely knit group is young men tend to congregate with young men and old men with old men.

When the woodpile reaches waist high, Kalam Singh is picked up, stretcher and all, dipped into the river for a ritual cleansing, and placed on the pyre. Two more feet of wood is layered on top of him. Afterwards dubala grass, a sacred and wild straw growing nearby, is stuffed in between the logs to serve as tinder.

The Baaman (Hindu priest) sticks a few sprigs of dubala grass of his own between the logs, says a prayer, and then signals to Shanu, Kalam Singh's oldest son, to light the pyre. Shanu walks over and picks up a burning stick from the already lit fire on the sand bar. When he returns, two elder Thakur clansmen walk around the pyre with him, instructing him where to ignite it, pointing to each and every bundle of dried grass.

As soon as Shanu touches the torch to the pyre, the hallowed sound of a conch shell echoes from the Shiv temple above the ghat. For the past 10 or 15 minutes, the holy man who takes care of the temple has been watching us from the cliff's edge, waiting for the exact moment the pyre is lit to blow his conch shell. He blows one long continuous breath, creating the characteristic hollow, haunting sound, which, not unlike bagpipes, travels far down and cuts deep inside towards the soul.

In Hinduism, the sound of a conch shell being blown is equivalent to the sacred sound of the universe, AUM, which represents immanent, transcendent, infinite reality. I ask the people seated near me what blowing the conch shell means in Pauri Garhwal. One man says it is a call to Yamaraj, god of death. Another claims the Baba blew the conch three times, not one, in honor of the three members of the Hindu trinity: Brahma, Vishnu, and Shiv. A third man says the blowing of a conch clears evil spirits from the air. A fourth offers a more elaborate opinion: "Blowing the conch shell rouses Shiv. He's not only Almighty god, he's master of the burning ghat—the giver and taker of life. We call out to him to let him know a dead person is coming because we want to move on to a better life and if Shiv doesn't come to take our spirit away, our next life may be worse than this life or we may not reincarnate at all, ending up caught in the hinterland between here and there."

It's not long before the funeral pyre is blazing, fueled by a gentle breeze, which, along with the scent of burning Oak and Pinewood, camouflages the smell of burning flesh.

For the next hour we talk amongst ourselves, periodically gazing over at the fire. There is some speculation Kalam Singh died of fright from witnessing the aftermath of the accident earlier in the day. Others suggest he succumbed to TB. Still others think he may have had a heart attack. They are all topics of conversation rather than concern. It really doesn't matter what Kalam Singh died of. No autopsy was performed. No police will be contacted. No government official will note his demise. His death might not be written in public records for 10, 20 or even 30 years; until his brother, sons or nephew need verification of their land holdings, a demand that may occur once every generation. Even if the situation arises, the local Patwari will only allude to Kalam Singh's death in the county land records by rewriting Kalam Singh's name as 'the late Kalam Singh Thakur' and making the new primary landowner Pratab.

Land is passed down from eldest male to the next eldest male in families extending out to the third, sometimes fourth, generation. In modern times, it's possible Kalam Singh's land will be passed down to his son rather than his brother, Pratab, however, it's rare and such arrangements are often verbal agreements, not legal ones. If by chance Shanu's name is written as the owner, it will be followed by his younger brother's name, as names are always written in birth order, oldest to youngest, making the latter a subordinate co-owner. Being a patriarchal system, a woman's name is not written in the land records, let alone her death.

Pratab and Shanu sit down on two large rocks by the river. Parvendar and Dinesh follow them, carrying scissors and disposable razors in their hands. Parvendar proceeds to cut the longest strands of Pratab's hair as short as he can, and then, switching to a razor, shaves the remaining hair completely off. Only the requisite one-square-inch lock of hair at the back of his crown remains uncut. Dinesh cuts Shanu's hair in the same manner. A Hindu tradition practiced all over India, the oldest male of a nuclear family must shave off his hair when his mother or father dies, albeit the youngest male can take the oldest males place if unusual circumstances warrant. Since the shaved head ritual generally extends to the death of one's brothers, sisters, sister-in-laws, paternal aunts, paternal uncles and paternal cousins, sometime later today several other Thakur clansmen will shave their heads, even some as distantly related as second cousins will shave their heads if they feel sufficiently close to Kalam Singh or particularly pious.

The heart attack theory leads our group to talk about life saving techniques. Besides myself, only one other man who teaches map reading in the army has ever heard of life-saving techniques, so the two of us begin to explain to those immediately around us what the

Heimlich maneuver and CPR are. A couple of men role-play the techniques.

An hour after the fire began, it's still going strong. The two elder Thakur clansmen who self-appointed themselves in-charge of the cremation, sporadically move logs around, fueling flames and knocking burned embers to the ground. About an hour and a half into the burning, they start moving Kalam Singh's charred body parts around too, checking to see what has burned and what has not. The skull and sternum are charred but still intact, so Kaakaa (Uncle) picks up a club and beats the two bones. Wood chunks, sparks and bone fragments fly out of the fire with every thump.

A few men from Chandpur, who had not come down to the ghat with the funeral procession, show up at the ghat while the cremation is in progress, each carrying a log from home to throw on the pyre. Those from surrounding villages who just found out about Kalam Singh's death after they arrived in Chandpur bazaar, pick up whatever branch or stick they can find on their way to the ghat, even if it's a flimsy twig, to toss on the fire. Some of them sit down with us and talk for a while. Others merely acknowledge us with prayer-shaped hands and a quick nod of their head as they wade into the river, where, facing the burning pyre, they scoop water into cupped hands and toss it into the fire, or symbolically in it's direction. They do this three times and then clasp their hands in prayer hand-shape, raise them to their chests for a brief moment, raise them in front of their faces for another moment and then walk away.

When the body is deemed burned and the fire almost out, the rest of us move into the water, a few people at a time, taking turns flinging water toward the pyre and giving our last 'Namaskar' to Kalam Singh. After everyone has completed the ritual, the Thakur clansmen, young and old, grab sticks and begin clubbing what is left of the logs and bones. Their feet sweep leftover charcoal chunks into the river and roll partially burnt wood into the water, giving them kick-starts to float downstream. Several catch on protruding rocks, causing logjams. Young men chase after them, jumping nimbly from rock to rock, as if it's second nature, to dislodge the wood. By the time clean up is finished, barely any evidence remains that a body was burned, merely a small, blackened spot on the sand and a few pieces of charcoal lying on the bottom of the river.

The boys and young unmarried men, with towels from home strung around their necks, head up river to bathe. The confluence of two rivers is revered but the burning ghats are feared. They are the favored stomping grounds of ghosts—people who have died and, because of the violent, painful or sudden nature of their deaths, their spirits have been disquieted, disrupting the normal process of reincarnation, causing them to be stuck in the hinterland, where they linger in strategic places like burning ghats, waiting to possess the most vulnerable, such as youth and people with 'weak' horoscopes (horoscopes foreboding bad news). Thus, to avoid unwanted ghostly encounters, which could change the course of their futures, boys and young men always bath in the river after a funeral to purify themselves, which is an effective means of repelling evil forces.

The rest of us wade through the water and walk back to Chandpur.

The cremation is over but not the funeral. For the next eleven days, Jankari Devi, her children, Pratab and his family, as well as Kalam Singh's first and second cousins and their families will perform mandatory rituals and restrict their diet, especially Shanu. As the oldest son (17 years old), Shanu has the heaviest responsible. He will distance himself from others and purify himself in several small but significant ways. He'll sleep in a separate room from his mother and siblings. Although a common practice in other parts of the world, in Pauri Garhwal it's almost unheard of and invariably disliked. His bed will be a mat of grass on the floor, which may or may not be covered with a cloth. He'll cook his own food, eating only rice with milk and sugar and drinking tea with boiled milk and sugar. Salt, spices and oil are strictly forbidden to eat for the next eleven days (if Shanu's mother had died, milk products and oil would have been forbidden, restricting his diet to rice and lentils cooked together and black tea).

Shanu will not leave the courtyard in front of his house except to go to the bathroom or to the river to pray for his father. He may go to the river 3 days, 7 days or more, depending on the Baaman who'll perform the puja (worship ceremony) and on Astrology, particularly on which of the next 11 days are auspicious: On auspicious days they'll pray, on un-auspicious days they won't. Besides reciting Sanskrit passages, burning incense and offering sacred substances to god (i.e. local plants and cow products), a small, temporary rock temple will be built on the riverbank and pind will be performed. Pind as a verb means to pray at a river and offer balls of rice (and sometimes idols) to dead ancestors, primarily one's deceased parents. It's an important way to honor Kalam Singh and facilitates a smooth transition of his spirit into the afterlife, improving chances that his next life will be better than his last. Pind, the noun, is cooked rice, barley, sesame seeds, sugar and honey compressed together with the hands into what looks like golf balls. Shanu will place one ball of rice at a time into the river while the Baaman recites prayers. A few balls will be set alongside the river for crows to eat—people reincarnate into almost any creature in their next lifetime but crows have traditionally been used to illustrate this concept.

During the eleven-day mourning period, Kalam Singh's extended family on his father's side will not cook with oil nor eat salt. On the eleventh day, Kalam Singh's family will host a mid-day feast for Chandpur's Thakur and Rana clans, marking the end of the eleven-day mourning period. His extended family will then resume eating salt and cooking with oil and Shanu will stop praying at the river and go back to living and eating with his mother and siblings.

The restrictions do not end there however. For one year Kalam Singh's family and extended family will not cook deep-fried foods in their homes (many of them will not eat these foods either), participate in worship ceremonies or wed and the first major holiday after Kalam Singh's death will not be celebrated by his family nor by any other member of the Thakur clan. One year after Kalam Singh's death, his family will perform puja in his honor once again and feed the entire village in a ceremony called Barsi, the final funeral rite that will allow family members to resume eating deep fried foods, attend public worship and hold weddings.

Ancestors are revered like gods. In the future, whenever Kalam Singh's nuclear family holds a worship ceremony, a special prayer will be said for Kalam Singh. And every year during a fifteen-day period known as Sharad, a day will be set-aside for Kalam Singh on which Shanu will hire a Baaman to help him pay homage to his father and Jankari Devi will cook a feast for her family, the Baaman and Kalam Singh (his plate of food will be set on the back of their mud and rock fireplace for the day) and in Kalam Singh's honor leftovers will be fed to stray dogs, the family's cows and the crows.

Initially the road winds up and out of the plains in long gentle curves, eventually growing tighter and tighter, snaking back and forth, as it begins to hug the natural contours of each and every mountain. Twists and turns that block full views of most valleys, revealing them in small, remarkable increments, leading us into and out of different ecosystems.

To our right is Jim Corbett National Park, a sub-tropical jungle where Project Tiger, the first save the tiger program, started in 1973. The park also supports hundreds of bird species, leopards, bears, crocodiles, jackals, mongoose, monitor lizards, wild boars, rhesus macaques, langurs, deer and elephants. The latter is a perfect metaphor for the unspoken tension growing inside our car. We're eleven strangers scrunched intimately together in an SUV and everybody wants to know who the foreigner is, but nobody wants to dive into the verbal foray first.

I decide to break the ice: "Three days ago a government bus fell into a ravine near Gaucher. Thirty-eight people died on the spot or on their way to the hospital. Twenty-seven more were seriously injured. These statistics are from the morning after the accident and, since there are no hospitals in this part of the Himalaya capable of handling serious cases, many of those people probably died too. The [Indian] government compensated by announcing disbursements of 50,000 rupees ($1111) to the families of those who died and 15,000 rupees ($333) to the injured."

My news report elicits a cacophony of 'uh-huhs', exclamations and groans befitting the tragedy and launches the anticipated barrage of questions about the pale face and my replies, "I live in Chandpur village. I'm an American. I've been coming to the Himalaya for 34 years, living here for six, 4½ of those years in Chandpur village. No, my family lives in America. No, I have no sons; two grown daughters. I'm doing social work with the Jwalpa Devi Foundation [JDF]. No, it's not a foreign NGO. Five Garhwalis, one Gujarati and I started it up. We help handicapped people start businesses; set up recycling projects—buy plastic, glass, iron and tin from villagers and then resell it to garbage collectors; set up health camps in remote areas, etc. Yes, we can work all over Pauri Garhwal. No, we haven't done any work in Satpuli yet. No, I don't speak Garhwali, only Hindi. Yes, Pauri Garhwal is a wonderful place!"

Our conversation abates and our excitement diminishes into a comfortable camaraderie.

As the road climbs it hangs onto a steep mountainside, bordered on one side by a brush-filled rocky wall jutting into the sky and on the other side by a cliff dropping down to the river. It tapers down to a single lane fifty or more times because of landslides that have never been completely cleaned up; familiar mounds of dirt and rock that have sat in the same place for years. Even whole trees have slid down the mountain, miraculously finding a place to stand in the road.

We pass by a local maintenance crew. A couple of wiry men pick up rocks and tree parts by hand and heave them over the embankment. Another man tends a fire under a gigantic boulder, trying to bake it brittle. On top of the unyielding beast, his coworkers hack away with picks, ignoring the smoke wafting in their faces. Another crewman plucks a handful of leafy branches from a nearby bush to sweep up smaller debris.

After sixty kilometers the road turns permanently into one lane, which both directions of traffic must deftly share: We happen upon a jeep, slow down and veer onto our respective shoulders to maneuver by one another; an on-coming truck spots us in the distance, pulls off to the side of the road and waits for us to pass; we meet a vehicle head on, forcing both vehicles to stop and the other driver, prompted by either etiquette or our driver's defiant stare, to back up to the nearest pullout. Our horn blares at every bend. Nonetheless, we suddenly encounter a car on a blind curve, seemingly about to crash but, at the last second, adroitly swerve around each other. Two buses bring us to a standstill while they pass one another, the tires of the outer bus inching along the precipice.

A few mountains stretch dramatically from the valley floor into the sky but, in general, they're small, compact and squeezed against one another, gradually and collectively reaching higher and higher altitudes, ultimately becoming the snow-capped monoliths for which the Himalaya is famous. Wherever the gradient allows, small terraced fields have been carved into the hillside. During the rainy season they turn into verdant green stairways; some draped up, down and around entire mountains, creating 3-D special effects. In the center of fields or close by are villages, paced one to four kilometers apart. There are 3,450 villages in Pauri Garhwal, three-fourths with populations of less than 200 people and in the remaining fourth, 200 to 500 people. From a distance, the mud and rock hamlets evoke quaint, tranquil and romantic notions. Up close, poverty and the strength of human character glare back, raw and uncensored.

Everywhere temples dot the countryside: Towering cherry, apricot or parchment-colored domes filled with statues and photos of gods, burning incense and a holy man or two; man-size, white temples erected by farmers in their fields to please the god or goddess who has blessed their life with good fortune or doused it with despair; small roadside temples carved in rock and adorned with brass bells ringing and red flags waving in the wind; naturally occurring caves and strategically placed rocks, hidden from the unacquainted eye, harbor the requisite oil burning vessel and Shiv's trident inside; and, within the inner recesses of almost every Garhwali home, altars for daily personal prayer.

  Round, dark brown eyes watch as our car passes by, soaking us in from the roadside, a stall in the marketplace or bent over in a field; turning, straining, still staring at us in the distance. Mixed forests of Shisham, Sal and Bamboo give way to Pine forests and, in the highest passes, to Oak forests interspersed with Rhododendron trees, aflame with bright red flowers. Along ridges, mountaintops ripple across the sky as far as the eye can see. The most prominent views are of perennial, snow-capped peaks: Nanda Devi (7,817m), Trisul (7074m), and Kedarnath (6940m)—to name a few.

  Fellow passengers disembark here and there along the road, stepping down in busy bazaars or wandering off on trails, merging with the landscape. Four hours into our journey, I get out at Kherakhal, a crossroads five kilometers before Pauri, our district's headquarters, to wait for a commercial vehicle going in my direction. Twenty minutes later, an old-fashioned jeep shows up: Canvas-covered, doorless and bulging with people. The driver, who I know by face, orders a young man sitting in the front seat to get out and sit elsewhere. Smiling warmly, he willingly hops out to give me his treasured seat. I holler out to him and the driver, "Don't worry, I'll get in back" and climb over the tailgate, knowing I'll get jostled around by the lumpy and leaning road no matter where I sit. My bottom clings to six square inches of a wooden bench, obliging me to balance myself by holding onto a metal ladder leading to the luggage rack on the roof. A man standing on the stairs moves his leg over a few inches to keep from banging my fingers. Noticeably, no one shows any signs of being miffed by our cramped quarters.

One of the passengers sitting in back is Asha Devi. She promptly informs the other passengers who I am, where I live and the work JDF does, information about a third of them already know since we all live in the same general locale. They proceed to talk about me, as if I'm not here. I join in now and again to make clarifications, ask questions and to make sure the others realize I can communicate with them myself. This knowledge, however, has little effect on their habit of asking Asha Devi about me, rather than asking me directly—a pleasing twist to my unwanted notoriety, giving me a reprieve by shining the spotlight on Asha Devi, who appears to enjoy it. Seemingly, the only thing Asha Devi doesn't know about me is that I brought my car to a garage in Dehra Dun to get a broken window replaced, hence my return home today by jeep.

Asha Devi informs me that her husband has died and follows the news with a plea for help from our foundation. We've helped her before.

Three years earlier, having heard the entire village of Baijro was destitute, I went there to see for myself. After trudging two hours uphill, I talked with various people about their situations. Asha Devi was one of them. Her husband had been sick off and on for the past five years so he hadn't worked, giving the family no source of income. Their two-room house was in shambles: Its mud and rock walls cracked and crumbling, the wood rafters rotten, water leaked through the roof whenever it rained. Their bed was a pile of black shredded rags. There was no food in the kitchen, no seeds to plant next season's crops and no milk-bearing cow or water buffalo, vital sources of nutrition and fertilizer. As if things were not bad enough, four out of six family members had leprosy. Although it had not progressed to the point of rotted-off extremities, insensitive white patches blotched their skin, the veins behind their knees were enlarged and the disease had attacked Asha Devi's nose bone, making her nose slightly formless and bulb-shaped.

While the rest of Asha Devi's family sat outside, Asha Devi begged me to help. I assured her JDF would help her family set up a long-term moneymaking venture, but warned her that it could take awhile since other people were waiting for JDF's help ahead of her. Overwhelmed by her desperate situation and despite all common sense, I secretly handed her the only bill in my wallet, a 500-rupee note ($11.11) and told her to buy food for her family in the meantime and, knowing she had never seen a 500-rupee note before, I explained to her what it was.

Scarcely able to get the words out, "By the grace of god!" Asha Devi collapsed to the ground. I assumed she'd fainted until she started to cry. I bent down and hugged her awkwardly, a result of both the physical position we were in and because I was unsure of how she would respond to my affection. She sobbed uncontrollably for several minutes. When her tears waned, she reached out from where she half sat and half lay on the floor, touched my feet with the fingers of her right hand and brought them up to her forehead in a sign of humility, proclaiming in half breaths, "You're god to us. God will reward you for your kindness."

JDF eventually gave Asha Devi goats to raise, breed and sell; we've taken her family to the hospital on more than a few occasions; and, we've bought her children's school clothes and supplies and paid their school fees for the past two years. I often find myself in a catch-22 with her and other poor villagers though. Their basic needs are multiple. I want to help but it's impossible to do everything. We explain this principle and set limits, but sometimes to no avail. A few villagers keep coming back asking for more, especially those who have lived in extreme poverty.

A woman named Gayatri Devi came to me and asked me to give her my leftover 2" x 12" boards in order to build a bed for her daughter's future father-in-law. He would be staying in their home during the wedding and they had no beds, not even for themselves. I refused and her minor request became pivotal. At that moment I surmised Gayatri Devi had asked me for something at least a hundred times and to confirm my suspicions, as well as to keep a check on my sanity, I sat down that afternoon and wrote a list of all of the things Gayatri Devi had asked me for over the past two years. The total was 103. I or JDF had given Gayatri Devi and her family members numerous part and full time jobs, helped her secure a bank loan, took her husband to the hospital for TB treatment for a year, took her son for his broken arm, paid her children's school fees, bought their school clothes, gave the family sweaters and blankets to keep them warm in winter, and fulfilled numerous other odd and end requests. After about her 25th appeal, however, I explained to Gayatri Devi we couldn't help her anymore: "JDF does not have the resources to do everything for you, there are other people to help."

She continued to ask anyway, even though the answer from that day forth was no. After about her 50th request, I started telling her, "You're driving me crazy! Every time I see you coming, I want to run and hide under my bed!"

Gayatri Devi, undeterred, kept coming. The day I wrote the list to confirm my suspicions, I realized how befuddled and exhausted I was. The very next time Gayatri Devi asked me for something I told her, "No" and added, "From this moment on, I will never speak to you again and I want you to stop talking to me", a restriction probably neither of us had ever experienced in our lifetimes, and for the umpteenth time I explained to her why. On the one hand, I felt like a heartless scoundrel. On the other hand, I could no longer help Gayatri Devi. I really did want to run and hide under my bed every time I saw her—and still do.

To focus Asha Devi on resources other than JDF, I ask her if she's applied for a widow's pension. When she tells me she hasn't, I explain to her what it is: A 150 Rs. ($ 3.33) a month pension dispensed by the government to poor widows who have no adult sons. Since it's dispersed in six-month increments, it's a significant amount of money at one time, particularly when someone has no income. Besides, it's expected to double in worth within a few months.

I ask Asha Devi who Baijro's Pradhan is and explain to her that as the village development officer, he's responsible to help her file her pension form. Asha Devi tells me she doesn't know who the Pradhan is. Even though I know we can figure out his name just by talking amongst ourselves in the jeep, I conclude the chances of the Pradhan actually filling out Asha Devi's forms are now highly unlikely, based on their tendency not to complete the forms for people anyway but especially since she doesn't know who the Pradhan is, suggesting that her village, because of it's small size, shares a Pradhan from another village, which means he may not have the necessary familial or emotional ties to Asha Devi to motivate him to fill out and file her pension forms. The process incurs travel expenses and requires paying bribes to almost every single government official along the way, for inconveniencing them to do their jobs. Money Asha Devi does not have. It would mean the Pradhan would either have to take money out of his own pocket or illegally from the village development coiffeurs. Even if the money is not a deterrent, the red tape involved in filing the forms turns what should be a minor undertaking into a monumental task, creating dread in even the most hardy of souls.

If Asha Devi fills out the forms on her own, she'll have to obtain the forms, fill them out and then take them to the Pradhan (Village Development Officer), the Panchayat Mantri (Secretary under which there are several village development councils), the Patwari (county clerk-cum-sheriff) and the Tahseldar (sub-collector of district revenue and the boss of county clerk-cum-sheriffs) for verifications and re-verifications, stamps and re-stamps, of her circumstances, before she can actually file the forms. It wouldn't be so bad, except Asha Devi doesn't know how to read or write; doesn't know who any of these people are or where to find them; and none of them have regular business hours, appointments or phones, except the Tahseldar. He has a phone, but Asha Devi doesn't and she doesn't know his phone number and there are no phone books, no information operators or Internet service to look the information up. Asha Devi would have to make countless trips by bus or jeep, sometimes to far-flung places, back and forth, again and again, trying to catch each person, taking six months or longer to complete her paperwork. Once these individuals sign the forms, however, they can be filed at the social services office in Pauri, where it takes another year for the government to finish its in-house paperwork and decision-making process. If Asha Devi is deemed suitable and enough money has been allotted by the Central Government for another applicant, an acceptance letter would be followed a few months later by a check and, despite all of the application hassles, once the checks start coming there is usually no further ado and recipients frequently mention how grateful they are to have an income.

An hour later our jeep, almost empty now, arrives in Mausi bazaar from where I need to catch another jeep to take me further on to

Chandpur. As we clamber over the tailgate, the bureaucratic jungle clear in my mind, I turn to Asha Devi and offer, "If you come by JDF's office one day, we'll fill out and file the widow's pension forms for you."

Crouching down so as not to hit my head on the doorframe, I make my way into Chachiji's (respected aunt's) kitchen. Smoke billows out of the fireplace, forcing me to stoop even lower to avoid the thick layer lingering just below the ceiling. It's hard to see. The fire, the open five-foot high door hidden under a veranda and one tiny window barely provide enough light to illuminate the small room with mud brown walls and a soot-blackened ceiling. As soon as my eyes adjust to the dark, I slip into my favorite spot on the floor along the wall. Chachiji hands me a burlap bag to sit on.

She's sitting on the floor kneading dough in a giant-size pie pan and smiling with more than just a hint of satisfaction, declaring, "You've arrived!" The surprise in her voice and the delight spread across her face imply she didn't think I would show up to work in the fields today. It's my first time.

Reaching over with her clean hand, she picks up the teakettle and says, "There's a little left. I just made it." And then she pours the steaming hot tea into a tin cup, careful not to fill it more than half way in order that my fingers won't burn when I hold it.

Chachiji sets a round, flat-iron pan on top of her stove, a 2'x 2' x 1' high fireplace made from rock, mud and cow dung, set in the far corner on the floor. An assortment of half-burned sticks juts out the front, extending into the room. She shuffles them around, stoking the flames. From a stack lined along the far wall, she grabs a few more dried branches and sticks them into the ambers, producing a string of crackles and pops, infusing the room with the aroma of pine. The smoke stings my eyes. Impervious to it, Chachiji rolls dough into balls and pats them into flat pancake-size chapattis (unleavened wheat bread) with her hands. Only the older women still make them this way. The younger women and girls put the balls on round wooden boards and roll them out with miniature rolling pins. Either way, there's a knack to patting, rolling and flipping them with minute turns to get the perfectly round shape they almost always are.

Chachiji lays the flattened dough on top of the hot fry pan. Two minutes later, she picks it up with her fingers and flips it over. Two more minutes pass. Without checking for doneness, she grabs the bread and tosses it onto the hot coals. It immediately puffs up, filling with air until there's no more room, and then deflates. Chachiji reaches into the fire, flames lapping at her fingers, and pulls it out. She makes at least 30 chapattis while we sit and talk, a couple for her and the rest for the seven of us going out to the fields to plow and churn dirt.

While we wait for everyone to show up, Chachiji brings me into the next room to show me the butter she's making. It's another low-ceiling, first floor room used to store grains. Since there is no fire and the window is closed, it is twice as dark as the room we've just come from. Silhouettes of vessels lined-up against the back wall and sitting atop wood planks are barely visible: Large woven baskets caked with mud on the outside to keep moisture and mice out; garbage can size tin tubs; and an odd assortment of smaller recycled plastic and metal containers.

Daylight streams in on Chachiji's butter-making device, a cylinder-shaped porcelain urn (a modern version of the wooden ones many people still use) set near the door. It's filled a third of the way up with cream, skimmed off the top of boiled and cooled water buffalo's milk over the past few days. A three-foot long bamboo pole sticks out of the urn. The end used to churn butter has been split and several small pieces of wood crammed into the slits to keep them spread apart, making it look like a claw. Chachiji loops a rope attached to the wall around the handle to keep it from making exaggerated movements and then sits down on a gunnysack on the floor, braces the urn between her bare feet and, putting both hands on either side of the pole, rolls it back and forth between her palms, making what turns out to be a delectable butter and a naturally extracted buttermilk called chanch.

Character emanates from every inch of Chachiji's body. Wrinkles chiseled into her face tell the story of a woman who's worked hard all of her life in the hot Indian sun. Her usually bare feet are short and remarkably broad from a lifetime of not wearing shoes, probably a size 5 D. When she leaves her house, she wears a pair of worn-at-the-heel rubber thongs, although not necessarily so. Her feet are as tough as the best leather boots ever made. But just like leather cracks when exposed to harsh weather, so do Chachiji's feet crack during the winter months, leaving deep crevasses that are extremely painful.

One day she told me she had been a robust woman when her husband was alive and used her hands to outline a chunky woman's figure. She then pointed to her frail and tiny body, exclaiming, "But after his death this happened!" A split second later, her mouth dropped open and she simultaneously sucked in a gulp of air and raised her shoulders and eyebrows. It's an idiomatic expression characteristic of older Garhwalis, revealing Chachiji's own sense of pity and surprise at the toll living has taken on her body.

Her cheeks sunk inward when her teeth were pulled out two years ago, giving her that lippy-look when she closes her mouth. Her daughter's good intention to have her mother's rotten teeth pulled out and replaced by dentures was foiled by a Quack. He'd pulled all of

27

Chachiji's teeth out in one sitting, fitted her for cheap dentures four days later and then sent her home. Needless to say, the dentures don't fit, forcing Chachiji to chew with her gums. I've tried to convince her to go with me to the plains to a real dentist. She stubbornly refuses. Her excuse is she needs to stay home to take care of her grandchildren in order for the other women in her household to work in the fields unencumbered.

Chachiji lives in her faded green cotton sari or her royal blue one with the red border. Both are dotted with hundreds of tiny white flowers and just as many burn holes from ashes falling from her bedis (miniature cigarettes rolled in tobacco leaves). She wears her saris wrapped and pleated as saris are wrapped and pleated but, like all elderly Garhwali women in our area, instead of throwing the long end piece over her shoulder to hang down her back, she wraps her sari around herself one more time and then strings one end piece over her left shoulder and the other under her right arm, across her back and up to her left shoulder, where both ends are tied together in a knot. A cummerbund made of several meters of white, pleated cotton is customarily bound around her waist, giving her lower back support. The style has other benefits too. A pouch is automatically created in the front of her sari, allowing her to carry important items with her wherever she goes. In Chachiji's case it is invariably bedis, matches, her small change purse and a house key. Giving her saris a little more Garhwali flair, she hikes them up a few inches above her ankles to make it easier to maneuver while she works, exposing fancy frilled, albeit threadbare petticoats. About half of the time a long scarf, shawl or dishcloth is haphazardly coiled around her head two or three times, one end tucked into itself above her ear while the other end dangles down to her shoulder. Sometimes she just flops the material on her head without anchoring it down anywhere.

Her real name is Rami Devi. At 63 years old, she's not too old to work in the fields but she's been chronically sick for the past year, so these days she stays close to home, taking care of her grandchildren, cleaning the house and cooking for the two women and five children who live with her. There are no men. Her husband died 22 years ago and her three sons live and work in Delhi, 380 kilometers away. The latter have taken their male children with them. Schools are better in Delhi and emphasis is on boys getting a good education because they will be responsible in the future to earn money and take care of their parents when their parents are too old to take care of themselves.

Chachiji actually has one more son. He was raised in Delhi by relatives. He had been sick since birth and was still unable to walk when Chachiji's next child, the 6th, was born. At the time, Chachiji worked the farm and took care of her small children with the help of her husband's brother's wife. Both women's husbands worked and lived in Delhi. Then her sister-in-law was summoned to join her husband in Delhi, a move that would leave Chachiji behind to do all of the work herself. When her sister-in-law got on the bus to leave, Chachiji unexpectedly, even to herself, handed her sickly son to her sister-in-law with only the clothes on his back and spoke frankly, "Take him. If he lives, he lives. He'll die here." Her sister-in-law took him without hesitation and raised him as her own. He didn't walk until he was five or six years old. No one knows what his ailment was, although it was most likely polio, but everyone I've talked to is certain the cure was rubbing his legs everyday with hot mustard oil.

From the first moment I met Chachiji, we've been friends. Over the years we've spent long hours talking while drinking tea during the day and whiskey at night. She keeps me up to date on village gossip and tells me what life was like when she was young.

One of my favorite conversations with Chachiji took place outside her home on a holiday known as Ghee Sankranti (A mid-August holiday marking the start of one of three main harvest seasons). She had invited me over to her house, explaining, "On this day every year we eat khir [rice pudding] and ghee [clarified butter]. You don't have to eat khir but you absolutely must eat ghee. If you don't, you'll come back in your next lifetime as a ghandiyal!"

Although I knew Hindus believe that after death people come back to life as something else, depending on their deeds in this lifetime and previous lifetimes and on the influence of their ancestors (a process referred to as karma), I had never heard the Garhwali term before, "A ghandiyal? What's a ghandiyal?"

Chachiji raised her pointer fingers along each side her head and stuck them into the air.

"Oh!" I exclaimed. "I know what that is" and then marveled at how two diverse cultures use the exact same gesture to represent the devil. I assumed her warning was a metaphor and she was telling me that I'd be devilish—sinful—in my next lifetime if I didn't eat ghee on Ghee Sankranti.

Chachiji then directed her granddaughter to search under some rocks. The comment appeared so out of context, I assumed they had changed the subject and were talking about something else.

A few minutes later her granddaughter returned. "I found one!" She announced, grinning from ear to ear.

"Show it to Vicki." Chachiji instructed—Chachiji is the only person in all of Pauri Garhwal who ever calls me by my name.

Her granddaughter opened up cupped hands, exposing a small, caramel-colored snail. Chachiji repeated her earlier warning, "If you don't eat ghee today, this is what you'll become in your next lifetime, a snail!"

Unable to suppress my astonishment, I burst into uncontrollable laughter, bringing tears to my eyes. Everyone standing around burst out laughing at my laughter.

Pointing to the tentacles on the snail's head, a woman immediately changed our gay mood, stating in a serious tone, "In the hierarchy of reincarnated forms, a snail is the lowest form of life on earth."

Everyone around nodded solemnly in agreement.

Another young woman asserted, "This is what the people before us believed," as if it was not what people believe now. It's a similar kind of statement that many Garhwalis who live in the big cities make, "That's how the people in the village think," as if they don't think the same way. Yet, when I walk into their kitchens in the big city, they are cooking khir and eating ghee as if their lives depend on it.

When I returned to JDF's office, four male employees were waiting for me. I told them I'd been eating ghee at Chachiji's house and had learned what Ghee Sankranti is. They chuckled amongst themselves and then Biru commented, "Yeah, that's a local superstition," as if it's not his superstition. To get a better understanding of what this duel stance means, I inquired as to whether they had eaten ghee today. They all nodded affirmatively. Then I asked if they ate ghee every year on Ghee Sankranti. Again, they nodded. Satish, who is used to my probing about Garhwali culture, apparently understood my confusion, prompting him to speak up, "Madam, we can see the absurdity in such an idea, but we believe in our customs and in our ancestors so much that we will eat ghee on Ghee Sankranti our entire lives."

Chachiji gets up from her butter-making contraption and we go back to her kitchen. She begins to make a fresh kettle of chaa (black tea and boiled buffalo milk heaped with sugar) for us to take to the fields.

Premalata Devi arrives and, spying me, proclaims with genuine delight, "Oh, you've come!" She then wrangles a 25 Kg water pot off her head and sets it down on a low bench next to two other brass pots, while informing Chachiji she fed and watered their cow and water buffalo and cleaned the shed.

It was Premalata Devi that I had talked to yesterday about coming to work in the fields today. She's the wife of Chachiji's second son. Her native village is what people call 'backward', meaning it's not accessible by road, has few basic amenities such as access to electricity or a nearby water source, and most of its occupants are poor. The isolation of her village is reflected in her traditional values. She follows strict adherence to men and women's customary roles and breaks out into a shy, nervous laughter at the slightest variation. One day several men and I were sitting together, talking inside Premalata Devi's house, when I invited her to join us. She giggled. Her husband, taking a skewed version of my invitation, commanded her to sit down. She, still smiling from the giggle, sat on the opposite side of the room in the far corner with an uneasy smile for a full ten minutes, finally stealing away at the first opportunity.

Premalata Devi's shyness is tempered in a room full of women or when her and I are alone. She's amazingly candid and astute. Often when I ask Garhwali women questions, I have to explain the question and give examples of the kind of answers I am looking for. With Premalata Devi, I never have to explain. She comprehends my meaning and spontaneously elaborates without prompting. She even looks a little different than many Garhwali women: Her eyes are set wide apart and are slanted, like the Mongolian influence seen in the most northern districts of the Indian Himalaya; her is nose broad; her hair cocoa-colored rather than coffee bean, with a slight frizz to it; and, although she's slender by Western standards, for a rural Garhwali woman she borders on pudgy.

Once the milk-laden tea comes to a rolling boil, Chachiji takes it off the stove, crumples up an old piece of paper and stuffs it into the teakettle spout. She packs the unleavened bread, a potato-cauliflower curry she'd made earlier, seven tin glasses, and seven small tin bowls into a woven basket and seals it with a lid.

Upon hearing voices outside, the three of us head out onto the courtyard where Nisha Devi, her 7-year old daughter, Gita, and Chachiji's two granddaughters, 15-year old Kali and 12-year old Kuri are waiting to go with us to the fields. Chachiji puts the basket with bread and vegetables on top of Kuri's head and the teakettle in her hand. Premalata Devi goes into the storeroom and pulls out four sickles and two partially filled burlap bags. She hands the sickles to Kali and sets the bags on top of her head, one on top of the other. Kali makes some minor adjustments, otherwise the bags are form fitting and seemingly self-adhesive. Chachiji inspects the sickles and directs Premalata Devi not to give me the one with the broken handle.

We head towards the fields, serenaded by chirping birds. A short ways down the trail the smell of dung becomes potent as we near a cluster of sheds, one in which Kaakaa (uncle) houses his oxen and plow. We stop to pick up the latter, a wooden contraption with three fused parts: A six foot long 2 x 4 that runs horizontally between the oxen; a four-foot long 2 x 4 attached to the front, with ropes, neck grooves and wooden pegs to secure it to the oxen; and, jammed into the back end, a three-foot long slab of wood tapered at the bottom and a footstep carved into its side. Premalata Devi lifts it up with the help of Nisha Devi and centers the long beam on her head so that the heavier back end of the plow is slightly closer to her than the front end, balancing the weight. It's not too heavy for Premalata Devi to carry, just awkward, so she places her hand on it to keep it steady.

We walk a little further down the trail where we bump into my favorite munchkin, Ghunghari, near the spring. She's three years old and precocious! She's also cute. Her hair is cut short like a boy and when she smiles her eyes twinkle. She's carrying a small water jug on her head that she'd just filled with water at the spring. She halts in front of us, confidently removes her hand from the jug, letting it balance itself, and, pressing her hands together in prayer, politely says, "Namaste, Madam." She then grabs her jug again and marches off up the hill, as if she's on a mission. By this age girls begin hauling water, sticks and grass partly for fun, like playing house, but it also contributes to the family's practical needs.

As we round the bend beyond the elementary school, the fields come alive with people. It seems like every available man, woman and child has turned out to work. Everyone plows, plants and harvests their own fields, but villagers normally start and end their activities together: They start plowing on the same day, plow during the same time of the day and plow in the same area (i.e. everyone is working in these fields this morning, despite the fact they have fields in other areas that need to be plowed).

A shrill arises as villagers begin noticing my presence. Twenty to thirty people stop working and line up along the edge of their fields to watch as we go by. "Madam, are you going to work in the fields today?" A woman shouts affably and then, not waiting for an answer from me, turns to the people with me and questions them, "Is Madam really going to work in the fields today?"

"Yes," they assure her.

"You're a real Garhwali woman now!" Another woman shouts.

A few women become downright giddy and start reciting Garhwali for me to repeat: "mee puungaraa jaanuu chon" (I am going to the fields), "mee puungaraa maa dolaa phuudanuu chon" (I am breaking up clumps of dirt in the field), and "mee garhwaali seekhanuu chon!" (I am learning Garhwali). I oblige them by repeating their sentences, destroying every syllable and the natural singsong rhythm of the Garhwali language. Nobody appears to care.

While they playfully shout out Garhwali, we make our way to our first field, which is located in the center of where everyone else is working. Kaakaa is waiting for us, sitting on his haunches in the field and smoking a bedi, his oxen grazing nearby. He is only 55 years old but like Chachiji his face is scarred with deep-set wrinkles. He's slightly taller than most Garhwali's at about 5' 8". His tattered and beat clothing either reflect his character or give him character, it's hard to tell which. His hair always looks like he has just gotten out of bed. He's laid back but apparently he hasn't always been. According to fellow villagers, he used to fight with anyone and everyone, including his wife, who villagers say he, his mother and his father used to beat daily, always emphasizing the word 'daily'. I never met her. She ran away in the middle of the night 15 years ago. She resurfaced three years ago in Delhi's Garhwali subculture, happily remarried.

Despite Kaakaa's history, if I ever had to survive off the land in the Himalaya, I would take him with me. He can light fires without matches. He's the village expert on animals. He has worked the fields all of his life, giving him practical knowledge about the land and weather. He knows various uses of wild plants and trees; which ones you can eat, make rope from and use for medicinal purposes. He can build a sturdy shelter from sticks and grass. He's a great cook. Moreover, by all appearances, he doesn't require much to maintain, not even shoes.

He's got the better deal in this plowing-planting arrangement. He's part of the Thakur clan, but Chachiji's husband and Kaakaa do not share the same grandparents, so they are not considered to be from the same 'nuclear' family, making this plowing relationship more of a business deal than a family one. We'll plow and plant in both his and Chachiji's son's fields for free, yet Chachiji's family has to pay Kaakaa for his work; roughly 60 days (three plowing seasons) for 2000 Rs. ($44.45), breakfast and bedis every day he works and bottles of whiskey on demand.

Kaakaa helps take the plow off Premalata Devi's head and hooks up his oxen. They're gigantic white beasts, taller than a man, with long pointed horns and sagging necklines wrapped in brass bells that tinkle with every step. Although common in India, they stand out in Pauri Garhwal where short brown steers plow the fields. Kaakaa likes to go down to the stockyards on the plains to buy his animals because plain's livestock are usually half again as large as local ones and half the price. He says he doesn't mind the several days it takes to walk home with his new animals, even though most of it is uphill.

Lining the oxen up at the periphery of the field, Kaakaa holds the blade of the plow up in the air while coaxing the oxen forward a couple of feet, hollering "Chalo! Chalo! (Lets go! Lets go!). They obediently lumber forward. When the blade is perpendicular to the edge of the field, Kaakaa sets it down in the dirt, applying pressure to the single step carved into the back of the blade, sometimes with his foot, other times with his hand. As the plow kicks up clods of dirt, we follow behind with the dull, backside of our sickles, smacking the clumps, breaking them into fine dirt, and pick out rocks and weeds, tossing them into a gully skirting one side of the field.

When the oxen reach the end of the field, Kaakaa nudges them to turn, cooing "Le! Le!" and gently pushes the buttocks of one ox in the direction he should go. They dutifully turn and meander along the far edge of the field, enabling Kaakaa to finish plowing the rest of his line. At the end of the field, Kaakaa lifts the plow up out of the ground and, using it as leverage, directs the oxen into a wide about-face turn, again crying out "Take! Take!" Without a fuss and without needing to readjust their positions, the oxen wind up at the end of their turn with one standing directly over the previously plowed line and the plow blade perfectly aligned to begin plowing the next row. Calling out "Chalo! Chalo!" at their heels, the oxen move doggedly forward and the blade is again set back into the soil.

Even though the oxen plod along in an orderly fashion, Kaakaa must work hard to plow a straight line. Plows are heavy and unwieldy, the dirt rock-filled and the steers, despite all appearances, are hard to manage. When a novice plows or someone is using someone else's oxen for the first time, oxen predictably show just how unruly they can be: Lunging hither and thither, dawdling or refusing to budge. The other main difficulty of plowing is beasts and plows must continuously turn and maneuver in tight places. Fields are terraced, confined by drop-offs or walls and they're small, averaging eight or ten-feet wide by thirty-feet long. Even this is often not the true length of a family's field. Upon close examination a rock can be found in the middle of many fields, indicating the land has been subdivided amongst brothers, cousins and/or uncles. The one we're plowing has been subdivided between cousins, but since one cousin and his family live in Delhi, Chachiji's family plows, plants and harvests that cousin's fields, as if they are their own. It's a suitable arrangement for both parties. Abandoning one's fields is likened to abandoning cultural or ancestral ties, so even those who have permanently settled on the plains rarely sell their fields and rather than let them fall fallow, prefer them to be plowed. Chachiji's family periodically gives the cousin's family a few kilos of rice, lentils and vegetables as a token payment of their appreciation.

Tilling the soil under a searing sun, we talk about farming. Premalata Devi and Nisha Devi tell me a family of six eats the following rations every month: 40 Kg of rice, 50 Kg of flour, 30 Kg of potatoes, onions and other vegetables, 10 Kg of lentils or dried beans, 3 Kg of mustard oil, 5-6 Kg of sugar, 1.5-2 Kg of tea leaves, 1-1.5 Kg of spices and 2 Kg of salt.

Roughly speaking, an average Chandpur family owns 24 fields, albeit some have none and a handful of families have more. If rainfall is plentiful, a person with 24 fields can grow 100 Kg of rice a year. Minus 20 Kg set aside to be next year's seeds and 25 Kg of husk weight, that leaves 55 Kg of rice to eat per year. The requirement for a family of six is 480 Kg per year. Under these same conditions, a farmer with 24 fields can grow 130 Kg of wheat. Minus 15 Kg set aside for next year's seeds, it leaves 115 Kg of wheat to eat per year. The requirement is 600 Kg per year. The saving grace for villagers in our area is they grow millet to supplement this flour requirement. For those who do not have a cow or water buffalo—and once a year when everyone's animal's milk dries up—they must buy milk from their neighbors. A month's requirement is 30 Kg, which costs 360 Rs.

We figure an average family of six in Chandpur with 24 fields and good rain still needs to spend several hundred rupees a month just to buy the minimal basic rations mentioned above. In dollars, the amount is ridiculously low. In rupees, especially when a family has no other income, it's manageable only because local stores give rations to people in exchange for payment later—exacting hefty interest and lifetime obligations.

One and a half hours and three fields later, we're finished plowing and breaking up dirt in this area. Premalata Devi pulls out the two partially filled burlap bags. Reaching into one bag, she takes out a fistful of millet seeds and strolls across the field, jerking her raised fist back and forth, as if she's rolling dice in slow motion, letting a few grains fall from her hand at a time. After she finishes tossing millet, she plants black beans in a narrow strip of land she had left empty along the supporting wall, using her same rolling-the-dice method.

Kaakaa unhooks his oxen. Premalata Devi puts the plow back on her head and we all make our way back to the trail, heading farther away from Chandpur. The wide trail used to be the main access route to all of the villages in this area before the road was built in 1974, so it starts way before it hits Chandpur and extends long after it and rather than go straight up or down hill like most trails here do, this one is pleasantly flat, running parallel to the river 100 yards below and to the road 100 yards above.

The surrounding brush is dry and the land brown, as it is every year from December to June, until the monsoons arrive, heralding in a lush green. Mountains loom overhead, hugging our narrow valley on all sides, casting shadows. Pine trees dot their slopes, sprouting up in collapsed fields, gradually becoming thicker as they stretch upward, turning into full-fledged forests three-fourths of the way up the mountain, denude of undergrowth because of their needle's acidity and over-foraging. There are a dozen or so other indigenous trees scattered throughout the landscape, surviving the hatchet due to their utility or religious significance, such as Peepal, Timaru and Painyaan, and there are cultivated banana and orange trees. The latter are invariably planted near one's house for ease of nurturing, to enjoy their fragrant blossoms and "to make it difficult for others to steal their fruit."

A trickling stream crosses our path. Everyone washes his or her hands. When we arrive at the next field to be plowed, Kuri gathers twigs and shapes them into a mound on the ground, tucking dry grass in the middle and on top. She then places a few rocks around it to form a fireplace on which she sets the teakettle and lights the tinder. With the help of Premalata Devi and Kali, she pulls the food and wares out of the basket that Chachiji had packed earlier, divides the curry into bowls and distributes the bread.

While we eat, the oxen roam free, perusing the rock walls for grass to nibble on. Again we talk about farming. Villagers started plowing and planting three days earlier and, barring any rain, they'll continue to plow and plant for the next two to three weeks, depending on how many fields they own. They've just finished harvesting wheat and next month, in May, they'll harvest garbanzo beans, rai (a mustard leaf), mustard seed, coriander and barley. Some of the fields they'll plow during the next few weeks will remain fallow until June, when they'll plant jundalaa (from which they make brooms), green chilies, cholie (a cereal highly sought after by sweet makers and grown to trade with shopkeepers for rations), corn, eggplant and prasbeem (a vegetable when it's picked right away and a dry lentil later in the season).

    We clear three more fields after eating. There are a lot of weeds mixed in with the dirt, requiring us to gather them into piles to be burned. Because everyone in Chandpur and every other village nearby plows at the same time, these burn offs fill the sky with a thick smoky haze, lasting for days, even weeks at a time, some turning into wildfires that blaze out of control, through the fields, up the mountains and into the jungles, a phenomenon so common that every year there are at least a half dozen raging infernos threatening to burn down Chandpur or another nearby village. That's my take on the situation. While I lie awake at night, periodically getting up to check a fire's progress, my neighbors sleep soundly, seemingly never giving the fires a second thought.

    Mid-day we head back home. As we meander through the fields, we catch glimpses of Chandpur ahead in the distance, a cluster of 40 homes and just above them, lining the one lane road, fifteen odd businesses, servicing a dozen or so villages. The fields are almost deserted now except for a few stragglers. The thud of bats hitting balls and boys cheering a game of cricket emanate from fallow fields close by but out of sight. Our group strings out along the path. Premalata Devi and I bring up the tail end.

I'm pooped, filled with the kind of satisfaction that only hard work, fresh air and good company bring and dream of taking a cold bucket-bath when I get home, maybe even a nap. My reverie is tainted only by the fact the other women and girls will rest for a mere hour or two at the most, before they head back to collect grass and firewood in the forest, followed by a host of other tasks that will keep them busy late into the night, prompting me to ask Premalata Devi what she thinks about the arduous and seemingly unending work her and other women do.

She replies, "We work in the fields. We cut grass. We collect dung. We haul water. There's no choice in the matter. We do what our mother-in-law tells us to do."

She says it as a fact, not a complaint.

I then ask her what she thinks about the small amount of food produced from all of their hard work. Again Premalata Devi answers pragmatically, "We work hard in the fields all day and we get very little out of our work, not even enough to feed ourselves. What's there to think? This is the way it is in Pauri Garhwal."

*Chachiji died December 8, 2004

Monsoon rains pound down hard, turning steep village trails into muddy rivers and flat ones into puddles. Wind is thrusting today's downpour sideways, rendering my umbrella useless and guaranteeing I'll be soaked from the chest down before reaching my destination only one hundred yards away.

As I climb the hill between my house and Angita Devi's, my feet search the mud for rocks and tufts of grass to cling to. Last year during the rains, I slipped and somersaulted down this very slope, nose-diving into a patch of nettles. My cheek and forehead burned on contact and, even though I applied mustard oil to lessen the sting, I was plagued with a red rash and strange twitching sensation for the next twelve hours.

At the top of the incline corn stocks line one side of the trail and an orange tree and drop-off on the other, obliging me to plod through sludge. Brownish green guck oozes over my rubber thongs and between my toes. I'm slightly repulsed but not really. I'm getting used to stepping in dung, to monster-size spiders crawling on my wall and to a whole lot of other things that used to make me squirm. The most compelling reason for my indifference though is I know that when I arrive at Angita Devi's place, no one is going to care if my feet are covered with muck or that my clothes are dripping wet. If my hosts even notice, the most they will do is offer me water to wash my feet.

Sharti Devi and her two teenage daughters, Manjuna and Anjuna, meet me at the edge of the veranda. We clasp our hands in prayer and raise them up in front of our chins to greet one another. Sharti Devi and I say "Namaskar" and then I switch to "Namaste" to address the children, who respond with a more formal "Namaskar" and bend over to touch the tops of my feet, as they do to any older relative or fellow villager they haven't seen in a while.

No one notices my sorry state so I stick my muddy feet, thongs and all, into the rainwater pouring off the roof. Before entering the threshold of the innermost veranda, we all take off our rubber thongs and leave them in the middle of the walkway. Sharti Devi heads into the kitchen, the girls go into their bedroom and I walk over to the room where Angita Devi and her newborn son have been staying since his birth and in which the naming ceremony will be held.

Directly in front of the door, lying on the floor, are a stack of wilted nettles, a sickle and a small, hand-held fishnet. They've been lying there since the day the baby was born to keep ghosts from entering the room, particularly but not exclusively, invisible ghosts who render people unconscious, especially unblessed babies and people with weak horoscopes, a phenomenon referred to as 'being hit by the wind'.

I step over the talismans and enter the room. After Angita Devi and I say our 'Namaskars', I ask, "How is your baby's health and where is he?"

I have a special interest in his well-being. Three years ago Angita Devi's first child died during childbirth. Afterwards, her and Chachiji repeatedly told me, in no uncertain terms, the baby would not have died if I had been in the village. Although I knew it wasn't my fault, I felt bad. There was some truth to what they were saying. If I hadn't gone to Dehra Dun for a couple of days, I would have been in the village when Angita Devi's labor became troubled and would have driven her to the hospital in my car. Maybe doctors could have saved the baby. The following year, for the birth of her second child, Angita Devi went to stay in Delhi and had the baby in a hospital. A year later, for this third baby, I brought Angita Devi to the hospital for check-ups and, because Chachiji made me promise to stay in the village during the baby's estimated arrival date, I was here when Angita Devi went into labor. We took the precaution of taking her to the hospital for delivery.

Grinning from ear to ear, the proud mother reports, "He's fine," and then walks over to where he's sleeping and pulls him out from under a pile of blankets to give me a peek, jostling him around, waking him up in the process. He lies quietly. Like most babies he's adorable, although a thick circle of black kajal dots the side of his forehead, leaving the uninitiated to assume he has a large unsightly mole, when in fact the eyeliner will regularly be applied to his forehead during his first years of life to repel ghosts, curses and other evil forces.

He is also tiny, swimming in a much too large hand-me-down pajama. Since he's not wearing diapers, his clothes and the blankets surrounding him are soaked and soiled. Angita Devi changes them, burying him under a new layer of dry blankets, covering his head completely. It appears as if he might smother or, at the very least, roast to death but he does neither. Angita Devi too is uncharacteristically bundled in a heavy sweater, shawl and knitted hat. It is neither cold outside nor inside the house. Even if it was, villager's bodies seem to have a remarkable ability to regulate body temperature, adapting and tolerating extreme variations, making a shawl sufficient to keep them warm during winter and giving them the capacity to work long hours under a blazing hot sun.

Sharti Devi enters the room. She's strikingly thin, a condition accentuated by black hair pulled back in a severe, albeit elegant bun.

Her animated brown eyes appear to be talking to me, letting me know she's too busy cooking and preparing for the baby's naming ceremony to sit down and chat. She hands me a cup of tea. It's the only strict moray based on expediency in this lackadaisical backcountry: Guests are always and immediately served tea. It's such an important ritual that whenever I used to refuse tea, it caused uncomfortable and unnecessary haggling with my hosts, eventually persuading me to drink it in all future circumstances, whether I'm thirsty or not, just to keep the peace.

Because it's a special occasion, Sharti Devi also hands me a plate of dal pakora, a Himalayan delicacy made from ground black beans, gram flour and water, deep-fried in oil. While I eat and drink, a hundred or more flies buzz around me, whining in my ear and landing on my food or the edge of my cup whenever I pause.

Sharti Devi and Angita Devi are sister-in-laws, married to brothers who live in Delhi. Their husbands work and live on the plains because there are only a few jobs available in Pauri Garhwal: Government posts, shop keeping, teaching, jeep or bus driving, animal husbandry and small terraced farming. According to published statistics, 40% of the Garhwal population has left the mountains in order to find work on the plains or in the army. Included in this number are entire families, but it's the huge exodus of men that is most apparent: Villages are filled with women, children and the elderly. In Chandpur, the number of male head of households who have left is 47%.

Sharti Devi and Angita Devi's husbands come home four or five times a year for a few days or a week at a time to attend weddings, funerals and worship ceremonies. Every third year Angita Devi, Sharti Devi and their other sister-in-law, alternate living in Delhi for a year, to do the cooking, cleaning and child rearing. I've asked them and other women how they feel about living away from their husbands. They invariably answer with some version of the same rhetorical question, "What's there to feel? It's the way it is."

"Is anyone else coming?" I wonder aloud. The baby's naming ceremony is a necessary ritual, but not a formal one, enabling anyone to pop in any time, but there are so many of them no one would come unless they were invited or are close family members.

In her naturally soft-spoken voice Angita Devi replies, "No one else is coming."

"When Sharti Devi mentioned to me this morning the naming ceremony is today, I was surprised eleven days have already passed since your son was born!"

Angita Devi nods and smiles.

"Pungari Devi told me that years ago in Chandpur the Namakaran was held on the 21st day after a child's birth and in numerous villages it's still performed on the 21st day. And, if by chance the mother or baby are sick on the 21st day or it falls on an inauspicious day, the ceremony is postponed until the 31st day!" My voice gradually rises into an exclamation, incredulous a woman might be cooped up in a room for 31 days, leading me to my next thought, "You must be excited for the ceremony to be over so you can get back to your normal routine?"

Angita Devi smiles and gives me a barely perceivable nod. She's not much of a talker, at least with me, but she probably isn't sure how to reply to my last comment anyway. Although ordinary in my culture, it's strange in hers. Conversations about feelings are rare and this kind of introspection uncommon. Even though I know this, I can't help but assume she has an opinion about the impact the Namakaran will have on her. The naming ceremony is an imperative rite of passage enacted by all Hindus, but here in Pauri Garhwal it takes on even greater significance. From the time a child is born until the Namakaran has been performed, the mother and child are considered polluted and thus kept apart from the rest of the village. The naming ceremony, despite what its name suggests, is actually a ritual focused more on purifying the mother and child and blessing the child's future, than giving the child a name.

Living separately means different things in different villages. Chandpur is an affluent village, with many families sufficiently wealthy to have a large enough house that they can spare a room for a few weeks. Thus, many Chandpur mothers and their newborns spend those eleven days living in a separate room located in their house. To keep pollution of the room and people at a minimum, the room is prepared before childbirth and cleared of anything other people might need during the 11-day period in order that no one has to enter the room unnecessarily. If it's a bedroom, the people who normally sleep in it will remove their bedding and sleep in another room until the Namakaran is over. If the room contains anything that could potentially be contaminated by the mother and child's presence such as food grains, they are removed and stored elsewhere during the interim. After birth rituals are also done to help minimize contamination, such as dipping dubala grass in cow's urine (both sacred substances) and sprinkling the urine around the room or a new mother will drink cow's urine or symbolically touch it to her lips.

In at least half of the other villages in our district, mothers and their newborns live completely separate in their family's cowshed. Although it is a far stretch for a person from the modern world, for Garhwali women the stretch is not so far from their daily routine. They live intimately with their animals every day of their lives; bathing them at the spring, cutting their grass in the jungle, lugging jugs of water to them, cleaning their sheds and milking them twice a day. I have never had a woman tell me she couldn't do something because her child is sick, but I have had plenty of women tell me they couldn't do something because they needed to stay home to take care of a sick cow.

Living separately means more than just sleeping in a different room or in the cowshed. Except to bathe and to go to the bathroom, mothers and their newborns live the entire eleven days in their room or shed, rarely stepping outside, even into their own courtyard. A new mother is not allowed to cook or haul water for anyone other than herself, cannot eat or drink with others, nor touch or be touch by another person. She cannot pray, burn incense or go into a temple of any kind—not even within eyesight of one. On the way to go to the bathroom or to bathe, if there is a village temple (the emphasis is on 'village', as everyone has a temple in their house) located inside someone's house along the usual route, the new mother will take a different trail, even if it's longer or even if she has to blaze a new path, just to avoid being in sight of the temple. The mother and child must also bathe daily. The catch-22 is they cannot use the village's primary water source for fear they will sully it. In our village new mothers go down to the river to bathe and in villages where there is no alternative water source, other women in the extended family haul water to the mother and infant.

These confines are not completely alien to a new mother. Every time women menstruate they experience similar restrictions. Although in Chandpur they live in their normal circumstances, in some villages menstruating women live separately in the cowshed. No matter where they live, menstruating women, like new mothers, are not suppose to pray, go inside a temple, cook, or haul water, although when there are no other women in a household or all the women are menstruating at the same time, a menstruating woman is compelled to cook and haul water for her family. No one outside the family, however, would eat at her house if they knew she was menstruating, especially a person regularly possessed by a god or goddess. Contaminating them is deemed particularly inauspicious, so a menstruating woman is not allowed to go into their house either. In my immediate neighborhood that means out of seven homes, a menstruating woman cannot go into five of them.

I've asked Garhwalis why they consider new mothers, newborns and menstruating women to be polluted. They never mention bleeding as a reason. Their answers are inevitably, "It's tradition" or "Our ancestors believed they're contaminated so we do too."

"What have you been doing during the day?" I ask Angita Devi, curious how a woman who normally juggles 10 to 15 jobs a day occupies herself when she is suddenly confined to a room. Few people, if anyone, would have visited her before the Namakaran and there is no TV, no reading material and no phone to call a friend who also doesn't have a phone.

"Taking care of the baby."

"What do you do when the baby is sleeping?"

She reaches behind herself and pulls out a square patch of aqua-colored yarn with needles sticking out of it and replies, "Knit."

"What are you knitting?"

"A sweater for the baby."

When I stop asking questions, the deluge outside becomes apparent: A drone of raindrops strumming the ground; the pitter-patter on leaves; an intermittent 'splish, splash, splash, splish' of water pouring off their cement roof; and, the roar of the river filled to the brim with brown rushing water.

Sharti Devi's two teenage girls and Angita Devi's one-year old daughter burst into the room, shrieking and laughing. The former are chasing the latter around in circles.

A Baaman follows them in. He sits cross-legged on a grass mat in the middle of the floor. Also called a Brahmin, Purohit and Pandit, he's of the priestly caste, the highest caste in the Hindu hierarchy and the only caste allowed to perform most puja ceremonies. He's an ordinary looking Garhwali man, small in stature with a rail thin frame. His eyes are round, his face narrow and his slightly graying hair is cut short and parted on the side. He's wearing a loose fitting, cotton shirt down to his knees and baggy cotton pants. Both are dingy white, wrinkled and stained. Turmeric paste is splotched between his eyebrows. Stubbles on his chin reveal that it's Tuesday, the monkey-god Hanuman's day, a day many Hindus, whether Baamans or not, do not shave, cut their nails and hair, or eat meat and eggs.

Removing a roughly woven purse from around his shoulder, the Baaman takes out three verse books, a copper water vessel and a copper spoon, placing them on the floor in front of him. He orders Sharti Devi to bring him the remaining requisite puja items, rattling off their names, one after another. Since they are all typical puja supplies, Sharti Devi has already assembled most of the items in the kitchen, including leaves and flowers she and her daughters picked in the fields earlier in the morning. While she brings them into the room, the Baaman makes two geometric designs atop a four-inch high wooden stool, taking fistfuls of wheat flour and then rubbing his thumb against his fingertips, releasing a few grains at a time, methodically moving his hand back and forth over the same area, forming thicker and thicker lines. When he's finished making the lines, he fills the spaces in between with mustard-colored turmeric powder. The first yantra is a right-side-up triangle and upside-down triangle superimposed on one another and surrounded by a circle lined with lotus flower petals. The inner design, presupposed to be the Star of David in the West, always represents Ganesh, the elephant-headed god of good luck and new beginnings. The second yantra design, a rectangle with nine squares inside, represents the nine Vedic planets, a combination of planets and other important celestial bodies.

The Baaman sets a small clay bowl filled with mustard oil in the middle of the two yantras and fashions a wick by rubbing cotton fiber between his hands. He soaks it briefly in oil and then carefully lays it down in the bowl, making sure the tip hangs over the side. He grabs a fistful of cow dung from a large pile stacked in a pan beside him and plops it alongside the oil diya. Opening a box of incense, he removes all twelve sticks and sets them upright in the dung. In what looks like a giant, round cake pan, the Baaman mixes clarified butter, barley, sesame seeds and sandalwood powder. On another plate, he places a smidgeon of uncooked rice on one side and turmeric powder on the other. By the time he's finished with his preparations, all of the necessary puja items are spread out on the floor in front of him: A small bowl of yogurt, separate piles of kunjala leaves and dubala grass, turmeric powder, marigold flowers, the clarified butter, sesame seed and barley mixture, a 17-inch round brass bowl filled with rice, a square-shaped, metal container with short legs and handles and filled with splintered pine wood, a miniature copper jug filled with Ganga water and a tin, handless jug filled with cow's milk.

Signaling the start of puja, the Baaman lights the cotton wick and then, lifting the incense half way out of the dung, he squeezes their tips together and lights them as well. Their sweet fragrance quickly permeates the room, infusing me with a sense of well-being, inexplicable even to myself but not unlike the feeling elicited by a wood fire on a snowy evening.

Angita Devi picks up the bundle of blankets in which her son is wrapped and sits down on the floor beside the Baaman, setting the bundle in her lap. I sit down next to her. Sharti Devi remains in the kitchen to cook lunch, while the children play in another room.

The Baaman begins to recite Sanskrit, an ancient Indian language, used almost exclusively in religious rituals, like Latin during Catholic rituals. Angita Devi and I don't understand a word he's saying, except for when he says names of gods or well known phrases. We get the gist of what's going on, however, as the components of puja are standardized, varying only slightly depending on a Baaman's style and the focus of a particular worship.

He dips his copper spoon into holy water from the river Ganga, pours it into his cupped hand and then lets it drop to the ground. He pours the next three spoonfuls into his hand and drinks them, one at a time. The fifth and final spoonful he lifts up past his face and over his head, purposely dripping water onto himself and into his hair as he moves his hand upward. Remaining seated, he begins sprinkling water in the direction of the small stool where the yantras are and around the room, showering Angita Devi, the baby's blanket and I. Finally he turns to Angita Devi and begins putting spoonfuls of water into her cupped right hand. Having done or seen this ritual hundreds of times in her lifetime, she knows exactly what to do, mimicking the Baaman's actions without prompting, cleansing away impurities, like sins and evil forces that may interfere with puja or life, hers or her son's.

The Baaman reads from a worn puja booklet. Holding it in his left hand, he tosses, alternately, kunjala leaves, marigolds, cow's milk and curd with his right, in the direction of the Ganesh yantra. Puja invariably begins by paying homage to Ganesh, before paying tribute to several other gods. Not only because Ganesh gives boons for success in new ventures and removes life's obstacles, but also because his mother, the goddess Parvati, mandated it.

After Parvati made Ganesh from residue on her body, she told him to stand guard and not to let anyone come near while she bathed. Her husband, the god Shiv, came along and wanted to join her. Ganesh, not recognizing his new father, wouldn't let him. Shiv, not recognizing his new son, cut off Ganesh's head. When Parvati found out, she was furious and demanded Shiv fix Ganesh's head. He did, but instead of giving Ganesh his original head, he gave him an elephant head. Some people propose Ganesh's original head had been flung so far away when it was chopped off that it was lost and the only other head around was an elephant's head. Others propose the elephant head was specifically chosen for the unique qualities it represents, such as wisdom and discrimination. Regardless, after his head was replaced, Parvati wanted to make sure her son would never be taken advantage of again, so she declared his importance by mandating that all puja begin with homage to Ganesh.

When the Baaman finishes offering items, he alternately places kunjala leaves and marigolds into Angita Devi's hand, which she tosses in the direction of Ganesh's yantra whenever the Baaman points his finger towards the floor, cueing her in accordance with what he's saying in Sanskrit. Eventually he reaches a threshold—a point that seems to be reached by all Baamans during puja—when he either no longer thinks it's necessary to dole out items one at a time or just gets tired of doing it, so he pushes the remaining piles of foliage and flowers in front of Angita Devi, enabling her to help herself whenever her hands are empty. Pointing his finger again and again, the piles dwindle until depleted, coinciding with the Baaman's completion of reading passages in his booklet, 'Ganesh Puja'. In the end, half of the leaves, flowers, curd, milk and water cover the yantra and the other half lay scattered across the floor.

The Baaman starts reciting a new series of Sanskrit verses and throws rice around the room, towards us and toward the yantra, producing faint, repetitive 'pings', as they hit hard surfaces. He calls out the names of Shani Dev (Saturn god), Budh Graha (Mercury), Surya Dev (Sun god), Mangal Graha (Mars), Sukra Graha (Venus), Chandra

Dev (Moon god), Brihaspati (Jupiter), Rahu and Ketu. Astrology plays a crucial role in Garhwali's lives, determining whom they can marry, when they should start a new business, which day a holiday falls on, a person's destiny and everything else in between, so besides paying homage to the Vedic planets as gods, the prayer is also being said to appease these celestial forces; to keep them from negatively affecting the horoscopes of those of us present, especially the newborn's.

Angita Devi watches on dispassionately, her stance reflecting neither ennui nor disrespect for the necessity of ritual, merely a state of being as common here as it is rare in America. I too have seen this rite performed dozens of times before, robbing me of the excitement of the nouveau, but never rendering me disinterested. On the contrary, Garhwali rituals fascinate, mystify and ignite a fire in me, not of religious fervor but of intellectual zeal, a desire to understand the beliefs behind the ritual, to understand Garhwalis, inducing me to scour their myths and minds, painstakingly extracting bits and pieces of information because Garhwali faith precludes the need for a rationale, for philosophy. Their knowledge and insights arise from custom; traditions reaching back to revered ancestors and gods; an intimate, un-shattered, sacred bond, which I appreciate but can scarcely comprehend by virtue of being modern—prostrate to science and the future.

The Baaman periodically doles out handfuls of rice to Angita Devi, which she, in staccato back and forth hand motions, tosses in the direction of the planet yantra. Eventually he places the entire plate of rice in front of her, like he did with the leaves and flowers, for her to pick up whenever her hands are empty. She continues to offer them on cue. Just before he finishes reading his last prayer, he instructs Angita Devi to scoop up all of the remaining rice and throw it onto the planet yantra, while he reads his last line.

With the second part of puja complete, the Baaman inquires as to whether Angita Devi's mother, father and grandparents are alive or not and what their names are. She lets him know her mother is still living, but everyone else died long ago. He tells Angita Devi to quietly pray for them. While she does, he chants their names aloud in the same way he did the names of gods. He then asks about her husband's dead ancestors and calls out their names too, followed by a short five-minute reading from a prayer booklet.

Standing up, the Baaman rearranges the items spread out in front of him on the floor. The stool with yantras on it, which had been the focal point of puja until now, is set aside and the portable fireplace with pinewood stacked inside becomes the new tool for worship. Once he lights the fire, he sets the ghee, barley and sesame seed mixture and a large ladle in front of Angita Devi and resumes reciting prayers. On cue, Angita Devi scoops dollops of the mixture into the fire. As each scoop falls into the flames, the Baaman, Angita and I bellow "Swaahaa," an exclamation stated specifically when offering items in a fire, most often ghee, to the gods. We pray to the 330 million gods collectively; the 16 Devis (Goddesses); the 7 Matrikas (Mother goddesses who fought evil); Brahma, Vishnu, Mahesh (Shiv), Lakshmi and Ganesh; Nag and Nagin (male and female snake gods, respectively), Bhaironath and Narsingh Devta.

The more ghee Angita Devi drops into the fire, the more it spits and smokes. Despite the door being wide open, the top half of the room quickly fills with smoke. The three of us continue with puja, as if nothing is amiss, theirs a genuine indifference and mine feigned. Ten minutes or so later, Sharti Devi, returns to the room to check on things and opens the window shutters, creating a cross-breeze, to let fresh air in and the dense cloud out.

When the ghee mixture is exhausted, the Baaman stops reciting prayers. He quickly makes a turmeric paste by adding water to the powder he had set aside on the plate earlier. Leaning over, he applies a small circle of paste to Angita Devi's forehead between her eyebrows. At the same time, Angita Devi casts her eyes down toward the floor and raises her prayer-shaped hands chest high to receive his blessing. The Baaman picks up a few grains of rice and presses them onto her forehead, on top of the turmeric paste. Half of the grains fall into her lap, seemingly unnoticed. Angita Devi lifts the blankets, exposing her sleeping son. The Baaman applies tilak to his forehead and then to mine. He walks out the door to apply it to Sharti Devi and the other children's' foreheads as well.

The naming ceremony is over. Angita Devi is now free to interact with her family and friends: To pick up and lovingly tend to the children, to brush the teenage girls' hair or to have her hair brushed by them, to gossip at the village spring with the other women; to eat and sleep with her extended family. All activities she enjoys doing. Yet, she doesn't jump up and down with joy. She doesn't holler out, "Halleluiah!" or whisper, "Thank god!" under her breath. She doesn't give the slightest indication that she is pleased to be getting back to her normal routine, except for the almost imperceptible nod she'd given me earlier. And the thing is, it could have been Bhuri Devi, Raki Devi or any other Devi that made this transition today and the response would have been the same.

We all leave the room. On the veranda, the Baaman sits down on a burlap bag. Behind him, stuck to the wall, are two mounds of cow dung with dubala grass sticking out of them. Around each dung cake are four miniature blobs of dung arranged together in distorted, circular shapes meant to resemble a rough outline of Ganesh's image. The symbol, with or without Ganesh's outline, denotes a "happy house," representing not the occupants' state of mind, but rather suggests the house is free of evil forces.

Off to the Baaman's side, lying on the floor, is a recycled plastic bag filled with rice and a new kurta-pajama (long cotton shirt and baggy pants), part of the Baaman's payment for performing the Namakaran. There is no set fee per se, however, the usual payment includes some combination of at least one cooked meal, a set of clothes, a few kilograms of uncooked rice or flour, a shawl, sugar, fruit, lentils and money. Any amount will do, however, 11, 21, 51, 101, 201, 501 and 1001 are all auspicious numbers so donations are generally made in these denominations, although it is unlikely the Baaman will be given anything over 101 Rs. for this short ritual. During larger worship ceremonies, Baamans are given more money and more and bigger things, such as a cow.

Sharti Devi gives the Baaman a plate of garbanzo bean curry, potato and green bean curry, deep-fried unleavened bread, plain unleavened bread and Halva. Rice has also been made but Garhwalis of the Pandit caste, whether Baamans or not, do not eat rice cooked by people from outside their caste and Sharti Devi is from the Rajput caste. When I ask why the restriction is limited to rice, the explanation repeatedly cited is 'tradition'. When I pressed a man once to give me an educated guess, his opinion was, "Rice is wet and therefore dirty."

After the Baaman eats his meal, the children, the two women and I sit down on the kitchen floor to eat. The women would not normally eat with me because custom warrants they feed guests and men first, then children and then themselves. I generally keep to custom, frequently eating with the men, but I don't know this Baaman so I wait, refusing to eat until they join me.

We all dig in with our right hands, our plates resting on the bare floor. They sit in yoga posture and I on a 9" x 15" x 4" high wooden stool, like the one on which the yantra designs had been made. Normally I sit cross-legged like everyone else on the floor but, on the rare occasions someone offers me one of these stools, I take it. It's difficult for me to sit in yoga posture and eat. Garhwalis have spent their entire lives sitting on the floor in this manner, so their legs lie completely flat with their knees touching the ground, allowing them to easily lean forward over their plate of food and to sit for hours if necessary. My legs fold, but my knees waiver high off the ground, eventually breaking into a full-fledged shaking frenzy if I sit in the position too long, and since my feet are not neatly tucked under by shins, my plate sits far away, resulting in food dropping into my lap or onto the floor on the way to my mouth.

"What's the baby's name? I ask between mouthfuls.

"He hasn't been named yet."

"When will you name him?"

Angita Devi hesitates and smiles shyly. Sharti Devi jumps in to explain, "After the Baaman gives us a sound."

"Oh yeah, sure, you haven't been told yet, huh?" I respond knowingly. Although I must still frequently probe such unusual statements, asking what seems like a hundreds questions to fully understand what a person is saying, in this case I already know what Sharti Devi is talking about. Before a child is named, a Baaman consults his horoscope book to ascertain a syllable associated with the baby's exact time of birth. Once he tells the family the sound, the family comes up with an appropriate name (i.e. if a baby is born under the syllable 'RA', his or her name may become Rajendar or Rajeshwari). Sometimes when the syllable is deemed too restrictive by parents, they solve the problem by giving the child two names, the required one and a preferred one, either one becoming the child's legal name, depending on which one is written in the child's school records.

When we finish eating, I say good-bye and start for home. Angita Devi hollers out behind me, "Don't be mad!"

The parting comment used to cause me a great deal of consternation. I'd wonder what had transpired during my visit for my hosts to think I was angry, even asking them outright if something was wrong or else I'd spend our parting moments reassuring them I was happy with my visit. It took several times of people saying it and several times of me trying to set things right with my hosts before I was finally able to put the statement into its proper context. When Anita Devi says, "Don't be mad!" I hear, "Hope you had a good time!"

Roopkund is an isolated glacial lake in the snow-capped Indian Himalaya (pronounced Hĭ-maa-lāy). Along its shore lie three hundred or so well-preserved dead bodies, which can be partially seen a few months every year when the snow melts. Scientists continually study the remains, trying to determine who the people were, when they died and what caused their deaths. The latest suppositions are they died around 500 to 600 years ago, they are from two distinct ethnic groups and the cause of death was possibly blunt trauma to their skulls. Previously the skulls were believed to have been crushed after their deaths from repetitive rock avalanches in the area, however, the newest hypothesis is that baseball-size hail rained down on the group, crushing their skulls and killing them. This theory coincides with local folklore. Villagers believe the remains are of people who were on a pilgrimage in honor of Nanda Devi when they got caught up in a horrendous storm and died.

Nanda Devi is a local goddess. Her unique status as the daughter and sister of the Himalayan people is imbedded in the custom of newly married girls going off to their husband's village to live and their subsequent trips back to their native village to visit family and friends. A girl spends her entire life in intimate relationships with the same unchanging faces, rarely going outside of her own village. After marriage, she moves away to a completely new environment. The drastic transition is mitigated through multiple visits back home to her native village during her first few years of marriage. The protocol is almost always the same: A male from the girl's family goes to the girl's new village to bring her back home for a visit and later brings her back to her husband's village. An escort is essential and an invitation or visit initiated by her family is highly valued. To celebrate her visit and send her back to her husband's village with fanfare, the girl's family makes arsi (a traditional Garhwali donut made of ground rice, brown sugar, and water mixed together and deep fried) and distributes it to fellow villagers on the day she leaves. In addition, to insure a daughter will be allowed by her husband and in-laws to come visit again, as well as to keep good relations between the two families, after every visit, a daughter is sent back to her husband's village with 5 Kg of arsi, 30 Kg of rice or wheat, and, if her husband's family is poor, clothes for the children and money.

These visits to one's native village are cherished, so when Nanda Devi got married and didn't go back to her native village to visit family and friends, she felt alone and lonely and languished in her predicament. She had gone to live with her husband, Shiv, a major god in the Hindu trilogy, on Mount Kailash, an uninhabited mountain located deep in the Himalaya. Shiv was often busy saving the world or meditating and, contrary to custom, Nanda Devi's family neither sent Nanda Devi an invitation to return home nor did anyone come to visit her.

Meanwhile, Nanda Devi's family back home was having troubles of its own. There was no money. Family members fell ill. Storms raged. The water source dried up and crops failed. To find out the cause of their plight, Nanda Devi's mother, Menavati, went to a Baaman and asked him why they were experiencing so many problems. The priest told her calamity had struck because her daughter, Nanda Devi, is homesick. When Menavati arrived back home, she told her family what the Baaman had said. Heet, Nanda

Devi's brother, took off straight away for Mt Kailash. The trail was overgrown from lack of use, requiring him to hack his way through the brush with his sword. Upon reaching Mt Kailash, he escorted Nanda Devi back to her native village. She was overjoyed. Water started flowing in her family's spring again. Everyone's health was restored. Crops were bountiful and the dreadful storms ended.

Every twelve years tens of thousands of pilgrims reenact taking Nanda Devi back to her husband's abode after her historic visit to her native village. It's a 280-kilometer roundtrip trek through numerous villages to the shrine of Nanda Devi at lake Homekund on Trishul Mountain. The pilgrims are accompanied by an idol of Nanda Devi adorned in jewels and a four-horned ram as far as the lake, where the ram is let go to continue the rest of his journey to Mt Kailash alone. The event is known as the Nanda Devi Raj Jat.

The pilgrims caught in the storm at Roopkund were on a similar journey. The King of Kannauj, a city on the Indian plains, decided to make a pilgrimage in Nanda Devi's honor. He brought a huge entourage with him, including his pregnant wife, servants, dancers and musicians. When they reached Roopkund, they should have dropped Nanda Devi off to continue the journey to Mt Kailash on her own. The King, however, wanted to go further and insisted everyone continue traveling with him, including his wife, his newborn (born during the trip), the musicians and the dancers. Newborns and their mothers are considered polluted until the appropriate time period has passed and puja has been completed and musicians and dancers were strictly forbidden to go beyond Roopkund, so as the troupe trekked passed the lake, Nanda Devi became angry at the King's lack of respect for propriety, creating a horrendous storm, killing everyone at Roopkund in its wake.

Nanda Devi first arrived in our area of the Himalaya several generations ago in the hands of a man from Kuransi, a village five kilometers from Chandpur. He had gone on a trip to Chamoli district where Nanda Devi's native village is. While walking along a river, he found a butcher knife called a thamolo and brought it back to Kuransi. During the next big worship ceremony in Kuransi, Nanda Devi possessed someone and started to dance. She explained to everyone who she is and how she had come from Chamoli with the knife. Since then Kuransi villagers have worshipped Nanda Devi. They built a temple in her honor, in which the knife was placed and can still be seen today.

Every year Kuransi villagers commemorate Nanda Devi's birthday, Nandastami. Sometimes they observe it quietly with nine days of private puja for the families who share Nanda Devi as their deity. Other years these same families host a huge fair in which hundreds of people from villages all around Kuransi honor Nanda Devi through puja, dance, and sport. Whether it's a quiet event or a fair depends on what Kuransi families and their Baamans deem is best for the well being of their families, what Nanda Devi dictates and on practical matters such as having enough money to host a big celebration. Roughly speaking, the fair is held every three years.

This year Nanda Devi's birthday is celebrated with a fair on September 12th (the dates of Nanda Devi's birthday and all other Garhwali religious events change every year according to changing astrological conditions). Throughout the morning, people arrive in Nouta village stuffed in, on top of and hanging out from behind commercial jeeps and buses. From Nouta a trail wanders down to the river and up the next mountain to Kuransi, a large village of over 100 families spread out over the entire upper hillside. Today the trail is packed with one continuous line of people, stretching from the road a full kilometer up the steep hill to the top of the village where the fair is being held.

Directly in front of me is a girl in her late teens or early twenties. When she first discovers I'm behind her, she frequently glances back at me with a wide-eyed, darting look of alarm, as if she thinks I might sneak up behind her and attack. Each time she looks my way I smile, trying to alleviate her fear. She has obviously never seen me or any other foreigner before. She's wearing a black velvet choker inlaid with eight squares of gold and intricately carved dangling gold earrings, announcing her recent marriage and, because many villagers living along the road system have given up this traditional style necklace for an all gold one, it also gives her away as someone from a remote village.

When she finally decides I'm not a threat, she smiles back. During the next stretch of the trail, she and her woman companion stare at and talk unabashedly about me. The other woman is quite a bit older, maybe 40 or 45 years old, and not quite as wary as the younger woman. She's totting a basket on top of her head and, despite turning around at least a dozen times to look at me, sometimes swiftly, it's never necessary for her to reach her hand up to balance it. Inside the basket is rice and bananas she's brought to donate to Nanda Devi. Almost everyone coming to the fair will donate something: Flowers, fruit, rice, incense, cheap jewelry or 10 rupees. In return, they'll receive a blessing of tilak in between their eyebrows. Although donated items are later distributed to the people in Kuransi hosting the program and Kuransi villagers apply the tilak, the donations are to Nanda Devi and the tilak is a blessing from Nanda Devi.

Three-fourths of the way up the hill my friends and I, tired and sweating, step off the trail into a courtyard where an elderly woman is pounding rice. Although she's a stranger, we know warm Garhwali hospitality means she won't feel in the least put out if we ask her for a glass of water and Garhwali's penchant for socializing just about guarantees she'll be delighted we've stopped to chat. She gives us each a glass of icy cold, spring water and jumps into conversation as if we're old friends, informing us that she intends to roast the rice she's pounding to make a snack called khaajaa. She and several other Kuransi villagers have made or are in the process of making several special treats for Nanda Devi's birthday: Wheat seeds soaked in water until they sprout and are then roasted and pressed into balls; roasted barnyard millet; unleavened wheat bread made with brown sugar and fried in oil; wheat halva (wheat, clarified butter and sugar cooked with dried fruits); and arsi. Because they're made in honor of Nanda Devi, all of the treats are blessed food, so although the families of the women and girls who make the treats will eat some of the treats themselves, they're making them primarily to distribute at the end of the fair to the people who become possessed by gods or goddesses. The only exception is arsi. It is reserved for those possessed by Nanda Devi only and for guests who are in-laws of Kuransi villagers, both gestures in the spirit of giving arsi to one's daughter to take back to her husband's village.

The old woman turns to me and asks if I remember her. I don't, so she reminds me, "You and I danced together during the last Nanda Devi festival!" And then good-naturedly adds, "People have been teasing me ever since!"

We head up the hill and within ten minutes arrive at the courtyard where the fair is being held. It's a typical courtyard made of huge slabs of rock inlaid in mud, but unusual because of its large size, 100 ft long by 30 ft wide. The house is also huge and remarkable. Its most striking feature is the elaborate woodcarvings covering most of its façade: Ornate swirling designs and geometric shapes, lotus flowers and elephants. Built 150 years earlier by a wealthy government administrator stationed in Kuransi, the architecture is also unique, influenced by British occupation at the time. It has only one door, which leads to a spacious courtyard inside, from where the multiple rooms are entered. A wooden stairway and balcony wraps around the entire courtyard, providing access to the second floor.

Propped up against the front of the house and spread out in a semi-circle are eight elderly Garhwalis sitting cross-legged on the ground, their foreheads plastered with turmeric paste and rice. Amongst them is a man named Amman Prasad Sundriyal. He lives with his wife, his four sons and their wives and his grandchildren in a house located not even fifteen yards from where he's sitting. He looks haggard. A Nanda Devi prayer session lasted all night last night, so he probably didn't get much sleep, but it's more than just being tired. Amman is always casual about his appearance: He's unshaved; his huge, black plastic, eyeglass frames have been broken and taped in the same three places since I met him four years ago; he's wearing a dingy white Nehru cap and tattered, mismatched clothing; and his bare feet are gnarled, making him look more like someone living on skid row than the highly respected Devi/Devta Baaman that he is.

Amman performs almost exclusively a special worship ceremony known as Devi/Devta Puja (goddess/god Worship Ceremony). It's different from all other Hindu worship ceremonies in that Garhwali is spoken and the puja's primary aim is to invite gods and goddesses to attend the ceremony—or another way of putting it is gods and goddesses are the ceremony. The hallmark of god's presence is possession. Possession is when a Devi (goddess) or Devta (god) enters a person's body, creating a trance state in the person, expressing themselves through conversation and 'dance' (repetitive, stereotypical and often dynamic movements). Dancing or talking done by a possessed person is recognized as actions by the gods themselves, not the possessed person. Nanda Devi's birthday celebration includes a series of these Devi/Devta Pujas, particularly but not exclusively, for Nanda Devi, her husband and her brothers. Without their presence, worship would be incomplete, like an honored guest not showing up for the festivities. Conversely, the more possessions that occur during the ceremony, the happier god is and the better the outcome of puja will be.

Spread out in front of Amman are sacred items and tools of the Devi/Devta Puja trade: A container of cow's urine and one of cow's milk, a brass pie-pan with two separate mounds of rice and turmeric inside, incense, a drum and two drum sticks, a bronze torte-like pan, wood charcoal in a brass ladle, Ganga water in a copper vessel, a copper spoon and a goat-hair blanket. He folds the roughly woven blanket in half and lays it in front of himself. He shapes gummy incense into a cone, lights it and sets it down in the brass pie pan, alongside the mounds of rice and turmeric. As Amman sprinkles Ganga water, milk and cow's urine around the blanket and over the people sitting nearby, he chants aloud. First he appeals to ghosts, any and all ghosts, not to disrupt the ceremony by possessing people. He then offers prayers to Bhoomi Dev (god of land), asking him to bless the blanket and surrounding area. While he prays, Amman places small piles of rice and turmeric paste at the four corners of the blanket and, after he has the barely lit wood-coals replaced with fresh hot coals from someone's fireplace, he moves the coal-filled ladle in circles over the blanket, wafting smoke above it and into our faces. During his incantations, Amman recites the names of a variety of gods, inviting them to the ceremony. He mentions supreme gods first such as Shankar (Shiv), Narayana (Vishnu) and Bhagwan (Krishna), followed by Nanda Devi and her four brothers: Ghandiyaal, Heet, Binsar and Latu. Dozens of more names ensue. By the time he's finished, he has recited the names of every single Devi/Devta who possesses any of the hundreds of people present at the fair—information Amman inevitably knows.

Amman picks up his dhonr (a small hourglass-shaped drum made of goatskin and wood, with numerous small bells fastened inside its concave sides), thumps it a few times to test its resonance and then, setting it in his lap, begins to play, smacking the left side with his hand and striking the right with a stick. A man seated next to Amman joins in, playing Amman's khansi-kee-thali. Made of bronze, it looks like a torte pan, is held like a tambourine and beat with a drumstick. Together they play a fast repetitive rhythm, reminiscent of a drum roll. Periodically Amman belts out a line or two of song.

Gods can show up at any time for inexplicable reasons, but normally it happens during a religious ceremony and in a place expressly prepared for their presence. A sanctified area is both an invitation to gods and goddesses to come to puja, as well as the perfect environment for them to talk and dance. One of the other main triggers of possession is the hypnotic beating of the drum and khansi-kee-thali. Sometimes, however, purifying the environment and strumming are not enough to get Devi/Devtas to show up, so Baamans use a series of strategies to coax them into coming. They sprinkle more cows' urine, cow's milk or Ganga water around to ensure the sanctity of an area. They tell stories about gods who they know possess people in the audience, using themes of sadness or courage to create emotion in the listener. They taunt people in the audience who regularly get possessed or taunt the gods who possess them. If all else fails, they bring out their special beat-it-out-of-him Devi/Devta tool. It looks like a medieval torture device; a short-handled iron rod with three one-foot long chains attached, each chain containing a dozen or less iron pieces that look like thick fishing weights, connected together by iron links. Baamans whack people with it as a last ditch effort to elicit Devi/Devta possessions. It usually works.

It didn't take much to get this Nanda Devi crowd possessed though. Many of them have attended days of Devi/Devta puja leading up to Nanda Devi's birthday; the first puja occurring nine days before Nandastami on the blackest night of the month, an auspicious day to begin activities, and again on the seventh, fifth and third day before Nandastami, and from the third day on, puja has been held every day, including all night last night. Consequently, many of the participants have been in and out of possession for days, putting them into dazed holding patterns in-between pujas.

A 50-something-year-old man sitting in yoga position next to me is one of them. He's dressed in a gray woolen vest and pants, both completely covered in turmeric paste, as are his face, hands, hair and feet. His bloodshot eyes are glazed over. He's chain smoking bedi cigarettes, holding them as if he's smoking a chilam (a straight clay hash pipe held in cupped hands close to the mouth). Although this style of smoking is not totally unusual, the fact he's doing it during Devi/Devta Puja, the repetitive nature of his smoking, his exaggerated puffing style that creates smoke clouds all around him and a body covered in turmeric paste, all suggest he's possessed by Shiv, Nanda Devi's husband. Shiv's known for indulging in chilam smoking and covering his body in ashes.

Kitty corner from me sits a woman in her 80's with a cherubic face and two remarkable features. One is her jewelry. She's wearing a thick, round, elaborately carved choker made of pure silver and 25 or 30 silver large hoops lining her ears. The latter are so heavy they make her ears droop forward. The other feature is she's as close to the living dead as is humanly possible. She never moves, not even twitch, and never makes a peep. Her face is expressionless and plastered with turmeric paste, including her eyeglasses, which she obviously can't see through, but what's even more noteworthy is it seems as if she doesn't know that she can't see.

Two women in their late thirties or early forties suddenly appear, dropping onto the blanket on their hands and knees. They murmur, mutter and moan, dancing in unison, raising their fists high up into the air and slamming them back down onto the ground. Each time their hands move upward, reaching toward the sky, their heads flop back and then jerk forward again, almost hitting the blanket when their fists come down to the ground. One of the women has let her hair down and applied oil to it and to her face. This is stereotypical of the goddess Kali. Even without the oil as a clue to her identity, the woman's hair is uncannily reminiscent of Kali's hair: Black, waist-long and incredibly full. Her vigorous movements cause her sari to fall down from her shoulders. She either doesn't notice or doesn't care, so while she moves up and down a woman sitting nearby wraps the sari back around her and tucks it into itself to prevent it from falling again.

The woman with Kali is ghastly thin and her teeth rotted and narrow. Her hair had been pulled back into a ponytail at some point, but numerous strands have escaped the rubber band and now stick out helter-skelter. Her eyes are closed. She's making movements similar to Kali, but her head tends to rock back and forth while it moves up and down, causing her head to hit Kali's shoulder several times. Neither appears to notice. They repeat their same movements about twenty times until both suddenly fall backwards, as if they've lost their balance, and, catching themselves with one hand, they stand up and stagger away still in trance.

A middle-aged man who's sitting along the edge of the blanket starts hopping up and down while seated cross-legged. Although there are several of us sitting near him, he never makes eye contact, despite looking directly at us. He hops in place for a few minutes and then, while still seated in yoga position, hops away using his hands to propel himself forward. Nanda Devi's brother, Heet, does this stereotypical movement.

Besides possessed people coming onto the blanket to dance, there's a score of possessed people dancing in the sanctified area stretching from where Amman is sitting to 20 feet in front of him, collectively promenading around and around in one large circle.

Two old women dawdle together; slightly twisting their bodies this way and that, faintly bowing in every direction they turn, giving the impression they're in no hurry to go anywhere and don't know where they're going anyway. Draped over their heads, hanging down alongside their faces, are plain white dishcloths, which they rub back and forth through their hair. These ladies are possessed by Nanda Devi. She likes to place cloth (usually her sari end or long neck scarf) over her head, as well as rub her hands through her hair.

Dressed in a white dhoti (cotton sheet worn by men and tied between the legs) and a long, cotton shirt stained with turmeric, a man in his 70's, a Mahatma Gandhi look-alike, moseys around the circle, sluggishly moving his torso up and down. He smiles, dances and moseys for an hour non-stop. In his right hand, he's carrying an iron rod, one end razor sharp and pointed toward the sky. He's barely moving so the rod hardly seems like a dangerous weapon, but several times while he's dancing his more rambunctious, possessed companions hug him passionately, causing him to sway uncontrollably and consequently his rod too. The god Heet possesses him. The rod represents the sword Heet used to bushwhack a path to Nanda Devi's house on Mt. Kailash. It can be seen towering above the rooftops of village homes in which there's a Heet temple.

A woman in her early thirties appears to be the youngest person possessed. Her hands are clasped on the crown of her head, while her upper body gently sways from side to side. She's not responding to anything going on around her, not even when a possessed 35-year old man dashes into the circle from the un-possessed audience, pushing and shoving her and everybody else in his way. He moves across the sanctified area and about four feet away from the Devi/Devta blanket takes a flying leap, landing on top of the unsuspecting people sitting in front of it. Amman glances at the guy over the top of his glasses, continuing to play his drum uninterrupted. The people he slammed down on top of give him dirty looks while rolling him off their bodies. The man ignores the visual cues and squirms back on top of them. He is trying to get to the blanket, the most sanctified place for gods to dance, but he's pushed away again. This time he leaps into a standing position and runs off. He gets about 20 feet away before he's tackled to the ground by a couple of fellow villagers. They hold him down for a moment and then lead him away.

A neighbor of mine from Chandpur is shuffling half-heartedly around the circle. She's obviously not possessed. For one, she normally dances ardently when she's possessed by Nanda Devi and secondly, if she was possessed she wouldn't acknowledge me, which she does. She smiles wryly and rolls her eyes up and back, as if her and I are standing across the room from each other at a party and she's telling me with her facial expression that she's bored stiff. A man clutching a tray of cheap beaded necklaces, glass bangles, and assorted rings donated by attendees, approaches her and places a necklace around her neck. He then spends the next several minutes trying to squeeze too small of bracelets onto her wrists. She finally picks the right size bracelet off the tray and puts it on by herself. Whenever Nanda Devi dances, whether it's at this festival or any other time, the devout adorn her with necklaces and bracelets, even their own highly valued jewelry, and give her brothers rings.

One young man with brown bushy hair sticking wildly out in all directions is dressed in a thin white pajama pant and turmeric paste. His bared chest is shockingly hairy. He jumps up and down like a pogo stick with his arms raised, flat palms toward the sky. This too is one of

Nanda Devi's brother's conventional dancing styles, either Ghandiyaal or Binsar.

Donning a Nehru cap, kurta-pajama and a gray vest with a Nehru collar, a stout man with a broad smile traipses around the circle singing songs. He's carrying a plate of turmeric paste and rice, smearing handfuls of it across anyone's forehead he can, the possessed and un-possessed alike. Reaching out, he blesses me as well.

During my first year in Chandpur, I probably would have found god possessions bizarre, assumed villagers were under the influence of some kind of drug or written the ritual off as primitive nonsense, categorically interpreting the possessions using psychological models, for lack of a better paradigm, but I was not privy to these kinds of cultural secrets in the early days. I don't think it was a conscious effort by anyone to keep me out and I was certainly doing what I could to be involved, it's just the way the culture unfolded itself, a slow evolution which has made me wonder on more than a few occasions how Cultural Anthropologists do their work in a mere year, without a pre-existing language base or intimacy?

There are potentially as many different possessions as there are gods and goddesses and potentially as many gods and goddesses as there are people—even more. The number of potential gods extrapolates because many gods come in multiple forms. According to Amman, there are 33 different Narsinghs just in our immediate locale, not including the rest of Pauri Garhwal, let alone all of India or the world. In Hindu holy books, it's written that there are 330 million gods. Modern Hindus say this number is a metaphor for god living inside all animate things. Garhwalis tell me there are 330 million gods.

There are personal gods, family gods and clan gods. These Devi/Devtas are both well-known gods from the Hindu pantheon and local Himalayan gods, the latter are often Hindu gods with local names, albeit not always. They come in all guises, from the fearful nature of Kachyaa to the pleasant nature of Dudh Dhari Narsingh and everything else in between. Some gods are multifaceted like Nanda Devi, who is primarily a benevolent goddess, yet prone to bouts of wrath.

Today gods and goddesses are called forth to honor Nanda Devi on her birthday, so the focus is on dance and celebration. Otherwise, Devi/Devtas other favorite activity is to talk, and these gods and goddesses were unquestionably talking up a storm during the nine days of puja leading up to Nandastami. Devi/Devta puja is essentially a way of keeping in touch with the gods. It allows villagers to find out what the gods are thinking, as well as what needs to be done to keep them pleased and it's the gods' way of connecting with people, letting them know what's on their minds.

Gods talk to anyone: The possessed person, someone else or a whole group of people. Their specialty is pointing out problems and telling people what they must do to get rid of them. Sometimes the problem is known such as an illness, conflict or poverty. And the superficial cause of the problem is known—you're poor because no one in your family has a paying job, but besides these practical factors (and Astrology), the underlying cause of all Garhwali's problems is god is displeased. No one has a job because god is angry. A Devi/Devta, through a possessed person, clarifies why he or she is disgruntled. Although the reasons could potentially be anything, usual causes are lack of prayer, a curse, a dead relative or conflict with others.

Sometimes a person isn't aware there's a problem, so it's the Devi/Devta's job to inform them. During one family puja in Chandpur, the family god Narsingh possessed an elderly woman. Narsingh told everyone present that they were performing family puja together, as if there was unity between them, but in fact, there was no genuine unity between the three nuclear families attending. He told them puja couldn't and wouldn't be fruitful without a heartfelt bond. Upon hearing this, the Baaman took a container filled with holy Ganga water and moved it in clockwise circles over the heads of each person in the three nuclear families, down to the youngest grandchild. Then the eldest male from each family took turns drinking the holy water. The elders assured Narsingh they were united in their relationship and in their prayers to him by verbally telling him so and by pulling a few rupees out of their pockets, touching it to one another's hands and then placing them on the small temporary altar in front of them, essentially becoming a donation to the Baaman, an act accruing kudos with god.

Problems are never solved. They're cured. The cure is often determined and related to a person by a Devi/Devta during possession. This advice is always followed if possible, usually according to a Baaman's interpretation. If a Devi/Devta does not tell a person how to cure his or her problem, the person asks a Baaman or a Soothsayer what the remedy is. Cures vary widely, but always include puja ceremonies, and often include some combination of fasting (which means restricted food intake, not no food), goat or chicken sacrifice, tantra-mantra (folk rituals), making amends in relationships, building a temple or, if it's already built, purifying its contents by washing them in the Ganga (a sacred river).

If Devi/Devtas don't show up in the form of possession, it means something is wrong and god is unhappy. The corollaries are the puja being performed will not bear fruition and god is not watching over and taking care of his flock. Sometimes gods do stop possessing: Personal gods come and go. Family and clan gods, however, always come back to possess someone. Who these gods initially possessed within a family or clan and why is unknown because the first possessions happened so many generations ago, but since their arrival, they've stayed. Although they can possess several people, more often than not they possess the same person repeatedly until the person dies. After their death, they possess someone else—if not in this generation, then in the next.

I ask a Garhwali man what would happen if Devi/Devtas didn't show up and possess people. He retorts, "It's a moot question. They've always come and they'll always come." I push him for an answer, emphasizing the question is hypothetical. He thinks about it for a moment and then he says, "It would be the end of Garhwali culture."

A mere 25 feet from where the Devi/Devtas are dancing, men and women who are not possessed dance to the lively beat of contemporary Garhwali songs. Thirty boys and men swarm together like bees, bouncing off of one another's bodies as they half-dance, half-saunter around in a circle, their arms raised and wrists twisting in the air. A few men are drunk, predictably leading to a scuffle; one man takes a swing at another. It is short-lived, as others jump into the fracas and pull the two apart. Away from the rowdier male crowd, a handful of women stroll around in a uniform circle, dipping their bodies low and moving their arms as if they're doing the breaststroke in mid-air. At center stage is the band; two men playing drums and one playing an 18-key child's piano.

A murmur rumbles through the crowd, informing everyone the swayamvar, an old time competition for the bride, will begin soon. Music and dance programs come to a halt shortly thereafter. Kuransi men haul off the repository of donated items that have been stored next to the swayamvar pole; numerous burlap bags overflowing with rice, rupee notes, bananas, flowers, cucumbers, ears of corn, jewelry and other odds and ends. A couple of Kuransi men wielding wooden clubs try to split the courtyard crowd apart to make room for the upcoming procession. There's nowhere for us to go. We stand wall-to-wall people on the courtyard. A few people have the luxury of sitting on the balconies, rooftop or in nearby trees, but most people on the side slope are standing, crammed together like us on the courtyard. The only way to make more room is to squeeze closer together, which we do.

The perpetually smiling Gandhi look-alike who'd carried the iron rod when he danced leads the procession. His demeanor has completely changed. He's now solemn and serious, rapidly waving a twig with a small piece of red cloth tied to one end back and forth in front of him, clearing the air of demons, ghosts and curses. Two women follow him, both sporting sprigs of barley in their hair, identifying them as people who've become possessed during the fair. Barley, besides being grown for animal fodder, is a 'pure' substance, its sprigs used during puja ceremonies and holidays such as Basant Panchami, to denote happiness, bountiful crops, and sanctity.

Behind the women is another man swishing a stick, this time with a small patch of white cloth attached to it. Behind him is the Kuransi Headman who also happens to be one of the patriarchs hosting the fair. His head and body are covered with a wool blanket, as are the smoking wood charcoals he's bearing in a metal pan. It's a mystery how he can see. Seven or eight young men follow him; each carrying brass bowls on their heads containing offerings to Nanda Devi: Incense, sweets and jewelry. A thin white cloth is draped over their heads and the bowls, covering the entire upper part of their bodies, leaving only their legs clearly visible and making them look like a white caterpillar with black, spindly legs.

At the tail end of the parade is a man carrying a bhankour, a musical instrument in the shape of a long, 3-inch diameter, copper pipe, which gradually widens into a large mouth, similar to the horns most people associate with Bhutan monks. This one is 3 ½ feet long, however, some are as long as six feet and in other districts of the Himalaya they are curved like saxophones. These instruments are played exclusively for special pujas, customarily reserved for and kept inside a clan deity's temple. Oddly, this man is neither playing it nor attempting to play it.

The silent procession promenades around a pole in the middle of the courtyard, purifying and sanctifying the area for the marriage competition, locally called the Patti Lutane. The pole towers a staggering 30 to 35-feet high. Kuransi villagers had cut down a shorter, more practical tree but while they were setting it up in the courtyard yesterday it fell and broke in half. The replacement was hurriedly cut down last night, stripped it of its bark and branches and hauled from the forest on young men's shoulders. This morning, sacred kunjala branches were wrapped around the entire pole and ears of corn and fat local cucumbers were sporadically affixed to the branches, prior to planting it in a deep hole and securing it with compacted dirt.

After several uneventful revolutions, the procession heads back across the courtyard from where they came. The club-wielding Kuransi men in charge of crowd control push us back from the tree once again, triggering a mad dash by young men toward the pole. A dozen or more cluster together at the bottom, only three or four actually manage to mount it. As they begin to shimmy upward, the men still standing on the ground seize their shirts and pant legs to prevent them from climbing further or, when possible, pull them all the way back down to the ground. Those who cling to their position find themselves being clambered over by the men below, who use them as ladders, scrambling up their legs and over their backs to reach higher positions on the pole. It's a futile tactic. The men they've just climbed over grab their leg, foot or any other body part and drag them back down the pole. Everyone's goal is to retrieve a cloth bundle from the top of the tree. Inside are several items for Nanda Devi: A gold wedding necklace, roasted rice, roasted wheat, arsi, bindi, incense, sindhor and bracelets. Whoever reaches the bundle first is declared Nanda Devi's husband and given 11 Rs. (25 cents) and a basket of arsi.

Eventually one young man breaks away, out of reach of the others. At times the cucumbers and corn help him to move higher up the pole, but just as often they're a hindrance, requiring him to stop, pick the vegetable off the pole and toss it to the cheering crowd before climbing higher. A grin takes up half of his face, no doubt reflecting a reasonable assumption that he'll reach the prize before anyone else since he's out of reach of the other men, still battling amongst themselves. He gets about fifteen feet off the ground when two middle-aged men, who had been sitting on the roof of the house watching his ascent, leisurely get up and grab a couple of buckets they had filled earlier in the day with a mixture of water, cooking oil and soapy shampoo lather made from the sap of a Bhyunl tree. Towering above the aspiring young man ascending the pole, they take turns hurling the mixture on top of him, drenching his whole body. He clings desperately to the pole, but the kunjala branches have also been saturated with the slick substance, so they, along with the young man, slide down the pole in slow motion, all the way to the bottom where his waiting comrades mercilessly yank him off the pole.

The bottom half of the pole up to a height of fifteen feet is now completely bare and slippery. The hapless group of men can't even grasp the pole, let alone scale it. A few men take breaks and are replaced by other men fresh for the challenge. Others change from their shorts into jeans and long pants, believing heavier material will help them cling to the pole better. They climb a few feet up the trunk only to slip back down just as easily as everyone else. Most of the young men don't give up, however. Instead, they become fighting mad: Tempers flare, shirts and pants rip and slugging fellow competitors becomes the new tactic.

Their rambunctious pushing and pulling movements cause the upper part of the pole to sway back and forth. My friends and I head to the far side of the courtyard in case it's necessary to escape a falling tree. We no sooner arrive at our new position when we spy a dozen or more wooden clubs flailing in the air, mercilessly hitting competitors on the pole, as well as the men gathered around its base. The crowd surges backward. The people standing along the edge where we'd been standing a couple minutes earlier fall ten feet into the field behind them. Being hardy Garhwalis, no one appears to be hurt. Even though our new place is safer, we too have to scramble up a nearby steep slope and cling to its precarious angle. Luckily the crowd stops moving as quickly as it had started. Clubbing, however, continues.

Half of the clubs belong to overzealous friends who are clubbing their climbing friend's competitors. Crowd control people are wielding the remaining clubs, hitting the overzealous friends to get them to stop clubbing climbers and to get them away from the base of the pole. Amazingly, the contestants who are being clubbed keep trying to scale the pole, ignoring the thumping they're getting, as if they're being hit by spongy snurf bats. About ten minutes after the clubbing began, it stops. Beating each other with fists, pulling each other down off the pole and climbing over each other persists.

Finally, 45 minutes into the competition, a new young man jumps onto the pole and scales it at incredible speed. It all happens so fast that his fellow competitors miss the chance to grab him and hold him back, leaving them dumbfounded and the audience astounded as he climbs higher and higher. His climbing technique is unique compared to the other men's style, who all hug the pole with their arms and legs and shimmy up by reaching their hands up above their bodies, grabbing the pole and lifting the rest of their body with their arm strength, the way most of us would climb up a pole. The new young man, however, squeezes only his thighs against the pole, stretching the rest of his legs out horizontally into the air and, although his hands are holding onto the tree, his whole body leans back to arms length. In this half-laying down position, he hops up the pole.

By the time the men on the roof throw the soapy, oily water on him, he's already reached the kunjala branches higher up on the tree, giving him something to hold onto. Coupled with his technique, it keeps him from slipping down. He climbs higher than the roof and sits upright, throwing corn and cucumbers to the throng below. The crowd goes wild: Whooping, clapping and whistling. Even his fellow competitors are cheering him on.

The boy is exceptionally poised, obviously unafraid. A rumor circulates that he's an electrician's helper and, having no machines, trucks or ladders to hoist him up electrical poles, he scales them the old fashioned way. When he starts to climb higher, the men on the roof caution him not to. The tree trunk narrows significantly halfway up, making the upper part of the tree unsteady and implausible for any one to make it to the top without it breaking. The men assure him he's the winner and then solicit his help to secure two ropes to the trunk for them to use as support when they take the tree down. After the young man ties the ropes to the tree, he sits there soaking up the limelight for another five minutes or so before coming back down to the ground. His peers pick him up and parade him around the courtyard on their shoulders.

Nandastami is over. People begin walking home. Kuransi men have the arduous task of taking down the pole, a slow, inch-by-inch undertaking. The ropes the young man had secured to the trunk are used in the initial stages of leaning the tree sideways and then shorter tree poles, lashed together to form v-shaped supports during the raising of the tree, bear the weight of the tree as it gets closer to the ground. About thirty-minutes pass before the tree is removed from the ground. A man hurriedly places a black female goat inside the hole left behind. Another man just as quickly grabs the nape of her neck and chops off her head with two whacks of his butcher knife. The empty hole is a "messenger of death," so the goat is sacrificed and its blood dripped into the hole to purify it and please Nanda Devi. The goat is then partially roasted over an open fire and distributed to Kuransi villagers as blessed food.

Meena sits quietly composed. There are no tears, no smiles, no nervous laughter; not a hint of the monumental changes she'll experience in the coming days. Sitting next to her is her future husband, Sandeep, a man she's never met before. Even now, as they sit side by side, they haven't really seen each other. The bride's eyes are cast downward and her face shrouded in a crimson scarf trimmed with billowing gold fringe and the groom's gaze is set stiffly ahead and partially hidden by strands of fake marigolds hanging down from his shimmering turban.

They look like a King and Queen out of an old Omar Shariff movie. Meena, radiant in a flowing pomegranate red sari embroidered with gold thread, is extravagantly adorned as the goddess Lakshmi. On her head is a gold-plated tiara with delicate strands draped across her forehead. A 3-inch diameter gold hoop is strung through her nose and supported by a chain wrapped around her ear. Bell-shaped gold earrings dangle alongside her face and a broad, intricately designed gold choker is fastened around her neck. Twenty or more red and amber-colored glass bangles run up and down both arms, clinking every time she moves. Diminutive silver chains hang around her ankles and two silver bands decorate her toes. In addition to the jewelry, Meena's lips and nails are painted cherry red, her eyes outlined in thick black kajal, and her hands and feet stained with mehindi (ochre-colored ink drawn in swirling designs).

Sandeep is no less dazzling. He's wearing a canary yellow western style shirt and pants, with a slightly softer yellow waistcoat. His sockless feet are dressed in brand new white plastic shoes. Garlands of fresh marigolds and ten rupee notes hang around his neck down to his waist, the latter fanning out in all directions, suggesting a man of wealth. His fingers are adorned with multiple rings: A solid gold engagement ring, a moonstone set in silver, a topaz set in gold and a piece of a black stallion's horseshoe fashioned into a band—the last three rings, dictated by horoscope, ameliorate life's trials and tribulations, as well as Sandeep's character flaws. To top off his outfit, he's wearing black eyeliner, red lipstick and a heavy coat of face make-up.

Sandeep's father found Meena through a friend of a friend who lives in Meena's village. The friend played the role of matchmaker, imparting cursory information about Meena to Sandeep's father and about Sandeep to Meena's father. At 18, Meena was of marriageable age and capable of doing the house and farm work she was needed for and Sandeep, at 28 years old and holding down a job, was deemed a suitable husband. Since their castes and sub-castes were well matched, Meena and Sandeep's horoscopes were taken to a Baaman to find out if the two of them and their families would be compatible. The Baaman determined they would be, so an engagement party was set up through intermediaries.

Sandeep could have gone to the party to meet his bride-to-be but, like most grooms, he opted not to go. Instead, his father, the Baaman and a few of his father's close friends and clan members went to the party. Sandeep's father brought a box of laddu (a sweet) for Meena's family and a sari and a choker made of gold for Meena. Meena's family gave Sandeep a gold ring and a set of clothes and gave his family a water pot, a dough-kneading pan, a large gunnysack filled with rice and 501 rupees ($11.13). During the engagement party, Meena and her Baaman prayed. Sandeep's father and his entourage drank tea and ate sweets. Afterwards, they were plied with whiskey and snacks until a feast for them and Meena's fellow villagers was served. By the end of the evening, Sandeep's father and Meena's father, along with their respective Baamans, decided on a wedding date according to auspicious days and everyone's schedules. It was set for eleven months later.

After climbing straight up hill for an hour, I arrive at the bridegroom's village, Bijoli. It's a collection of a couple dozen mud and rock, mostly two-storied homes and lacks basic conveniences: There's no electricity, no roads, no nearby water source, no school and no marketplace. What it lacks in amenities, however, it makes up for with warm hospitality. Seemingly the whole village has turned out to say 'Namaskar' and kindly proclaim how wonderful it is that I've come to their village.

A soft-spoken man with darting eyes takes charge of my luggage and instructs me to follow him. He doesn't introduce himself, but I assume he's my Chandpur neighbor's brother and the groom, Sandeep. He leads me to the courtyard in front of his house and sits me down in the only chair in sight. The entire village follows. They huddle together, sitting on the courtyard floor, the surrounding rock wall and on the stairs and open veranda of Sandeep's family's home. For most, if not all of them, it's the first time they've ever seen a foreigner. While Sandeep's father and I talk, the onlookers seemingly examine every inch of my body and listen to every word spoken; a self-imposed silence occasionally broken by giggles and whispers. One brave soul in the audience finally asks me where I'm from, inciting everyone else to join in, asking a salvo of questions: "Are you married? Do you have children? No sons? Where are your daughters? Are they married?

They're not married yet? They live alone? Where's your husband? How do you like Pauri Garhwal? Is it a better than where you're from?"

Eyes light up and double in size, incredulous at some of my answers.

"Mothers and fathers don't arrange their children's marriages?" a young girl repeats, obviously wondering if she misunderstood what I said.

"No we don't arrange marriages for our children" I reiterate and elaborate, "Boys and girls choose their own husbands and wives. They choose the person they love to marry."

Throughout our discussion question marks remain on their faces. It isn't that they think I'm lying, per se, it's just that what I'm saying is so outrageous, it's difficult for them to conceive: Hot water automatically comes out of pipes? Machines wash dishes and clothes, as well as dry them? Rooms heat up with the flip of a button?

As we talk a whirlwind of service greets the other wedding guests and I. We're offered cold water from the spring, and then tea with spicy, salt snacks and biscuits. When tea is finished, a plate overflowing with cigarettes, bedis, matches, large sugar granules, licorice seeds and betel nuts is brought around. A Baaman follows the plate, applying a blessing of vermilion paste and rice to everyone's forehead. The groom's brother accompanies the Baaman, handing each guest a plain white envelope with a crisp 10-rupee note inside (23 cents). As an afterthought, someone brings us dal pakora and arsi. Made the day before every wedding in both the bride and the groom's villages, they're distributed to fellow villagers, guests and, during the wedding, informally exchanged between the two families.

Sandeep's mother, Channa Devi, hovers in the doorway of their house watching us. She's schizophrenic and depressed. The local interpretation is 14 years ago she drank milk laced with a derivative of the marijuana plant and her mind has never been the same. Whatever the etiology of her condition, most days she hangs around the house apathetic and anxious.

The first time I met her was several months ago. I had taken her to Pauri Hospital to see if medications were available to help her function and feel better. She threw-up the entire two-hour car ride going there and was just as miserable the entire ride back. Rural Garhwali women and children are not used to riding in vehicles, traveling in them as little as a dozen times during their lifetime, resulting in them easily becoming carsick and exacerbated by the winding, potholed and warped roads that toss them around like rag dolls, making women and children hanging out of windows, throwing-up, a common occurrence. It is so common here that not a single jeep or bus could ply the roads for one full day without vomit dripping down it's sides.

After the guest welcome, Sandeep's youngest sister, 15-year old Kumari Santoshi, escorts me to my room. Since she's the only sister still living at home, she does almost all of the family's copious housework and farm chores herself. Her mother is often either unable or reluctant to help her. Sandeep can't help because he works on the plains in a bicycle factory, coming home a mere one month, at the most, a year. Although her other brother and father could help, as they both live at home and are unemployed, they don't because a strange cultural phenomenon occurring over the past two to three generations has robbed them of their role as farmers. In this part of Pauri Garhwal (and I do emphasize 'in this part'), men doing household or farm chores is frowned upon—with the exception of plowing fields, fixing terraced walls and chopping wood—so instead of helping the females harvest crops, cut grass or milk cows, unemployed men often spend their days idle; roaming around the village talking and playing cards.

I once asked my neighbor, Lakshu, about the anomaly and this was his answer, "If we [men] do farm work, we won't educate ourselves and look for more rewarding jobs. We'll have no chance of making money…, no chance of advancing ourselves and our families."

At the time, his reasoning made no sense to me. At 27, he had been unemployed his entire life and in the meantime his mother and wife could have used help with their abundant workload. He recently landed a job as a school teacher, however, radically changing his family's economic situation, opening up a whole range of possibilities for his children, drastically easing the burden on his wife, turning him into a confident, capable man before my eyes and essentially throwing any doubts I had over his 'advancing strategy' into the wastebasket.

Sandeep and Meena, as is often the case, are getting married because another woman is needed to help Kumari Santoshi do the housework and farm chores. Meena will not live with Sandeep. She'll live with her in-laws and will see Sandeep when he comes home for special occasions, once or twice a year.

My accommodation is a private room in Sandeep's next-door neighbor's house. It's spotlessly clean. Mud and cow dung have recently been applied to the floor and walls, giving the room a fresh appearance, like a new coat of burnt-orange paint. Furnishings consist of a worn wooden side table and an old plastic one, a large tin storage chest, a 2-foot long calendar hanging on the wall (several years old, but coveted because of its colorful picture of the goddess Saraswati on it), a kerosene lamp and two wooden cots. On each cot are one-inch thick mattresses, one-inch thick pillows and one army blanket. Sleeping on them is like sleeping directly on boards. It's a fact, not a complaint. I wouldn't dare complain. Beds and bedding are luxuries in Pauri Garhwal with many people being forced to go without. I went into a two-room house recently in which the sleeping room was completely bare except for a pile of gunnysacks in the corner. I asked the young, motherless girl what the gunnysacks were for and she replied, "We lay half of the gunnysacks on the floor to sleep on and the other half to cover ourselves up when it's cold."

In the evening four male guests, Sandeep's father, his uncle and I meet in an upstairs bedroom in Sandeep's house and sit bunched together on two single beds. A coffee table is brought in and placed in front of us. While we talk, we drink whiskey and eat sliced tomatoes and cucumbers heavily sprinkled with salt and freshly ground red chilies.

Sandeep's uncle passes around the wedding book for guests to sign. We're expected to write down our names and how much money we're donating to the groom, a record Sandeep and his father will keep to determine how much money they must give to a donator's son or daughter's wedding in the future. Most guests will give 11, 51, or, at the very most, 101 Rs. Donations to a groom are minimal because his wedding expenses are minimal. He pays his pre-wedding expenses (cost of prayer items, food for his wedding guests and one village feast), his Baaman's fees and transportation for his entire wedding party to and from the bride's village. The bride's family pays for everything else. Her family's expenses, which include food, a dowry and puja, run anywhere from 40,000 Rs. for the poorest of the poor to 200,000 Rs. or more for an average family—Meena's is an average family. To put these amounts in their proper perspective and get a more accurate view on how the expense affects the family's pocketbook, rupees should never be translated into dollars but instead evaluated as if they were equivalent to the dollar (200,000 Rs. equals $200,000 dollars). And since many, if not most people have no savings, living from month to month, weddings are financed with loan upon loan from family, friends and shopkeepers; by cashing in on every favor ever owed; and, relying on close family members to pay for their customary share of responsibilities. The latter (brothers, married sisters and their husbands, first cousins, uncles, aunts and grandparents) are expected to buy major dowry items or pay for major expenses and although they have the option of refusing, there is tremendous social pressure not to.

Detailed donation records are kept for the bride's wedding guests as well. Meena's father and brothers will be expected to contribute at least the same amount back to the donator's daughter or son's wedding and if it's a relative who donates money to Meena's wedding, Meena's family will be expected to give double the amount of money written in the donation book to the relative's children's weddings. Thus, donators often look at their donations as investments for their children's future wedding expenses, as well as an important way to keep good social relations.

We're served a dinner of unleavened bread, rice, potato and bottle gourd curry, curried black lentils and Halva (a desert made from browned semolina, ghee, sugar, and water with a handful of raisins, cashews and/or coconut mixed in). The meal is simultaneously fed to Sandeep's fellow villagers sitting outside on the courtyard floor. Afterwards a band plays lively Garhwali tunes and the men dance until midnight.

In the morning I awake to Sandeep's aunt knocking on my door. She has brought me a cup of tea and a jug of cold water. I drink the tea and then walk outside with the water to the far edge of the rock and mud quadrangle. Standing there, with my new neighbors looking on, I wash my hands and face and brush my teeth. A man is washing up nearby. In addition to washing his hands and face and brushing his teeth with a twig from a Neem tree, he clears his throat with gusto, creating a wide range of spitting, hacking and gagging sounds. For the uninitiated, it sounds as if he is choking to death. He's not. Enacted all over India, it's related to the Ayurvedic practice of consciously and thoroughly cleaning oral passages in the morning.

An hour after a breakfast of curried cabbage and chapattis, everyone gathers on the courtyard for Sandeep's prenuptial ceremonies.

The Baaman sits down, cross-legged, on a burlap bag. Sandeep comes out of his house carrying his own gunnysack and sits down on the ground beside the Baaman. He is told to cover his head, so someone quickly hands him a clean handkerchief, which he haphazardly throws on his hair. Spread out on the ground in front of them are standard puja items and Ganesh's yantra design atop a four-inch high stool. The only difference is, beside the traditional wheat-colored outlines, the Baaman has placed a single betel nut in the center of the yantra and. added a second outline of bright red sindhor to give his design a little flair, reflecting this particular Baaman's flamboyant style.

As soon as he lights the oil-saturated wick and gummy incense, he begins to recite Sanskrit prayers and, dipping his copper spoon into his copper water pot, pitches water around the courtyard, sprinkling those nearby with its holy contents. He then leads Sandeep through a water purification ritual; putting spoonfuls of water into his hands, which Sandeep drops on the ground, drinks or tosses over his head. Afterwards he prompts Sandeep to follow suit. Still chanting, the Baaman tosses various items (yogurt, flowers, etc.) on or in the direction of the Ganesh yantra, periodically placing items in Sandeep's hand and cuing him with a nod of his head to toss them.

Four elderly women, standing in the front row of the watching crowd, start singing auspicious mangal songs in two part harmonies. They sing praise of Ganesh for the full 20 minutes of puja. Their gravelly voices coupled with the singsong rhythm of the Garhwali language create a hallowed chanting melody, sung as loudly as the Baaman speaks.

The Baaman ties rodis, bundles of yellow cloth around the wrists of Sandeep's immediate family and a few of his mother's relatives who have come from distant villages, tying the male's rodis on their right wrists and the female's on their left. Inside each bundle are 1½ rupees and a betel nut. The betel nut represents Ganesh, the god of good luck and new beginnings, symbolizing best wishes for Sandeep's future. The yellow cloth represents Vishnu, the preserver of life and a major god in the Hindu trinity. His numerous incarnations (Rama, Krishna, Narsingh, etc.), or rather the stories of his incarnations, illustrate the basic tenets of Hindu thought. The coins represent Lakshmi, goddess of wealth, symbolizing hope for material wealth in Meena and Sandeep's future.

Switching to a new series of Sanskrit phrases, the Baaman mixes turmeric, curd, Ganga water and rice for the next ceremony, the Haldi Hath (literally meaning, Turmeric Hand). The old women stop singing and the three musicians, who until now have been sitting quietly on the far edge of the courtyard, begin to play a bagpipe, a dholak (barrel drum) and a damoul (round drum). These men, their fathers and their father's fathers have been the musicians for Sandeep's family for several generations. Every family in Pauri Garhwal has a corresponding Harijan family of musicians who play music for their religious activities. This same protocol goes for Baamans. Every Garhwali family has a family of Baamans who perform their religious rites. The father of the Baaman currently performing Sandeep's wedding rites performed Sandeep's father's wedding rites and the Baaman's grandfather performed the wedding rites for Sandeep's grandfather and so on. These binding relationships have been intact for so many generations, no one can tell me when they began. They are obligatory, making use of another Baaman family, except under extenuating circumstances, rare.

The Baaman sets five bowls of watery turmeric mixture in front of Sandeep, along with a ball of red string, a plate of turmeric paste and foot-long dubala grass separated into two bundles, each bound together with red string. Sandeep adjusts his sitting stance from yoga position to sitting on his bottom, pulling his knees up to his chest and leaving just enough room in between the two to prop his elbows on his thighs, allowing his hands to rest easily above his knees. His palms held upward, the Baaman dusts them with turmeric powder.

Throngs of people watch as Sandeep's eldest sister bends down in front of him (usually it's the mother who goes first but Sandeep's mother did not participate). Without saying a word, they simultaneously apply turmeric paste to one another's foreheads, followed by the Baaman tying red string around their wrists. Sandeep's sister picks up the bundles of grass, one in each hand, and dips them in all five bowls of the turmeric water and then methodically pats Sandeep's feet, knees, hands, shoulders and head with the dripping wet grass, for a total of three times. When she's finished, she sets the bundles down where she found them. One by one, people walk up to Sandeep and enact the exact same ritual his sister had; closest family members first, followed by more distantly related family, friends and fellow villagers.

The Haldi Hath is being carried out this morning for Meena in her village as well. For brides, the ritual is experienced more as a poignant good-bye than the purification ceremony that it is. Brides will essentially leave their family and village forever. As family and fellow villagers come up and go through this silent ritual with the bride, women often break down crying, typically mothers, and once a mother starts crying, several elderly women tend to join in.

After everyone present goes through the Haldi Hath ritual, several people, young and old, jump up and crowd around Sandeep.

Without pause, they grab the remaining turmeric water and paste, rowdily pouring, throwing and rubbing them on Sandeep's body, drenching him from head to toe, coloring him mustard yellow, in an auspicious ritual cleansing called a Mangal Snan. A few men quickly encircle him with a gray, wool blanket, creating a curtain behind which Sandeep changes into a brand new yellow kurta and white pajama pant, the traditional Garhwali male wedding attire until this current generation relegated it to being worn during pre-wedding rituals only, preferring to wear a tuxedo during the wedding ceremony, attire adopted from the plains.

When Sandeep reappears from behind the blanket, his hair and body are still wet and mustard-colored. He purposely does not wipe the turmeric off his body. Because it is a holy substance, the leftover residue clinging to him is a good omen. Besides, it makes skin color look lighter and many Garhwalis find that appealing.

Now that the Haldi Hath and Mangal Snan purification rituals are complete, Sandeep will not leave his courtyard until he leaves for his wedding, for fear that he might become contaminated. After a bride's Haldi Hath and Mangal Snan, her brother lifts her up onto his shoulders and carries her to the threshold of her house to keep her from becoming sullied by touching the ground. These precautions and rituals are not conducted to help the bride and groom reach higher states of purity. They are done to help them maintain a pure enough state to keep ghosts, curses and demonic forces at bay. During a wedding, a bride and groom are more vulnerable to evil than they might otherwise be. Thus, Sandeep and Meena must take additional precautions to protect themselves: They must go through several purification rituals just to maintain their normal equilibrium.

While wedding pictures are taken of the groom and the guests who gave him garlands of money, the Baaman prepares for the next ritual, Arti. He sets five small white candles on a tin plate and draws designs around them using red sindhor, turmeric powder and flour, including an AUM symbol—the number three with a tail sticking out it's back and a dotted crescent above.

Sandeep and the Baaman stand face to face. The Baaman lights the candles and, grasping the plate with both hands, moves it in vertical circular motions in front of Sandeep, reciting Sanskrit and purposely wafting smoke in Sandeep's face and in the space in front of him, purifying the air and Sandeep. The Baaman then hands the plate to Sandeep's father. When he finishes rotating the candles in front of Sandeep, he passes the plate to Sandeep's brother, who passes it to the next person in line. All the while, the Baaman recites Sanskrit and the musicians play background music.

After about the fourth or fifth person performs Arti, a man watching the activities unexpectedly starts rubbing his legs and arms, moaning and writhing, as if he's in extreme pain. It's Sandeep's mother's brother, who recently retired from the army. Slightly hunched over, he slaps at his body, flailing this way and that around the courtyard. No one pays significant attention to him except the musicians. Upon noticing him, the bagpiper stops playing and the drummers change their beat to a fast, hypnotic rhythm.

Less than five minutes later a distantly related aunt of Sandeep's spontaneously starts twirling like a Sufi whirling dervish. She spins around in circles, her arms alternating between stretching straight out from her sides and bending at the elbows, bringing her hands back to her chest. Her jaw becomes firm, almost rigid, and her eyes have stopped focusing, making it appear as if she's seeing through everyone and everything she looks at. She shakes her hair down from its bun and rubs her hands through it, repeatedly combing it back. It flows outward in the wind created by her feverish spinning. Without pausing, she suddenly switches to jumping up and down, holding her arms stiffly at her sides, pushing her body as high off the ground as possible with her toes, extending her head up into the air, several inches above her normal height. A moment later she throws herself down onto the courtyard, onto her hands and knees, precisely where the wet turmeric mixture poured on Sandeep earlier had formed a puddle. The front of her sari gets soaked. She swings her head around and around in circles, brushing her hair against the ground, soaking it as well. Moments later she springs back up and begins spinning like a twirling dervish again, her arms alternating between extending straight out to her sides and bending at the elbow, this time to run her fingers through her hair at regular intervals.

Meanwhile, people take turns moving the candles in front of Sandeep, not giving the slightest hint something is amiss. Sandeep is calm amidst the ongoing activity, maybe even pleased. Gods showing up to his wedding in the form of possessions is a good sign.

The drums beat fast. The whirling dervish continues twirling, pausing periodically to gyrate her upper body, as if she's doing the hoola-hoop. The army man continues grimacing and rubbing various parts of his body, sometimes halting midstream to hold awkward catatonic poses, only to return again to brusquely rubbing his body. His possession is not a full-fledged possession, but rather a possession trying to happen, which is not such a good thing—a god stuck trying to manifest itself is not a happy god. Knowing the Baaman is busy, a bystander takes it upon himself to help the army man. He goes into Sandeep's family's kitchen and brings out a long-handled ladle filled with burning fire ambers from the fireplace. The Good Samaritan moves the smoldering fire in circular movements in front of the retired army man, wafting smoke onto his body, trying to purify him and the space around him in order to induce the desired full-fledged possession.

After Arti, the Baaman proceeds directly to the next ritual, filling a handleless jug with Ganga water. He moves it in clockwise circles above Sandeep's head, and then pours the water in the four directions around Sandeep; first dribbling it to his left, reaching over his shoulder to dribble a little behind him, to his right and then in front of him. The Baaman then tips the jug above his own mouth, never touching the container to his lips, and pours water into his own mouth, affirming to Sandeep he is pure of heart and sincere in his wish for Sandeep's future, essentially proving it by drinking the purifying water to keep evil away. A parade of people follow suit, taking turns performing the water ritual in Sandeep's honor.

    Out of the blue, an old woman who's just finished pouring water in front of Sandeep, half hands half drops the container into the next person's hands. Grabbing Sandeep's head, she rubs her hands energetically, back and forth, over his mustard-stained hair. Her own head simultaneously revolves around and around in irregular circles. Shortly thereafter, she shifts to hopping up and down, small spurts of geriatric fervor made remarkable only because she continues to hold Sandeep's head between her hands, causing it to jolt back and forth with every bounce. His face remains expressionless the entire time.

    A man whose been watching the activities from a nearby veranda, starts hopping violently up and down while still seated in yoga position. To make sure he doesn't go flying off the veranda, two men rush up the stairs, grab him under his armpits and quickly bring him down the stairs, where they set him on the courtyard floor. He hops up and down vigorously for a few more minutes and then yelps like a dog that has just been kicked, flies backward onto the courtyard and passes out. It looks as though he has cracked his head on the courtyard rock and knocked himself out. This idea, however, does not appear to enter anyone's mind but my own. The man lies there unattended until he regains consciousness several minutes later.

    As the water ritual winds down, the Baaman turns his attention to the possessed people. He prepares a tray of turmeric paste. While trying to apply a small circle of it to the army man's forehead, the army man grapples with the Baaman for the tray. Leaving one hand glued to the tray to fight the battle, the army man plunges his other hand into the paste and smears it across the Baaman's entire forehead. After wrangling the tray free from the Baaman, he runs off to where the rest of the possessed people are dancing and plasters their foreheads with paste. The whirling dervish snatches a handful of paste off his tray and begins plastering it across the foreheads of anyone within her reach, including Sandeep's.

The old woman who had clasped onto Sandeep's head earlier disappears. Another elderly woman takes her place. She has just begun the water ritual when she too abruptly drops the container. It crashes to the ground, spilling water. Like the first old woman, she rubs Sandeep's head energetically with her hands, stroking his face and smiling like the Cheshire cat. As the plate of turmeric paste passes by, she scoops up a handful with one hand and, while still holding onto Sandeep's head with the other, proceeds to wipe the paste across Sandeep's forehead and onto the shoulders and chest of his brand new shirt. She finally lets go of him and strokes her turmeric stained hands gently through her own hair, followed by an involuntarily quaking of her body and a sudden outburst into song, swaying back and forth like a caroler at Christmas, in apparent joy.

An old man begins strolling back and forth across his veranda nearby, barking like a bear. At regular intervals his legs jerk straight down, like a wooden toy soldier's and his arms spring rigidly in a downward slant on either side of him.

Without warning, all of the possessions come to an abrupt halt, within a minute or two of one another. There is no apparent reason for the swift change, although it does to some degree coincide with the ending of the water purification ritual. The people who had been possessed and infused with energy now look dazed, hung over and exhausted. They move around slowly, going through motions like zombies. One drinks water. Another mechanically ties her hair in a bun.

The drummers glance around to ascertain if there are any ongoing or potential new possessions. When they decide there are not, they stop playing their drums. The crowd dissipates.

Weddings are measured in terms of a one-day wedding or three-day wedding, regardless of the fact a one-day wedding is actually a three-day affair and a three-day wedding is a five-day affair. If this were a three-day wedding, the wedding activities would have ended here for the day and tomorrow Sandeep and Meena would be married. This is considered a one-day wedding, however, so one hour after the water ritual ends, the groom's wedding party gathers in front of his house to travel to the bride's village for the marriage ceremony. The wedding party consists of most of the village's men and boys and myself. Women and girls rarely travel with a groom to participate in his wedding. Two reasons cited for this practice are, "It's always been done this way" and "The trails are too long and arduous for women to manage."

We head downhill. The groom and his friends lead the way. Sandeep's Baaman follows close behind, swishing a chaunr gai above Sandeep's head and around his backside. Protruding out one end of a copper handle are numerous coarse hairs from an animal's tail, making the instrument itself look like a tail. The hair is variously attributed to a cow, a "wild cow" or an antelope. No matter what animal it actually belongs to, swishing it above and around a person wards off evil.

The band follows playing popular Garhwali tunes. Every 50 feet our procession stops to dance. The leisurely pace is perfect for the steep and rocky trail, allowing us to descend carefully, as well as gives us ample time to take in the far and wide view. Boys sporadically let off firecrackers. They're not the typical firecrackers that go 'put, put, put'.

Firecrackers in Pauri Garhwal are miniature sticks of dynamite, each one exploding in a loud 'ka-Boom!'

A hired bus is waiting at the bottom of the hill to take us to the wedding. Taped to the windows are yellow pieces of paper with the hand written message, "Sandeep weds Meena."

The bride's village is 15 kilometers away on the same dirt road, making the trip short. Once we arrive, the groom leads the way again. At the start of the stairs leading from the road up to Meena's village is a cement archway on which is written the village's name, 'Nakuri', and 'welcome'. A reception of teenage girls singing welcome songs is milling around underneath it. They apply tilak to Sandeep's forehead and place a homemade garland of orange marigolds around his neck. They then adorn his father and his uncle in garlands and tilak. Just as the trio moves forward, however, the girls block the entryway, preventing the rest of us from following. They demand we give them 501 Rs. to continue onward. The groom's father jokingly claims highway robbery and bargains them down to 101 Rs. After receiving the money, the gladdened girls apply tilak to our foreheads and we all continue our journey up to Nakuri. It's hardly a ten-minute stroll from the road to the bride's house, but we stretch it out another 20 minutes by dancing every few feet and exploding bombs to let our hosts know we're coming. It's fashionable for grooms to make long, drawn-out, noisy entrances to their weddings, as well as to be late.

The broken cement, rock and mostly dirt trail has been swept clean of cow manure, dried grass and other debris. White powder, normally used to make whitewash, has been strewn along the rough edges of the walkway. It's the Garhwali equivalent to a red carpet welcome. The main venue, a large red & white tent with the sides rolled up, has been set up in the quad outside the bride's house. We sit down under it in plastic chairs rented for the occasion. A half-dozen, multi-colored tinsel balls glitter overhead. The bride's house has been freshly whitewashed and sky-blue paint applied to the doors, shudders, and trim. With leftover paint someone has drawn AUM symbols, lotus flowers and written 'Welcome' on the front wall facing us.

Sandeep's future father-in-law, a large, affable man, greets us. Smiling warmly, he clasps his hands in prayer-shape, raises them to his chin and slightly bows in the direction of anyone whose eyes meet his. He asks Sandeep to join him. Sandeep takes off his shoes and stands in front of him. A Baaman blows a conch shell three times, clearing the air of evil forces and announcing to the gods and fellow villagers that Arti is about to begin. Generally performed at the end of puja ceremonies or as a special veneration to god, it is performed today for Sandeep because as a groom, he represents the god Vishnu throughout the wedding ceremony. The bride's father rotates a ladle with burning wood coals, circling it vertically in front of Sandeep, and begins to sing Arti in a splendid alto voice. It's a nine-stanza, Sanskrit rendition addressed to all gods, praising their greatness and pleading for their help in leading a religiously righteous, trouble-free life.

When Arti is finished, the groom glances around, looking for his shoes to put back on. They're missing. One of the young girls stole them with the intention of demanding a ransom before returning them, but the bashful groom doesn't say a word. Instead, he sits back down in his chair, barefoot.

In one corner of the courtyard the bride's dowry is displayed for everyone to see: A matching wooden sofa set (a coffee table, a low-set couch and two low-set chairs); a hand-run sewing machine; a free-standing metal closet; pots & pans, two single beds held together by a queen size headboard; a brass water jug and a small calf. These are standard items given to every groom's family. Occasionally dowry is openly discussed amongst the bride and groom's families, and the latter may request cash instead of gifts, but just as often hints and custom form the basis of a dowry's content. In addition, because this is

103

the bare minimum of gifts, money will most likely be or has already been given to Sandeep's family as well. Outlawed in 1961 by the Indian Government, dowry is still absolutely mandatory.

More dowry is sometimes demanded from a bride's family after marriage. Although common on the plains of India, it does not appear to be a common practice in Pauri Garhwal. Nonetheless, it did happen to a Chandpur girl who was married to a Garhwali man living on the plains. Shortly after their marriage, he quit his job and began demanding money from the bride's family. Initially he asked for money to help pay his monthly expenses. Then he demanded money to buy a motorcycle. The last I heard the husband was demanding hundreds of thousands of rupees to start his own business. In the interim, the groom occasionally beat his wife to elicit the bride's family's cooperation. The bride's family, however, has obviously become fed up with the groom. A couple of months ago when he came to visit his in-laws in Chandpur, the bride's grandfather slapped the groom around in the middle of the bazaar.

The groom's party is served lunch. As honored guests, our meal is brought to us on tin plates: Rice, sweet rice (rice and brown sugar), red lentil curry, potato and eggplant curry and halva. We hold our plates on our laps with our left hand and eat with our right. Afterwards, a young man brings a jug of water around and pours it over my hands while I rub them together to clean them of food and curry stains, the rinse water and debris falling onto the courtyard unnoticed.

A hodgepodge of twenty or so of the bride's relatives, guests and fellow villagers meander into a nearby fallow field and sit down on the ground in a circle. A young boy walks around the circle and places dried leaf plates and tin cups on the ground in front of each person. His companion follows behind with a jug, filling the glasses with water. Off to one side of the field a Baaman cook hovers over two giant-size mud and rock fireplaces that were built three days earlier to accommodate the huge 15 and 20 Kg cooking pots. He scoops rice out of one of the pots and puts it into a manageable 3-gallon container, which he then carries around the circle, doling out mounds of rice onto people's plates with his hand. Village men normally cook feast food, but there are a few occasions when a Baaman is hired to cook it, one being the day the groom's party goes back to his village and because this is a one-day wedding, we'll all go back to the groom's village today. As a member of the Brahmin caste, food cooked by him is 'shud', a connotation similar to kosher or halal.

The Baaman makes four more rounds of the circle, each time dishing out a different food: Sweet rice, lentils, curry and halva. The boys and the Baaman then walk around the circle offering water and seconds. Those who have already finished eating wait for those who are still eating to finish their meals. When everyone is done, they all stand up and leave together, depositing their wilted plates into an overflowing box and stacking their tin cups on a nearby table, where boys are frantically washing them with water to give to the next group of stragglers into the field.

During a lull between eating and the actual wedding ceremony, male members of the bride's extended family carry dowry items down to the road to load and tie on top of the bus. Later, Nepalese porters and friends & family of the groom will carry the items up the long hill to Bijoli on their heads, shoulders and backs.

A group of young women, unmarried friends and relatives of the bride, gather in a corner under the tent and begin to sing. Their loud unrefined voices, coupled with the nursery-like rhymes of the song, make them sound like a classroom full of children singing. The lyrics, in a blend of Hindi and Garhwali, are a lengthy version of the old saying, 'Your mother wears army boots!' Except the taunting is aimed at the groom's father and to a lesser degree at the groom and his guests. Its roughly 40 refrains of two rhyming lines each; the first line denotes an activity in the village, thrown in just to rhyme with the second line, which is the tease:

> "Sugar cane is eaten in our village.
> Father of the groom, Rakesh Khanna."

Rakesh Khanna was a famous Indian actor. The line suggests the father of the groom is phony like an actor. Sugar cane is ganna, which rhymes with Khanna, both of which come at the end of the sentence.

> "Grass is cut in our village.
> Where are the groom's intelligent friends?"

> "Logs are cut in our village.
> The groom's father is a letter box."

Like mailboxes are stuffed with letters, so the groom's father stuffs himself with food—in other words, he's a glutton.

> Pakora are cooked in our village.
> Drag the groom's father outside, lash him
> with nettles and throw him in the field!"

A young boy from the groom's party playfully hollers out, "We'll lash the bride's father and throw him into the field!"

After the song, Sandeep, his father and their Baaman head into the room in which the bride and her family have been doing puja off and on all day. Meena, her father and her Baaman are already seated on the floor in the middle of the room. Meena and Sandeep still cannot see one another, however, because a sheet is being held up between them. Both Baamans simultaneously and in concert conduct puja: The bride's Baaman administers her puja and the groom's Baaman administered his. When puja is finished, the curtain comes down.

Meena's father lifts her thumb and places her hand in Sandeep's hand. The bride and groom stand up and separate white cloths are wrapped and tied around each of their waists. Afterwards the end pieces of the two separate cloths are bound together, joining Meena and Sandeep, who then walk outside with their Baamans and families to the vedi.

Earlier in the day, on the far side of the courtyard, the Baaman marked off a rectangular area, about 6 ft X 4 ft, which he, the bride's father and other family members then prepared for this final wedding ritual. In one corner stands a transplanted 7-foot tall banana tree, roots and all. Commonly used as a pillar to define sacred spaces, the banana tree, in this case, also symbolizes Meena's father's wish for her to live a fruitful life. In the other three corners are cut pine trees on which bundles of sacred painyaan, banyan and mango tree leaves are hung. There's a large pit dug in the middle and stacked with splintered pinewood, forming the focal point of the ceremony. Colorful carpets are strewn on the ground around it for the bride and groom and their Baamans to sit on. A carnival red canopy stretches behind and above where Sandeep and Meena sit, shading them from the sun and creating an elegant backdrop befitting a King and Queen, or in this case, the goddess Lakshmi and Lord Vishnu.

As per custom, the bride sits on the left and the groom on the right in front of the fire, their respective Baamans positioned at their sides. The fire pit is lit and more puja enacted: Dollops of herbs and clarified butter are dropped into the fire, water and rice fly, red strings are tied around wrists and tilak applied to foreheads.

Then the Aag Kee Kasam (Fire Oath) ritual begins. Sandeep and Meena repeat promises to each other and promenade around the fire together, still bound by the cloth. Seven rounds around the fire represents the seven reincarnated lifetimes they will spend together, as well as their seven promises to one another, albeit in Garhwal seven is figurative and promises include instruction as well.

Meena acknowledges Sandeep as Lord Vishnu. She tells him he must feed her and bring his money home to her. In return, she promises to be spendthrift. Sandeep tells Meena she is now a member of his family. She must talk to him in a nice way and keep good spirits during bad and sad times. Meena promises Sandeep she will do what he commands and keep a good spirit. Sandeep promises to provide Meena with anything and everything she needs. He tells her that as beautiful as the goddess looks in all her finery, he too will provide Meena with the things that will make her look as beautiful as a goddess. Meena tells Sandeep when he is sad she is sad. She promises to care for his animals. She then explains to Sandeep that there are six seasons. As the seasons change, their needs will change, so they must change with the seasons and Sandeep must give her what is appropriate for each season. Sandeep promises to give Meena what is appropriate for the season. He also promises to take Meena with him wherever he goes. Meena promises not to go with another man and promises to follow a righteous religious path. As both a promise to and request from Lord Vishnu, they simultaneously vow to have a rewarding life together, promising their behavior between one another will be pleasant and that they will not fight. They finish the Aag Kee Kasam by walking around the fire and reciting in unison "With Agni [Fire god], the Baamans and our family and friends as our witnesses, this is a new beginning. Whatever we did wrong in our past, from this moment forth will be forgotten."

Sandeep applies red sindhor to the part in Meena's hair, declaring her a married woman.

It takes another couple of hours before the married couple and groom's party arrive back in Bijoli. Upon arrival, the village women and girls gather around to greet the new member of their community. At Sandeep's house, Meena washes the feet of all the women in his household by scooping water from a bucket with cupped hands and pouring it over their feet. The new couple, Sandeep's family and their Baaman perform another round of puja. After the initial standard rituals, the Baaman recites the story of Narayana (an incarnation of the god Vishnu), called Shri Satya Narayana Kathaa (Honorable True God's Story):

> "Narada [a famous Hindu mendicant], while traveling through the three worlds [heaven, underworld and earth], was struck by how sad and distraught people living on Earth are. He went to Lord Vishnu and asked him what he could do to help ease their burden. Vishnu told Narada to spread the word of god and teach them to pray to him, including the necessity of giving and eating blessed food as part of their prayers.
>
> The first person Narada came upon on earth was a poor Sadhu. He was a pious mendicant who owned nothing and begged for his food, but no matter how much time he spent begging, he barely collected enough to feed himself. Narada told him the story of Shri Satya Narayana and encouraged the Sadhu to pray to Narayana and offer bananas and other fruits as prasad. The Sadhu took his advice. He prayed to Narayana and offered prasad. His situation miraculously changed. From that day forth he prayed to Narayana, who provided him with ample food, giving him more time to devote to his religious pursuits.
>
> A Woodcutter came upon the Sadhu and noted his prosperity. He asked him how he had become so

prosperous, while lamenting about his own situation. He barely earned enough money selling wood to feed his family, let alone indulge in luxury. The Sadhu told the Woodcutter about god and suggested he pray to Narayana and offer prasad. The next day, the Woodcutter spent his meager earnings on puja supplies and prayed to Narayana. From that day forth he prospered and vowed to pray to Narayana for the rest of his life."

Their prayers continue late into the night. Afterwards Meena indulges Sandeep's family in a game adopted from the plains. Because her head has been shrouded in a veil, Meena's face has not yet been fully seen by anyone, so a few members of Sandeep's family take turns giving Meena small gifts in exchange for a peek at her face. Sandeep's sister gives Meena a homemade garland of flowers, so Meena lifts her veil, giving her two new sister-in-laws a peek. A male cousin offers her a ten-rupee note. She obliges him as well.

The next morning Meena goes to the village spring in Sandeep's village with Sandeep's aunt and her sister-in-law to perform a ritual called Pandera Dikhain, meaning 'show the spring'. Meena lights incense and applies turmeric paste to a rock near the spring, blessing the spring as she would someone's forehead, and then presses her hands together in prayer and brings them up in front of her chin, giving further respect to the water source, silently acknowledging that from now on she will take her water from this spring and confirming it by filling a brass jug with water and carrying it on her head to her new home.

After breakfast, Sandeep and Meena head back to Meena's village alone—contrary to the more common scenario where the groom's mother, father and other friends and family members often accompany the bride and groom. Sandeep and Meena are served tea before the Baaman conducts another puja ceremony. Meena's family's Baaman tells them another story from Shri Satya Narayana Kathaa:

"A merchant, watching a devout King perform puja one day, asked him what he was doing? The King told him he was praying to Narayana because it provides wealth, progeny and good tidings to those who pray to him. The merchant went home and told his wife that if they have a child they must perform Narayana puja. His barren wife miraculously gave birth to a girl child a short time later. Despite his good intentions, however, the Merchant postponed performing Narayana puja. In the meantime, his daughter grew up and married.

One day the merchant and his new son-in-law were returning home from a business trip. As they passed through a great kingdom, dusk fell. They could not afford to stay at an inn, so they fell asleep on the side of the road. While they slept, two thieves snuck into the King's palace and stole boxes of gold and jewels. During their escape, the King's guards chased them and just as they were closing in on the thieves, the thieves dumped the treasure on the side of the road near the sleeping merchant and his son-in-law and ran off. The King's guards arrived on the spot and, assuming the sleeping men were the culprits, hauled them off to jail.

In the meantime, the merchant's wife and daughter had become destitute and were forced to beg to feed themselves. Then one day his wife remembered her husband's unfulfilled promise to pray to Narayana. The women spent their meager earnings to buy puja supplies and prayed to Narayana. Narayana heard their prayers. During a dream, Narayana informed the King that the merchant and his son-in-law were innocent and urged him to let them go. The King, awed by the presence of god, not only let the merchant and his son-in-law go, he atoned for mistakenly incarcerating the pair by giving them the stolen treasure.

On their way home, they crossed a wide river in a boat. The boatman giving them passage asked what was inside their heavy chests. The merchant, fearing he would be robbed, lied and told the boatman it was grass. When they reached the other side of the river and off-loaded the chests from the boat, the merchant noticed how light they had become, so he opened them. The treasure was gone and in its place was grass. Realizing the boatman was god, he apologized for lying to him. God accepted his apology and restored the treasure.

The wife and daughter were in the middle of performing Narayana puja when they heard the merchant and his son-in-law were crossing the river. The daughter abruptly ended puja, forgetting to eat prasad, and ran down to the river to meet them. Her father and husband appeared to have drowned. Narayana reminded her that she hadn't finished doing puja and had forgotten to eat prasad, so she ran all the way back home, finished puja and ate prasad. When she returned to the river, her father and husband were waiting, along with their treasure chests filled with gold and jewels."

When puja is finished, they pass the rest of the day casually together, giving Meena's family and fellow villagers a chance to get to know Sandeep and Sandeep a chance to get to know them. They eat a special meal with Meena's family and spend the night in Meena's village.

The next day when Sandeep and Meena are leaving to go back to Sandeep's village, Meena starts to cry. She sobs uncontrollably all the way down the trail. Sometimes she wails so loud it seems as if she wants the whole world to hear her pain. Sometimes she cries so hard she can't walk. As she passes by elder women, they offer her words of encouragement and farewells: "Everything is going to be alright," "There's no need to cry," and "Go now."

*Meena died one year later while giving birth at home. Her son lived. Sandeep waited the customary one-year mourning period and then remarried.

At first it looks like blood splattered across my kitchen counter. As I get closer, I realize it's sindhor. The fire-engine red powder lying atop pine green and black marble appears much darker than it really is, especially in the dim morning light, and high humidity from incessant monsoon rains has caused the otherwise fine grains to clump together in pools. But what's it doing inside my house?

A moment passes before it dawns me. The neighborhood children are the culprits! They probably found the ubiquitous powder lying around in one of their homes and while playing, threw it on my back wall, causing residue to accidentally blow in through my open window shutters.

The neighborhood children are notorious for making a mess outside my house. They use dirt, pencils or whatever else they can get their hands on to scribble graffiti across the entire front wall, as high up as they can reach. The reasons for their behavior are perfectly clear. First and foremost, the children are six years old and younger, prime drawing-on-the-wall age. Another reason is their favorite place to play in the courtyard is on my veranda. And there, compared to the dark mud and rocky contours of their own houses, my smooth, cream-colored walls must scream out to be drawn on. Last but not least, their mothers spend their days working in the fields, milking cows and collecting grass and firewood in the jungle, leaving the children unattended for hours at a time, obliging them to monitor their own behavior, as well as to entertain themselves. A dearth of toys must make it challenging. In the four and a half years since I've lived in Chandpur, I've seen nine toys: One plastic doll; one tricycle; one stuffed dinosaur; two kites; one flute made from a hollowed out barley stock; cricket supplies (which our foundation bought for Chandpur's cricket team); an assortment of crayons, colored pencils and coloring books, which I bought for my three neighbor girls in an attempt to refocus their drawing talent; and, a homemade wire contraption called a car, which is actually a piece of wire bent into a circle and connected to a straight piece of wire by a small loop. A child holds onto the straight piece and when he runs, the circle (a.k.a. tire) rolls along the ground.

When I first moved in, I was appalled by the children's behavior and indignant at their parent's lack of control over it. I never said anything to the parents or the children, but I said plenty under my breath. I would go outside occasionally and scrub my walls in front of them, hoping they'd get the hint. If they did, they never let on. Everyone was indifferent about the children drawing on my wall, as well as to my wall's perpetually unsightly appearance. Over time, it became less and less important to me too. Now the children have endeared themselves to me to the point where it really doesn't matter anymore. Instead of fretting, I keep a spare can of paint in my storeroom to paint the wall now and again.

I'm certain there's sindhor on the wall. It's just a matter of whether there's a little or a lot, and whether the children have thrown it on just the back wall or on the side and front walls too. I jump up on the counter and peer out my kitchen window to assess the damage. All I can see is a sprinkling of sindhor clinging to the window grate, so I head upstairs and hang over my sundeck railing to get an unimpeded view of the wall. There is nothing on it! I hang over the side railing. There is nothing on that wall either. Puzzled, I go back downstairs to examine the powder again, racking my brain for an explanation.

As I start to make my morning coffee, I'm flabbergasted by what goes through my mind next. It wasn't a child who had tossed sindhor in my house. It was an adult. Someone has purposely thrown it in my window to cast a spell over me!

Garhwalis practice a variant of Hinduism called tantra-mantra (pronounced tăntăr-măntăr). In the West it's referred to as Tantracism, packaged as sexual practices and defined using complex mystical definitions, with words like enlightenment dangling at the end. In Pauri Garhwal, it boils down to people doing ritual prayer and animal sacrifice to control things in their daily lives. The sindhor on my counter represents a wish solicited through a tantra-mantra prayer ritual and was placed inside my house to facilitate the prayer's outcome.

The person who threw sindhor in my window either wants something from me or wants to wreak havoc in my life. Regardless of the motive, he would have blessed or cursed the powder in a similar manner: He would have gone to a temple with the powder, lit incense, told god his desire, promised to sacrifice a goat in the god's honor if his wish is fulfilled, applied a circle of powder to the middle of his forehead between his eyebrows and then took the remaining powder away to be tossed in my window later.

If someone tossed sindhor in my house because they want something from me, the possibilities are endless. Wanting something from me is just another way of saying they want something from our social service agency and because we live, literally, on the front lines of the war on poverty, those wants are many—although rarely frivolous.

It's equally possible someone's aim is to wreak havoc in my life. Curses do not necessarily involve deep-seated animosity. A minor altercation or unprovoked jealousy can elicit a curse from someone. A

Garhwali man explained it to me this way, "Garhwalis don't tell one another to their face that there's a problem between them. They don't try to resolve it. They gossip about the person behind his back, pull pranks on him like steal something out of his garden or they put a curse on him."

Mentally I narrow down the list of people who might want revenge. Two names and an entire group of people come to mind, all from Chandpur village.

The group of people is the entire Rana clan. For several generations, the Rana clan and the Thakur clan have lived together in Chandpur. Being of the same caste, these two groups live in harmony like close knit relatives. Daily they visit each other's homes and work side by side in the fields, sharing the intimacy of their lives. They attend each and every function of the other clan's: Weddings, funerals, feasts and worship ceremonies. Sometimes, however, the tension between the two clans grows until a divide is created. The hallmarks of the divide are the two clans completely stop attending one another's ceremonies, they stop eating one another's food and village meetings come to a dead halt. It starts with a dispute between a few individuals from the different clans and a couple of angry, outspoken men. They call a meeting of fellow male clan members and convince them their clan needs to break with the other clan. Majority does not always rule. It takes merely a few forceful people to assert the decision has been made and the break will happen. After the meeting, the men go home and announce to their families a divide has occurred. There may be some initial grumbling, but there is little further discussion. From that day forth, people from the opposing clans purposely avoid or severely limit interacting with one another.

Although these splits may happen as seldom as once in 10 or 15 years, the most recent one occurred a year ago. The Rana clan broke with the Thakur clan. According to the Ranas, there are two reasons for the split. One reason is they are fed up with Parvendar Singh Thakur's behavior. When he drinks, which is often, he's a bully. He either openly commits pranks like piling bricks up in the middle of the road to block traffic or he becomes aggressive, threatening to beat people up, break down their door, or kill them. Generally, only the rare person who commits these kinds of offenses against a community is ostracized from a village, along with his immediate family, but because the entire Thakur clan has been unwilling to ostracize Parvendar, the Rana clan blames the entire Thakur clan for not controlling his behavior.

The second reason is the Ranas believe it was traitorous when Thakur clan members did not support the Rana's political candidates during recent local elections. The worst offense was after a powerful Rana man's wife announced she was running for Jilla Panchayat (District Council Member), a woman from the Thakur clan announced she too was going to run for the position and did.

A third reason not cited by the Rana clan, but whispered among the Thakur clan as the real reason, is our foundation, JDF. Thakur clan members believe the enmity between the two clans stems from the downfall of the Rana clan's prestige, political power and economic strength. Several people from the Chandpur Thakur clan work for JDF, including the Director. From good work throughout the district, JDF's reputation has soared and with it the status, popularity, and confidence of JDF's staff. They also earn good money, giving them economic freedom to build new houses and, most importantly, to no longer depend on the moneylenders, the Ranas.

Rumors now circulate among the Rana clan, such as "JDF employees are making political statements!" and "JDF personnel are going to government meetings to find out what development schemes are available to the community!" The allegations are innocuous, but the way Rana clansmen say them is as if JDF is conspiring against them and Thakur clan members take these seemingly minor comments as personal assaults.

Tension between the two groups is at an all time high. If it's someone from the Rana clan who is trying to cast an evil spell, it's probably not directed towards me per se, but towards JDF. JDF conducts all of its business from the bottom floor of my house, where the sindhor was thrown in.

It could be Anu. He worked for JDF for almost two years until he was fired about a month ago. A bright, resourceful man, he unfortunately has had a life long penchant for lying, drinking and stealing. He went too far when he stole money from JDF meant for a patient, and worse, because of his alcoholism, he neglected the patient, Vinod Singh.

I met Vinod Singh one day while standing outside Mausi hospital. He approached me and humbly introduced himself. Like someone reading a resume, Vinod Singh recited his credentials: "I'm extremely poor, my mother is dead, my father is terminally ill, and I don't know how to read or write."

A small 35-year-old man, Vinod Singh didn't look a day over 20. His sparkling brown, friendly eyes and neatly cut short hair were strikingly incongruent with his dress: A dirty, water-stained shirt hanging down below his knees, no pants and no shoes. My first impression was that he's mentally ill.

Continuing in a soft-spoken voice, he informed me that he had heard JDF helps people get medical treatment, buy medicines, etc. He intimated he too wanted to go inside the hospital, but stated that he didn't have the two rupees (4 cents) needed to pay the entrance fee and asked if I would pay his fee. I asked him why he needed to see a doctor and he replied, "I can't stop urinating."

Although the statement again made me think he's mentally ill, I invited him to go with me and another patient into the hospital.

A man sitting at the registration table made a snide comment, "Don't you wear pants like a man?"

Vinod Singh remained mute and continued smiling, his composure attesting to the fact he'd dealt with people making fun of him his entire life. Outside on the uneven ground it was not easily noticed, but while we waited in line to purchase the admit slip, a puddle started to form underneath Vinod Singh. The stench of urine also became apparent.

The doctor's response after examining Vinod Singh was, "We can't do anything for you here."

Vinod Singh passively accepted the news. Not understanding the full extent of his problem, I solicited an explanation and a referral to where he could get treatment. The doctor described Vinod Singh's penis as severely deformed and confessed he had no idea who could fix it.

Two years, four hospitals, 2,800 kilometers, 1.3 lakh rupees ($2,889), a dozen doctors and one 15-hour long operation later, Vinod Singh stopped urinating for the first time in his life. The doctors had connected his urinary tract to a stent, allowing him to urinate through a tube whenever necessary. Vinod was elated. For the first time in his life he was invited into people's homes, he attended weddings and he got a job.

It was during Vinod Singh's hospital stay we fired Anu. He had stolen 5,000 Rs. meant for Vinod Singh's healthcare and left him unattended on several occasions for days at a time. It was a big offense. Hospitals in India require a family member or friend to live in the hospital with a patient to do everything for a patient that a nurse does in modern societies, including clean up bowel movements, change bandages and run back and forth to the medical store to buy all the patient's medical supplies (medicines, syringes and bandages). Without an aide, a bed-ridden patient is helpless and unable to receive treatment.

Anu liked his job. He would do almost anything to get it back, even if it takes putting a spell over me. Conversely, he could just as easily have thrown the sindhor in my window as an act of revenge, hoping to wreak havoc on JDF or on me.

It could be the Chandpur Headman who tossed the sindhor in my window. A couple of months ago, he had threatened to put a curse on me.

Lila Devi came to my house and uncharacteristically jumped right into the heart of the matter, "You shouldn't complain about the Pradhan [the Headman] anymore."

"Why not?" I asked, unsure of where our conversation was going.

"He'll cause trouble for you," she warned.

"I don't care. As long as I know he or anyone else is stealing money or doing anything I perceive as morally wrong, I'll speak up. It's my nature, my culture."

I didn't need to explain to Lila Devi about the Pradhan's illegal activities. Everyone in the village knew he took village grant money meant to build houses for the poor and instead built himself a new house and repaired his brother's. They also knew he was taking money meant for village projects and putting it directly into his pocket. But corruption is rampant, particularly of government officials, so people accept it as normal behavior. Besides, the enormity of the problem, fear of curses, a host of cultural tendencies such as passivity and the high value placed on harmony with your neighbors, apathy, and the fact that officials higher up won't do anything about it anyways, usually landing whistle-blowers in a hundred times more trouble than the corrupt, all keep people from complaining about it. The Pradhan was mad because unlike everyone else, I was speaking up.

Lila Devi, visibly agitated, blurted out, "He's telling people in the bazaar that if you don't stop talking to government officials about him, he's going to caste an evil spell over you!"

I almost burst out laughing, but suppressed my urge out of respect for Lila Devi. She is genuinely afraid of evil spells. Everyone in rural Pauri Garhwal is. Evidence of their fear is everywhere: White rocks, iron tridents, timaru branches and potted cactus tower above the rooftops of almost every single house; villagers adorn themselves in copper bracelets, kajal tilak and hollowed amulets filled with sacred substances and secrets; and, during every religious activity, rituals are performed to purify the place of worship and the people attending. These acts or items are never described in terms of bringing good luck, to enhance normal levels of purity or as metaphors. Their explicit purpose is to ward off demons, ghosts and curses—intentional curses like the one the Pradhan was threatening and inadvertent curses like those caused by a house being within eyesight of a temple or from strong negative or positive sentiments.

Another way villagers avoid curses is by not saying or doing anything overt to provoke anger in another person. Because I was breaking this unspoken rule by complaining to government officials about the Pradhan embezzling funds, the Pradhan was trying to intimidate me into being quiet by threatening to put a curse on me.

My first contact with the Pradhan was when JDF was in its infancy. We were planning to build toilets in Chandpur's Harijan Basti (area where Harijan caste people live), so we held a meeting there to ask someone to donate land on which to build the toilets and to formulate a community-based plan. The Pradhan dominated the discussion, speaking loudly, negatively and non-stop. "We will not allow

JDF to build toilets in Harijan Basti!" he proclaimed, and then proceeded to accuse us of taking their money from the government to build their toilets. He likened it to stealing and demanded JDF give the Harijan community their money back and let them build their own toilets.

In the beginning, I thought it was a genuine misunderstanding and patiently explained to him it was my money, not government money, JDF would use to build the toilets. He countered my explanation with a new and even more bazaar accusation: "JDF plans to hook up dirty water in the toilets!"

We assured everyone the water JDF will hook up in the toilets will be the same spring water they drink everyday. The Pradhan then accused JDF of scheming with the Rajputs (fellow villagers but from the warrior caste) to hook up water in Harijan Basti toilets with the real intention of later taking away Harijan water rights to the village spring. JDF reminded everyone the water would be used for flushing toilets and showering only, not for drinking. Harijans would still haul their drinking water from the spring.

The Pradhan then proposed, "The Rajputs will poison the water!"

He made these allegations and no one opposed him except JDF staff, whenever we could get a word in edgewise. The Pradhan would not let the other members of Harijan Basti speak. If someone spoke in favor of the project, he interrupted and belittled their idea and when someone offered to donate land on which to build the toilets, he bullied the man, informing him and everyone else that he would not allow anyone to donate their land for the toilet/shower complex. What villagers heard between the lines was the Pradhan threatening to put a curse on anyone who did (casting evil spells is one of his favorite pastimes and everybody knows it).

The unconstructive meeting and mute stance of people from Harijan Basti forced us to temporarily cancel the project. It was resurrected in the ensuing weeks, however, because numerous people from Harijan Basti surreptitiously came to JDF's office and requested we build the toilets and one extended family quietly donated the land.

The Pradhan protested throughout the toilet's construction. Immediately after it was built, he threatened fellow Harijan Basti members with consequences if anyone used the toilets. In a startling turn of events, they began threatening him. They also collectively banned him and his family from using the toilets and even put locks on the doors to keep them out. JDF had to bring in the county sheriff and hold another meeting in Harijan Basti to ease tensions. We explained to people the benefits of toilets and emphasized what 'public' in public toilets means. The sheriff reiterated our comments and then threatened to throw anyone in jail who taunts, terrorizes or locks his or her neighbor out of the toilets. The toilet controversy ended there and then.

In case I didn't understand the gravity of the situation, on her way out the door Lila Devi warned me again, "Kachyaa is powerful and ferocious!"

She was referring to the local Himalayan god Kachyaa. He is primarily, although not exclusively, a Harijan caste deity who lives in almost every village in Pauri Garhwal in which Harijans live. In our village, he lives in a 1½ -foot square rock pile along the river below Harijan Basti. Kachyaa's only jobs are to exact revenge and eat corpses. Although no one I've talked to has actually seen Kachyaa, they describe him as "scary" because they've seen people possessed by him: Their hands become claws; they eat ashes, mud, and rocks; and, they engage in dangerous antics like hanging off high ledges or playing with fire. Not even a month ago, a man from a nearby village became possessed by Kachyaa and tried to drink a live goat's blood.

Villagers also have a sense of Kachyaa's prowess from the trouble he wreaks in people's lives after someone has caste an evil spell over the person in Kachyaa's name: Failed businesses, sick family members, bad luck, conflict, death and every other human malady known to man.

A musician from Kuransi who plays the drum and sings local folk histories narrated the following story to me:

> "During the early history of Pauri Garhwal, an important man's son died. Distraught and angry, he sought the advice of a Soothsayer. The Soothsayer told him the goddess Parvati had found a seed stuck to her dress and planted it in her garden. He informed him that it's now a fully-grown plant with branches and leaves. The Soothsayer directed the man to find the plant and cut it down. After finding the plant, the man struck it with an ax. Blood came oozing out. He struck it again. Milk poured out. When he struck it a third time, Kachyaa and his younger brother, Daundayaa, jumped out of the plant. From that day forth, people in Pauri Garhwal have quarreled and made enemies. Their enemies, full of anger and wanting to exact revenge, build temples to Kachyaa and pray to him to curse the person they are mad at. In this way Kachyaa's popularity has spread."

A few hours after I discovered the sindhor on my kitchen counter, two contractors arrive to give me a bid to fix my leaky roof. They're strangers to Chandpur, so as they enter my house, six young Chandpur men, enticed by curiosity and concern, follow them in. We're all milling around on my sundeck, assessing the water damage from the monsoons, when I notice Ganesh staring at the red stained dishrags I'd used to clean up the sindhor and afterwards had hung out to dry in the sun. Thinking he might assume its blood, I inform him, "It's not blood. It's sindhor. Someone tossed it in my window last night" and flippantly add, "No doubt trying to put a curse on me!"

The Chandpur men turn dead silent. They then begin drilling me about the incident, wanting to know exactly what happened, when and where. The last question sends us all down to my kitchen window to look at the scene of the crime. One by one, they take a look at my kitchen counter and window grate, both of which have been wiped clean. Talking amongst themselves, not to me, they comment: "She's going to have to do puja!" "She should go see a Soothsayer" and "We'll have to inform Bhai Sahab" (respected brother, referring to JDF's Director). One man, Gajendar, directs me to, "Keep the window [shutter] closed at night!" And in his next breath warns me, "You should always keep your windows closed at night!"

News of the incident spreads like wildfire. Everybody I talk to broaches the subject in hushed, funeral-parlor voices, "I heard sindhor was tossed in your window." And then they don't say another word, as if to talk about it further will make matters worse. Even Garhwalis living hundreds of kilometers away in Delhi hear about it. I consult a friend of mine, Shakambari Devi, about their reactions.

She explains, "People think you should consult a Bakhyaa."

"Why do they think I need to talk to a Soothsayer? What will he do?"

"He'll tell you who did it. Well...maybe not tell you who did it, but he can apprise you of things about the person who did it."

"Like what?"

"Like what the person's house looks like."

I think, 'All rock and mud houses look the same. How will it help to know what the perpetrator's house looks like?' I ask, "What good would it be to know who did it?"

127

"If you know who did it, you can figure out what to do about it. If the person cursed you, which everyone thinks he did, you can probably find out from the person which god he prayed to. The solution is for you to pray to that god for forgiveness. When that god dances in the village again, you can even ask him yourself how to make amends."

I'm taken aback for a moment, not sure if I misunderstand or not. "Are you saying the person who wishes someone ill tidings is not the blameworthy person, but the person who is cursed is? The cursed person is responsible for making amends?"

"Uh-huh."

"What kinds of things do people do to make amends?"

"The cursed person gives one or two kilos of rice or jangora (barnyard millet) to the curse-giver. When the rice is given and received it means any bad feelings between the two people have been resolved, and the mind and heart of the two people are clean and pure toward one another."

"Are there other ways people make amends?"

"The usual: Slaughter a goat, build a temple, pray. Go ask a Bakhyaa."

A couple of weeks later, shortly after dark, there's a knock on my door. Magan Singh, a Thakur clan elder, informs me he and another Thakur elder, Trivendar Singh, are heading out early in the morning to Tehri Garhwal. He explains, "We want to consult a famous Bakhyaa who lives there. We think the Thakur clan has been cursed."

I'm dumbfounded. The sindhor incident has gone from a spell cast over me to a spell cast over the entire Thakur clan. I'm also suspicious. Since I haven't gone to talk to a Bakhyaa, I suspect they really just want to find out about the spell over me.

"What's wrong with the Thakur clan?" I demand to know.

"People are getting sick," he bemoans.

Thinking he wasn't going to be able to come up with one name, let alone two, I push him for details. "Who's getting sick?"

He recounts them one by one, pausing thoughtfully between each incident. "Meenu's father suddenly died of stomach cancer...Gaju's mother's foot got crushed under a jeep tire the other day...Out of the blue, Bhabhiji [older brother's respected wife] died while dancing [during possession]...Vikram's father accidentally ate a piece of wire and now his stomach is torn open...Suru's mom is dead...The village has split apart..." He lingers on his last sentence.

My callous stance softens. He's right. Several Thakur elder's have either died recently or met with accidents and the split in the village has caused people to feel unsettled. I understand now how they've come to the conclusion a curse is the source of their problems, but what I don't understand is how sindhor tossed in my window has become the impetus for their journey? Even though he doesn't say it, I know they're going to talk to the Bakhyaa about the sindhor tossed in my window. I'm just not sure why.

Four days later Magan Singh and Trivendar Singh return. As I predicted, they had asked the Soothsayer about the person who threw sindhor in my window, however, the Soothsayer couldn't divine anything about the incident because neither of the elders could tell him important details such as which window the sindhor was thrown in, my age and so forth. What they did find out is that they were right. An evil spell has been cast over the Thakur clan and in order to break the spell the entire Thakur clan must have a three-day puja performed, as soon as possible. The elders waste no time in arranging it. The ceremony starts the very next day.

Ducking into the first floor room of Narendar Thakur's house, I sit down on the mud floor next to five other people who are already seated in front of the Baaman. He's chanting in Sanskrit and placing leaves and flower petals on top of a woman's head. After he finishes blessing her, he places leaves and flowers on my head too and applies a splotch of turmeric paste and rice in between my eyebrows. Since people during this part of the puja ceremony merely pop in to get blessed and then leave, I sit there for only a few minutes, then get back up and go outside.

Chachaji (respected uncle, Trivendar Singh) is crouched against the wall with his head cradled in his hands. When he glances up, I can barely believe my eyes. Chachaji, the vibrant 73-year old who never looks a day over 55 and who with extraordinary vigor labors in the fields every single day, now appears to be 90 years old. He's dressed the same as always in his long faded cotton shirt, pajama pants, a stained white Nehru-style cap and bare feet, but he looks completely different. His face bares lines I've never seen before. He whispers, as if he doesn't have enough energy to raise his voice to a normal volume, "The Bakhyaa told Mangan Singh and I the reason the Thakur family is experiencing so many problems is because someone has caste a spell over Bhaironath."

Bhaironath is the Thakur clan god who lives in a room in the house across the courtyard from mine. When the gods Vishnu (preserver of life) and Brahma (creator of life) were arguing over which of them is superior, their argument got out of control. Other gods summoned the third member of the holy trinity and the destroyer of life, Shiv, to intervene. By the time Shiv arrived, Vishnu and Brahma's weapons were drawn, so Shiv quickly erected a firewall between them. The wall stretched far up into the heavens and deep into the earth, thwarting their impending duel. Nonetheless, their argument remained. Looking at the formidable firewall between them, they decided whoever finds its end is truly the superior god. One went up into the heavens and the other underground. Upon return, Vishnu admitted defeat. Brahma, however, erroneously claimed he had found the end. Shiv, hearing Brahma's lie, grew angry. He pulled Bhaironath out of his angst and instructed him to kill Brahma. Bhaironath cut off one of Brahma's five heads, but before he could kill him, Brahma repented and Shiv forgave him. Brahma's life was spared and Bhaironath was born.

Bhaironath has eight major forms in Hinduism and, according to a local Baaman, Bhaironath has 32 different forms just in the Chandpur area alone. In popular literature he's depicted as an old naked sage accompanied by a dog, carrying the skullcap from Brahma's fifth head and a sword. The Bhaironath that lives in Chandpur is sometimes depicted as a naked sage accompanied by a dog, albeit in Pauri Garhwal he carries fire tongs, a timaru branch and a Trident, but more often than not, he's perceived as fierce and feared, like the Bhaironath who cut off Brahma's head, an image reflected in his blackened idol with barely perceivable features. In response to my queries about who Bhaironath is and why he's worshipped, villagers have replied:

"Bhaironath is a powerful god. He takes away our problems."

"He's dangerous! He dances in the cremation grounds."

"There is only one god, Shiv, but he's known by many names."

"We must worship him and sacrifice goats to him every three years, otherwise bad things will happen."

"Before we travel anywhere and before we get married, we always go to Bhaironath's temple to ask for his blessing."

"Our mothers & fathers, grandparents and their grandparents worshipped Bhaironath. For this reason, we worship him too."

"Outsiders do not know what a terrible force the gods are here in these mountains."

"Life is hard in Pauri Garhwal. We depend on Bhaironath to help us out. We have depended on Bhaironath as long as our forefathers can remember. Long live Bhaironath!"

Chachaji continues his lament; "The Bakhyaa told us that 25 or 26 years ago someone from Chandpur's Harijan Basti put a spell on Bhaironath. Because of the spell, Bhaironath can no longer see us and because he can't see us, calamity has fallen upon us. We don't know who cast the spell or why, but the Bakhyaa said whoever did it died within a couple of days of casting the spell." Heaving a sigh he paused, and then added, "It's the same kind of spell Iravanna cast over Hanuman in the forest."

The spell Chachaji is referring to is from the Hindu epic, Ramayana. The story recounts the life of Rama, the perfect man. Being an incarnation of the god Vishnu, he is worshipped as a god. His father was King of Ayodhya, a city in Northern India located on the banks of the river Ganga. The King was getting old and planning for his son Rama to become King but at the last minute, there was a change of plans. Because the King's second wife had saved him many years earlier, he had granted her two wishes to be bestowed whenever she wanted. She exacted them now. She demanded her son, not Rama, become the next King and she had Rama banished to the forest for 14 years because she feared the people of Ayodhya would protest the change of plans if Rama remained in the city. Rama, being a perfect son as well, complied with her wish. He, his wife Sita, and another brother, Lakshman, went to live in the forest. While in the forest they experienced a variety of adventures, including the kidnapping of Sita by the demon King Ravanna of Sri Lanka. Rama and Lakshman set out on a long search to find Sita. During their search, they met Hanuman, the monkey god. Extraordinarily strong, exceptionally intelligent and devoted to righteous causes, he became Rama's devoted companion. One night while Rama and Lakshman slept in the forest and Hanuman stood guard, Iravanna (the demon King Ravanna's brother) slipped past Hanuman, kidnapped Rama and Lakshman and whisked them away to the underworld. Hanuman had been totally awake and diligently guarding his charges, but Iravanna was a Tantrik Sorcerer. He put a spell over Hanuman, enabling him to slip by, right in front of Hanuman's open eyes, without being seen. When the spell wore off, Hanuman figured out what had happened. He went to the underworld, killed Iravanna, saved Rama and Lakshman, and the trio continued their search for Sita.

The Soothsayer had told Chachaji this same kind of spell had been cast over Bhaironath. Even though Bhaironath is living in Chandpur watching over the Thakur clan and they're right in front of his eyes, he can't see them because of the spell caste over him a quarter of a century ago and consequently he can't protect them either. Thus, bad things are happening to Thakur clan members. Hanuman came to his senses, figured out what had happened and saved Rama and Lakshman. The Soothsayer explained to the Thakur clan elders that only a three-day puja for the entire Thakur clan will clear Bhaironath's vision.

A blend of standard Hindu puja and tantra-mantra rituals continues all day with Thakur clansmen, women and children coming and going at their leisure. A large group gathers later in the day for a havan, the fire ceremony in which clarified butter, sesame seeds, and a sandalwood mixture are offered to god. Every Thakur family is given a handful of ashes and burned sesame seeds from the fire, a small branch from the timaru tree (a symbol for Bhaironath) and rot (unleavened wheat bread made from brown sugar, ghee, and anise seeds)—all blessed items that will be applied to foreheads, set on home altars and eaten, respectively. Even those who do not attend are sent bundles of blessed items wrapped in an old scrap of newspaper.

I miss the next two full days of puja. It is immediately deemed unsuccessful anyway. Thakur clansmen and the Baaman had buried sacred items down by the river on the last day of puja and that night someone went down to the river and dug the items back up—a sacrilegious act voiding the ritual's intent. Thakur clansmen whisper amongst themselves that it was Gobind Singh Rana (a fellow villager but often rival clansman) who unearthed the prayer offerings to thwart the Thakur clan's attempt to end the spell over Bhaironath and subsequently keep the Thakur clan vulnerable to life's ills.

Who or why someone put a spell over me is still a mystery. I've never told anyone, but since the sindhor was tossed in my house, several problems have arisen in my life. The worst I've had in over 25 years and the persistent kind, which keep me up at night ruminating about what I could or should do to make things better. Whenever my mind turns towards the curse as a possible source of my troubles, I burst out laughing imagining how my American friends and family would guffaw at the thought, and then I fall asleep.

"Whomp!....Whomp!....Whomp!" The sound reverberates across the courtyard, melting into faint thumping sounds emanating from other courtyards. Rajeshwari Devi wields the four-foot long wooden club as if it's a twig, swinging it up over her right shoulder with a hoola-hoop like gyration, lifting it straight up into the air before slamming it down onto the pile of millet lying on the ground in front of her, bending her torso all the way forward to keep the stick parallel to the ground at impact, in order to separate the chaff from the whey. She repeats this fluid, rhythmic motion over and over again without stopping until she realizes I'm watching her. She pauses to give me her customary quick nod and then holds the stick out in my direction. Breaking into an amused snigger she asks, "Do you want to thresh millet?"

"No thanks. I think I'd throw my back out the first time I raise the pole to do one of these numbers," I reply, while grossly imitating her hoola-hoop gyration and a ready-to-topple-over wobble.

Rajeshwari Devi laughs. She's a handsome woman. At 46 years old, she's robust and strong, with an air of nobility about her. She stands perfectly erect, a posture no doubt attained from carrying water, grass and wood on her head every day of her life since she was three or four years old. Wrapped around her head multiple times is a long, shimmering peacock blue colored scarf with one end tucked into the folds, securing it, and the other dangling down past her shoulder. The loosely applied turban would be seen as sloppy in any other context, but here it only adds to her regal appearance. It's also utilitarian; preventing the thousands of floating particles generated by threshing from landing in her hair, keeping her hair from falling into her face while working and it's a readily accessible tool used to bind firewood, fill with grass or form into a cushioned platform to set water jugs on top of her head. She's wearing an array of jewelry: A brass orb in her nose, brass hoop earrings, a black beaded necklace with a tin amulet, two silver toe rings, two silver anklets, several multicolored glass and brass bracelets and a round, red appliqué between her eyebrows, proclaiming her status as a married woman. They add to her beauty and royal appearance, but clash with the hard continuous labor she does every day, stealing away any telltale signs of being overworked.

"But I do want to talk to you," I tell her, without elaborating.

She looks at me intently and then shyly, her eyes glancing down to the ground periodically, patiently waiting for me to speak up.

Up to this moment, I am convinced Garhwalis made up the saying 'the more the merrier'. They have a strong sense of community and spend a good deal of their leisure time socializing, often in close approximation with one another, so close that their personal body space appears almost nil. Jammed packed jeeps appear to bring about even more camaraderie and shoulder-to-shoulder crowds seem to be sought after. Everyday at JDF's morning meetings, the first five male employees to enter the room invariably cram onto a small couch meant for three and all of JDF's female employees squeeze together on one bed-cum-couch, their bodies unnecessarily scrunched together despite the fact there are numerous other places to sit. This close spatial relationship extends into the night as well with several people normally sleeping in one room, often sharing beds (i.e. a girlfriend of mine sleeps on a 6 ft square floor with her four children and mother-in-law, all sharing the same bedding).

When I first came to Chandpur, women offered to sleep with me. They assumed I disliked sleeping because they're afraid to. I'd politely refuse and let them know I like to sleep alone and that I'm not afraid, a conversation that occurred multiple times before they finally stopped asking.

It dawned on me a few minutes ago that Rajeshwari Devi has been sleeping alone in her house for the previous three days. Her husband and eldest son live in a village far away where they run a small restaurant. Her daughter has gone to her grandmother's village for a few weeks to help her during the busy harvest season. And her youngest son, at my behest, is in Delhi to learn from JDF's accountant how to maintain a cashbook. Knowing how much Garhwalis dislike being alone, let alone sleeping alone, I'm mortified imagining how distressed Rajeshwari Devi must be. Thus, hearing her pounding millet on the courtyard, I rush outside to tell her I'm going to call her son home from Delhi immediately. As a prelude to our conversation, I ask her, "How are you getting along these days, staying in the house alone?"

She answers cheerfully, "Great! I like being alone."

I am momentarily speechless, her words a stark reminder how stereotyping rarely reflects an individual.

Suddenly a pressure cooker lets out a piercing scream from Kaneeka's house next door, leading Rajeshwari Devi to ask, "Have you eaten dal-bhat (lentils and rice) yet?"

It's a question I used to answer with drawn out, truthful explanations, including unorthodox ones like telling people I'd eaten curried vegetables and roti (unleavened wheat bread) or that I hadn't eaten lunch yet, both relatively shocking answers since everyone eats rice and lentils for lunch and everyone eats lunch who can afford it. Later on, I realize the question has the same kind of meaning as when the grocery clerk asks a person standing in the checkout line, 'How are you doing today?' The only appropriate answer is some version of 'I'm fine', regardless of whether a person is fine or not. Therefore, I answer Rajeshwari Devi's question with, "Yes, I've eaten lunch," even though I haven't had a bite of food all day.

Nisha Devi appears around the corner lugging a tub of washed laundry on her head. She's wearing a giant smile—the kind that lights up her whole face and makes anyone who looks at her feel a little better. Amazingly, Nisha Devi smiles like this every day all day long. Only laughter and an occasional scolding of her children break the monotony.

Her life circumstances make her sunny disposition difficult to understand. Her first husband left home nine years ago. I assume he ran away from the confines of village life and the lack of opportunity therein, rather than from Nisha Devi. Regardless, he's gone and his younger brother was unceremoniously appointed Nisha Devi's new husband. Her three children went through the terrible twos one right after the other. She has been breast-feeding continuously for the past ten years and could easily do so for another two years, until the youngest turns five. The family lives in a mud and rock house built several generations ago and owned by Nisha Devi's father-in-law, who lives with them. She and her husband share a 10 X 12 foot bedroom with their three children, two short single beds, one wooden table stacked with their belongings and one small freestanding metal closet crammed into the corner. The only other furniture in their house is her father-in-law's bed. They own all of the practical things they need like pots and pans, dishware and farm tools, but they have few additional personal items other than clothes. At night, they illegally hook up a wire to their neighbor's recently installed electrical line to generate one light bulb—when there's electricity.

Nisha Devi works outdoors 365 days a year. Six months of that time is spent in either the blistering hot sun or incessant monsoon rains. There are no machines. She plants, cuts, hauls, harvests and threshes all of her crops by hand. During this current season, she will harvest two types of millet, two varieties of rice, a cereal, four dried beans, eight different vegetables and two spices. In addition, she'll plant six vegetables, three spices, two grains and two dried beans. Being the only woman in her family, she'll do 90% of the work herself. Because fodder and fuel are not bought, Nisha Devi, goes into the jungle, almost daily, with a sharp sickle, negotiating dangerously steep slopes to cut grass to feed the family's livestock and climbs high into trees to cut wood to fuel their stove. She cleans the animal's shed daily; scooping urine soaked straw and dung with her hands and hauls it on her head to fallow fields for fertilizer.

It's not just what Nisha Devi does that's so remarkable, but the fact that everything she does takes a little more effort and stamina than what we're used to in more modern societies. When she gets up in the morning, there's no heater to turn on in the dead of winter. There's no running water, no bathroom and no sink. Every day she hauls six 25 Kg water pots on her head from the spring to her house and four more pots to the animals. There are no ready-to-eat pre-packaged foods and no refrigerators. She makes everything on the spur of the moment, from scratch: Bakes homemade bread twice a day, picks her vegetables from a field and grinds her spices between two rocks. There are no ovens. She has a Coleman-like two-burner gas stove, which I gave her, however, she uses it sparingly because gas costs money, choosing instead to cook on her mud and rock fireplace. There are no potholders, tongs or other nifty kitchen items. Nisha Devi sticks her hand directly into the fire at least 50 times a day. There are no washing machines or dryers, obliging her to carry her family's clothes down to the spring or river and wash each piece by hand, while sharing water rights with the other village women. To wash dishes, she takes them outside, cleans them with handfuls of mud and then rinses them with the buckets of water she has hauled.

Right there and then on the courtyard, I finally ask Nisha Devi what has perplexed me for years, "Are you as happy as you always look?"

I explain to her that if she is, she should tell the world her secret because a lot of people could use help in the contentment department.

She laughs her hearty laugh and replies, "Yes, I'm happy. But I also smile out of habit. I smile even when I'm mad."

At first, I take her answer to mean she has no secret to impart. Upon reflection, I realize that maybe being able to smile even when you're mad is her secret.

Nisha Devi lays out her laundry to dry and Rajeshwari Devi goes back to pounding millet.

The smell of simmering onions, chilies and coriander permeate the air. Kaneeka, who lives in the fourth and final house on our shared courtyard, is making lentils and rice, necessarily leaving her doors and windows wide open to allow smoke from her fireplace to escape the room. Eventually, she pokes her face out from the kitchen, smiles and then, stooped over, drags a huge, heavy brass container outside the door. She maneuvers it up onto her head and trots off toward her cow's shed. In the pan is reusable water, food scraps, discarded plant stems and leaves, vegetable peels and table scraps, including waste from the first rinse of everyone's dishes, which she is on her way to feed to their lactating cow.

Nisha Devi moseys around the courtyard checking on her crops, running her hands through the kernels and flipping them over to dry on all sides. After threshing, seeds, beans and spices are laid out on tarps and mandaros (large woven mats made from dried wheat stalks, hemp or Mala tree bark) to dry in the sun for three to four days, turning courtyards into mazes that must be navigated rather than crossed. One grain is the same millet Rajeshwari Devi is currently extracting from stalks. Its flour is used to make a thick flatbread, derogatorily referred to as 'poor man's bread'. It's a misnomer. The bread is delicious and because it generates body heat, practical to eat during the winter months.

Strewn across another tarp is a local variety of black beans, used primarily to make curried lentil, a staple eaten with rice, but it's also used to make two Himalayan specialties; dal pakora and, when ground and mixed with spices, it's stuffed into dough and cooked like unleavened bread, making a mouth-watering parantha called simply 'stuffed bread' or when referring to it using the above named flour, mandua-kee-roti.

Nisha Devi ducks inside a small room off the courtyard where her family's grains and tools are stored. She reappears carrying a six-foot long, four-inch diameter solid wood club, a flat, woven basket and a 15 Kg bucket, partially filled with un-husked rice that she'd soaked in water overnight. She pours a portion of the un-husked rice into a 6-inch deep by 6-inch diameter hole in the courtyard. Straddling the hole with her bare feet, she picks up the heavy pole and, grasping it with both hands in the middle where the circumference is slightly less, she raises it up in the air as high as her arms can reach and then slams it back down into the hole, onto the rice. She lifts it up and slams it down again and again, producing a loud thud each time and making it sound like Nisha Devi and Rajeshwari Devi are playing a waltz together with their repetitive, rhythmic threshing: "Whomp, thud thud, whomp, thud thud, whomp!"

Every time Nisha Devi strikes the rice, husks separate from the grains and with each successive thud, spent husks or kernels are ejected from the hole onto the courtyard, which was newly coated with mud and dung not even two weeks ago to keep kernels from falling into cracks. Between the up and down movement of her pole, she deftly brushes the husks off to the side with her bare feet and scoots rice back into the hole.

When Kaneeka returns to the courtyard, she pulls out her 6 ft-long pole, walks over to the hole and begins to pound rice with Nisha Devi. They both straddle the hole from opposite sides. Just as Nisha Devi lifts her club out of the hole, Kaneeka's club slams down onto the rice and just as Kaneeka's club lifts up, Nisha Devi's club slams down. They take turns lifting and jabbing their poles forcefully into the hole, one right after another in a synchronistic pounding so precisely timed and expertly executed, neither hesitates and there are no collisions. Every so often they stop to pull the semi-cleaned rice out of the hole, put it into the flat basket and pour more husked rice into the hole. After the rice is cleaned as much as possible by pounding, Nisha Devi begins tossing the husked rice into the air, using the flat basket, flipping it gently enough so that the heavy rice grains fall back into the basket, yet high enough for the remaining husk particles to be caught by the wind and blown away.

Kaneeka is helping Nisha Devi clean her rice just to help Nisha Devi clean her rice. At nineteen years old, she is community-oriented and mature beyond her years. The first nine years of her life were spent living on the plains in Delhi, the bustling capital of India with a population of over 14 million people. Then her mother died and shortly thereafter Kaneeka was given to her mother's parents to be raised in

Chandpur. Kaneeka had to learn Garhwali, learn village culture, make new friends, fit into a new family and learn how to do rigorous field and house work. Her grandparents were in their sixties when she came to live with them, so Kaneeka has always done the bulk of the labor.

Last year when Kaneeka was still in school and year-end exam results had been publicized, she proudly informed me she had passed her tenth grade exams at the top of her class. She wanted to celebrate but her grandmother was too ill. Her grandmother had become increasingly dizzy and agitated over the past year, eventually becoming so afraid of people that she spent her days lurking in the shadows of her house, hiding from everyone, especially me. The undiagnosed condition rendered her incapable of organizing a celebratory party for Kaneeka, as well as made it impractical to hold a party in her home, so Kaneeka asked me, "Will you throw me a party at your house?"

I was taken aback for a split second but then replied, "Why not?" It reflected not only the question I was asking myself, but also the linguistically equivalent statement as, "Sure!"

Several women were working in my house that day cleaning and painting, so I posed the question, "What should we do for Kaneeka's party?"

The room went dead silent. It was truly a case where if a pin had dropped, we would have heard it. I thought that maybe they didn't understand my question, so I rephrased it. Again, there was no response.

Finally, one of the girls suggested, "We should eat something."

"Good idea!" I encouraged. "What will we eat?"

"Samosas!" Someone else chimed in.

"And dipping sauce."

"Anything else, something to drink like pop? Pepsi?"

"I drank Pepsi once and got nauseous." Dikka recounted and then added, "For many villagers, especially children, pop is too strong.

If we get any pop, we should buy Limca or Fanta because they're not as strong. Most people will drink tea anyway."

"What else will we do?"

There was no reply. Their silence was puzzling. I was unsure of what Kaneeka expected of a party, but I thought for sure Kaneeka and the other women would know. I recommended we think about it over lunch.

After eating, we continued cleaning, painting and talking. Lakshmi Devi had clearly thought about the party during lunch, immediately declaring, "We should set up a TV and VCR to watch videos."

It was answered by a chorus of 'yeses'.

I volunteered to pick up a video machine and videos the next time I went to the city and had them write a list of video titles I should try to find. They wrote down eight tapes: Six depicting Hindu religious stories and two contemporary movies.

I urged them to think of other activities we could do during the party, reminding them that although I have electricity hooked up in my home, more often than not there is no electricity—either a line goes down or is purposefully turned off by the government because there are not enough megawatts to go around.

Kaneeka suggested we should "do a kirtan" (sing devotional songs). Everyone's faces were bright with excitement, nodding in affirmation. I unenthusiastically agreed. In my opinion, a fun party for a teenager didn't include singing religious songs.

"What about playing some games?" I offered.

Again dead silence.

Determined to make the party a fun event I pressed on, "What group games do Garhwalis play besides cricket and hide and seek?"

They looked around at one another in silence. Finally, Shakambari Devi asserted, "We don't play games."

"Oh! The perfect situation to learn something new!" I stated and to stimulate ideas, I elucidated on the kinds of games I played as a kid: Red light-Green light; Red-rover, Red-rover; and, Simon-says. The women seemed unimpressed, so I switched to adult games, elaborating on how to play Charades, giving numerous examples, intentionally trying to capture their attention. Their reactions remained muted. I figured maybe charades was too complicated, spontaneous and animated, so then I described how to play 'I'm going on a tiger hunt'. I was sure this game would be the right blend of mild complexity and fun. I lined everyone up in a circle. "We'll pretend like we're going on a tiger hunt," I announced, knowing they all knew what going on a tiger hunt in the Himalaya might entail. I expounded on the rules and gave examples of answers. We then went around the circle taking turns recounting the series of items being carried on the hunt, as well as stating the new item we intended to bring along.

The women and girls looked anything but enthused. In a last ditch effort to engage their interest and to get them to do something different, I suggested, "We don't have to go on a tiger hunt, we can pretend we're taking a trip to Delhi or Vaishno Devi Temple!"

Finally I asked them outright, "Do you want to play this game?" In the ensuing silence I added, "Or any of the others?"

A horrified look came over Kaneeka's face. Collecting her courage, she candidly, albeit haltingly, informed me, "We've never played these games, Madam…. People will not want to play them…. We better stick to singing religious songs and watching videos."

I glanced around the room. Everyone was nodding their head in agreement, obviously relieved Kaneeka had told me what they had probably all been thinking and feeling for the past hour.

We went on to plan who would arrange the samosas, tea, etc. Kaneeka and I spent two days going door-to-door, face-to-face, extending personal invitations. Because the village was in a political divide, the Rana women were not allowed to come. Their children came, however, as did all of the Thakur clan children and all of the Thakur clan women. Women and children are usually the ones who sing kirtans, except during formal religious ceremonies when the older boys and men join in with unbridled enthusiasm. Nevertheless, six or seven men showed up to play the instruments: The dholak (barrel drum), a chimta (looks like giant-size metal tongs and when hit against the hand or leg rattles similar to a tambourine), and a harmonium.

In any other language, the lyrics might have been solemnly sung, but the singsong melody of the Garhwali language and the fast, gay, lively rhythm produced the kind of songs that made me want to get up and dance.

We meditated on the foot of god, confessing that during our darkest days and with a trembling heart, we can step on a thorn, be burned by a flame and even leave the country, but we can never leave meditating on the foot of god.

We recounted the story of Krishna (the blue-bodied, flute-playing, man-god) frolicking on the banks of the Yamuna. How his ball rolled into the river and he jumped in after it. How his mother and fellow shepherds cried. How he had come upon the serpent, Kaliya, swimming in the river and how Kaliya had wrapped his coils around Krishna, intending to squeeze him to death. How Krishna transformed into a black giant, broke free from Kaliya's grasp and proceeded to dance tandava (the dance of anger) on Kaliya's 101 heads. And how Kaliya instantaneously recognized the glory of god and repented.

We pleaded with Shiv high atop Kailash to play his damaru (small drum). We marveled at Sheravali Mata riding her lion and Durga riding her tiger, proclaiming in every refrain we are their devoted worshippers. We praised Ganesh, the elephant-headed god who gives eyes to the blind, bodies to lepers, children to the barren, riches to the poor. We searched for Kal Nath Bhairon Baba, a longhaired god and son of Jhaali-Maali who drinks poison, carries fire tongs and wears a garland of skulls. We celebrated the mother goddess's garnet flying through the air, dropping into the lap of Shiv as Parvati, Brahma as Saraswati, Vishnu as Lakshmi, Rama as Sita, Raghunath as Radha, and Lakshman as Urmila. And we recounted how life lasts a mere two days—fire burns wood to ash, rain washes soil away and a clay water pot breaks when dropped—reminding ourselves the only thing perennial is Rama's (god's) love.

We sang, jammed and clapped for three hours non-stop, an hour longer than we had planned. The Kirtan was a hit! We ate samosas and drank tea and soda afterwards. There was one confirmed pop overdose in the form of a stomachache. We never did watch videos. There was electricity, but no one knew how to run the video machine. Someone had inadvertently pushed a wrong button, causing the play button not to work.

Just then, Raki Devi comes up the path carrying a water pot on her head. She is obviously on her way to fetch water from the spring, but having spied me standing in the courtyard, she starts meandering my way. Furtively glancing at Rajeshwari Devi, Nisha Devi and Kaneeka, all going about their chores, Raki Devi begins to plead for money in a semi-hushed voice. Her daughter's engagement party is in two weeks and she needs money to buy an engagement ring for the groom, to entertain the groom's father who will be coming to her home with some of his friends for the engagement party and to hold a feast for her clan.

I reply, "If I give you money, I'll have to give everybody else money, and I mean e-v-e-r-y- b-o-d-y!"

It's one of those lessons I'm continuously learning the hard way. When I came to Chandpur for my second visit nine or ten years ago, it was winter. Knowing people have few items to keep themselves warm, I distributed blankets, sweaters and shawls to the poor. I thought I was doing something kind and useful. Instead, I created a row. People who I didn't give anything to were insulted. Even though they knew the people I had given items to were poor and in great need of them, their sense of fairness would not let them shake loose of the fact that I had given gifts to some people but not to them. The fact they could afford to buy these items on their own had little bearing on their feeling left out.

I received the same kind of response when I hired people for various household jobs like doing my laundry. People made statements like, "You always ask Jankari Devi to do your laundry. When is it my turn?" In the beginning I replied by explaining that Jankari Devi is poor and has no source of income other than selling milk, so I gave her the job as another way to make money. This reasoning did not matter to them. Fortunately, their complaint didn't matter to me either, so we broke even on lack of empathy. When they made the same kinds of comments to Jankari Devi, however, she so disliked being harangued in this manner, she surreptitiously washed my clothes during the village's mid-day siesta, as well as took the clothes away from my house and brought them back to me under the cover of darkness. Although I now send my clothes to her whenever it's convenient, she still brings them back to me after dark and probably still washes them when the least number of people are at the spring.

Raki Devi says, "Oh," in response to my statement that if I give her money, I'll have to give everyone money. The expression is not one of surprise but means yes, I know what you mean or okay. She understands what I mean because she too shares the same sentiment; 'if you give something to one person you must give it to everyone'. Nonetheless, she continues to plead her case for money. I compromise by suggesting she start collecting firewood for me early this year and earn money that way. She readily agrees. Her enthusiasm reflects not only Raki Devi's desire for money, but also her personality. She is dirt poor and it causes her innumerable hardships, but it never seems to rob her of vitality. Given the slightest opportunity she bursts out laughing and her whole body gets in on her joy: Her eyes sparkle, her dimples flash and she'll suddenly double-over, catching her stomach with one hand while the other one unabashedly reaches out and slaps me on the arm or comes up to caress my cheek.

The following afternoon Raki Devi drops off a bundle of wood at my house. Without measuring, I can immediately tell many of the sticks and logs are too long for my small iron-bellied stove, so I ask her to cut the wood she's brought in half, explaining, as I do to her every year, it won't fit into my fireplace. I also let her know she doesn't have to cut it right now, "Whenever you're free, because I won't start using it for another month or two."

My 72-year old neighbor, who's been lying in the sun listening to our conversation, jumps up and comes over to where we're standing. In a gruff voice he retells Raki Devi what I'd just told her, "This wood is too long. Cut it in half!" A split second later, he commands her to "Cut it over there," adding, "We cut wood over there."

He meant the people who live on this courtyard cut wood in that particular spot, a fact Raki Devi has probably known since she was married and moved to Chandpur 20 years ago, making his observation redundant.

Raki Devi listens patiently and does what he says. She picks up a handful of wood and carries it over to the fire pit, per his instructions. She then starts to cut her first piece of wood, when he interrupts her, "No, no, no! Gather all of the wood into a pile here first, then cut it"—as if his strategy is important.

The more he speaks, the more irritated I become. My mind reels with unspoken snide comments: "Shut up you old fart," "Get off her back" and "She knows how to cut wood better than you do!"

Conversely, Raki Devi appears devoid of any negative emotions or thoughts whatsoever. She gets up, walks over to the remaining wood and brings it all over to the fire pit before she begins to chop. People have been telling her what to do and how to do it all of her life. As a child, it was her mother, father, older members of her extended family and older villagers bossing her around. In the second half of her life it has been her husband, her in-laws and her older brother and sister-in-laws. This is the normal hierarchy. The difference is my neighbor is a curmudgeon so almost everything that comes out of his mouth is crotchety. In general, the people who tell Raki Devi or any other Garhwali female what to do, normally speak in a dispassionate, matter of fact manner, like they're saying something as impersonal as, 'cows give milk', lacking the bite of statements dressed in feelings.

The Curmudgeon hovers over her shoulder watching her every move and whenever the slightest opportunity arises, he directs her on how to cut the wood, "Not like that! Hold the axe handle like this," "Cut it small," "Don't cut it on the knot" and "You're splitting it lengthwise. Cut it in half!"

Raki Devi remains unruffled by his brusque manner. She continues to listen and do whatever he says. On the contrary, my ego is banging its head against the wall. I know I can say something aloud to the Curmudgeon, like tell him to leave Raki Devi alone, but I don't. He's just trying to help. He has spent his entire life telling women and girls what to do and how to do it. For him this is his normal and necessary job. He would be devastated if I said anything. Raki Devi, I assess, could care less if I say something or not. It could even be embarrassing for her or maybe even grounds for a village squabble. Instead, unable to tolerate his comments any more, I go inside my house.

Raki Devi dutifully cuts all the wood and stacks it next to my fireplace. She then walks back outside to sweep the wood chips off the courtyard. She has a broom in her right hand and a dustpan in the left. Nevertheless, the old duffer, spotting her, rushes to her side and orders her to do the obvious, "Sweep up the wood chips!"

Of course, he doesn't stop there. "Put the wood chips in the chopping area. We'll burn them later." And before she has a chance to touch the broom to the courtyard, he begins pointing to individual woodchips scattered here and there and instructs her like one would a severely retarded person who is on a supervised work assignment, "Sweep up this one. This one. And this one."

I go back inside my house. When Raki Devi hands me the broom, I'm relieved my suffering has ended. Raki Devi has not been perturbed by his behavior in the least. But just in case I misunderstand her impassionate stance, I ask her outright how she feels about being commanded by the old codger on what to do and how to do it.

Raki Devi smiles broadly and says, "What's there to feel? It's compulsory," which in colloquial usage also translates to mean, "Why get perturb? It's the way it is."

When I mention to her I am furious, she giggles like a shy schoolgirl.

I consider myself to be a liberated woman. On an esoteric level, it means being free to pursue my own happiness. On a personal level, it means being able to make my own decisions about my life and my self. This self—ego—is always striving to be fulfilled even though I consider myself to be happy. Garhwali women do not totally lack an ego, but their ego demands are strikingly minimal compared to an American woman's ego. This stark lack of ego centrism has nothing to do with altruism and its essence is not captured in words like humble, meek or compliant, especially the latter two words, which, along with 'small ego', imply adverse states, when the rural Garhwali woman's disposition is anything but unfavorable. Day after day, month after month, year after year, I see it in action in Pauri Garhwal, forcing me to ask myself who is more liberated? Who is freer? Who is better off? The woman with the big ego clamoring for life to be the way she wants it or the woman with the little ego who accepts life as it is?

"Holi hai! Holi hai! Bang! Bang! Clang! Clang! Bonk! Holi hai!" A cacophony of noise wind its way down the trail behind my house, making a beeline to my front door. "Bonk! Bang! Clang! Rattle! Rattle! Holi hai! Holi hai!" The ragtime band of 5 to 9 year olds shouts again just in case I don't hear them coming, followed by another roar of their instruments, "Clang! Clang! Bang! Bang! Rattle! Rattle!"

I lean over my deck railing, creating a buzz of excitement, evoking more cries of "Holi hai! Holi hai!" Seven boys dressed in their everyday rag-a-muffin attire, faces plastered in red sindhor, stare up at me with wild-eyed excitement and an unbridled spark of hope that I, the trillionaire, will donate oodles of money to their band. One boy waves a flag made from a scrap of red cloth tied to the end of a stick taller than he is. Another boy, clasping a large tin plate from his mother's kitchen with sindhor paste clumped on top, keeps lifting it in my direction, silently offering to apply tilak to my forehead. The rest of the band holds an assortment of instruments: A small drum, a chimta, a khansi-kee-thali and two pot & pan lids, which they thwack whenever one of them is struck by the urge to make noise.

Ten days before Holi young boys form makeshift roving bands and parade from village to village or station themselves along roadsides, flagging down passing vehicles or brazenly stepping out in front of them, hollering "It's Holi! It's Holi!" Implied in the ritual is a

153

demand for money to buy Holi powders, candy and firecrackers. Donations are normally one or two rupees. I oblige the boys' fantasy by giving them a whopping ten-rupees (22 cents). Their faces light up as if they've just hit the jackpot. The boy carrying the tray of sindhor paste applies tilak to my forehead, after which they head back up the trail toward the road, banging on their instruments and bellowing, "Holi hai! Holi hai!"

The night before Holi, just as dusk settles in our valley, people carrying bundles of pinewood informally gather in the courtyard outside my house. Years ago this courtyard was designated the 'village courtyard' because of its large size and central location, so village meetings and celebrations are held here. Young men build a fire in the center of the yard while the rest of us watch. More people arrive with wood, tossing some of the pitch-laden pieces onto the fire, causing it to spit and crackle, and setting the rest aside for later. Before long, a bonfire is blazing in remembrance of Holika, the sister of King Hiranyakashipu. Hiranyakashipu was trying to kill his son, Prahlada, because his son worshipped the god Narayana more than he worshipped his father. In one of his bids to kill his son, the King solicited Holika's help. She had been given a boon by another god, guaranteeing she would not be destroyed by fire, so the King ordered his sister to take Prahlada into a raging fire to burn him alive. Holika, thinking nothing would happen to her, did as he commanded. Unexpectedly, Holika turned to ashes and Prahlada survived the fire unscathed, illustrating the doctrines, 'If you're devoted to god, nothing can destroy you and if you try to harm a devotee of god, you will be destroyed'.

There is no electricity so when darkness descends the night turns coal-black, causing the fire to glow supernaturally. Boys and girls grab pitch-laden, inner core pieces of wood and lay one end of the log in the flames. When the tips are fully ignited, the children pick the splintered logs up and begin twirling them around and around, creating fire designs in the dark. Two, ten, and then twenty 2-foot long sparklers whirl in the air. Sparks fly everywhere.

In the distance, a band can be heard playing 'Maithi', a popular Garhwali tune. The sound grows louder and louder as Barsu and his band show up on the courtyard to join in on the fun. They're no doubt also hoping dancers will tuck ten-rupee thank-you notes underneath the ropes tethered around their drums or, at the very least, offer them a shot or two of whiskey.

Barsu, like many musicians in Pauri Garhwal, is from the Harijan caste, making metal tools and pots & pans for a living. Playing in a band is a part-time job. He plays a variety of instruments, but tonight he is playing bagpipes—a remnant of the British Raj. The other four men are playing a dholak (barrel drum), a damoul (round drum), a chimta and an 18-key child's piano. Local musicians provide highly valued entertainment in a place otherwise devoid of frivolity. Beyond that, their playing and singing ability is usually amateur and often marred by one too many shots of whiskey, fourth-class equipment and bad uniforms. The irony is Garhwali music is some of the best music in the world; folk songs with fast, lively beats and song lyrics that accentuate the natural singsong characteristic of the Garhwali language, making the music remarkably melodic, not requiring knowledge of Garhwali to enjoy it.

Men and boys spontaneously start to dance. Lined up behind one another in a muddled circle, they saunter Garhwali style: Feet alternately lift up off the ground at a slight outward angle and come back down in the center of the body, keeping the dancer in a relatively straight line; torsos turn toward the raised leg, almost dipping before heading towards the other rising leg; arms bent at the elbows form lackadaisical goal posts that bounce up and down and sway back and forth with the torso; and, with palms facing the body, fingers rapidly fan inward, one at a time, and then fan open when wrists twist swiftly outward.

The women delay dancing, choosing first to size-up the situation, checking to see who is present. Some don't or can't dance in front of certain older relatives, especially older male relatives. Eventually four women, two girls and I start the women's dance program, following each other around in a small orderly circle. We dance similar to the men, except our lazy goal-post arms stretch out in front, one at a time like we're swimming the breast stroke in mid-air and some female hands, especially the older women's', are permanently cupped, rather than fanning. A few women and girls join our circle for one or two dances, but otherwise our group rarely expands beyond seven or eight, a striking contrast to the 30-35 dancing men and boys.

The hoopla winds down slowly and unceremoniously with women and children straggling home long before the dancing men do at midnight.

Early Holi morning, just as the birds begin twittering and the water buffalo with the weird sense of humor begins grunting, my neighbors are waking up to another day; opening shuttered doors, walking along the path and talking amongst one another. They are all familiar sounds, but there is something different about them today. Shuttered doors, which normally groan and scrape against the ground refusing to budge, fly open with ease. Plodding footsteps are quick and spry. Monotonous good-morning greetings turn into hearty welcomes. Everyone, heightenly aware that Holi can break out at any minute, scurries about to finish their bathroom chores and milk cows while time still permits.

Then just before the sun rises fully above the mountain ridge, Holi hits the courtyard behind my house. Anil steps into his house for a minute and when he comes back out, Surendar is waiting for him, standing flat against the wall near the door, holding three small, green plastic bags in one hand and a fist-full of fuchsia-colored powder in the other. Surendar throws the powder at Anil with reckless abandon. It falls onto Anil's shirt and cakes his hair and face, forcing him to blink repeatedly to keep the fine grains from getting into his eyes. Surendar laughs unmercifully and reaches into his bags for more powder.

A broad, shy smile leaps across Anil's face. He dashes back into the safety of the room he'd just come out of to retrieve his own stash of Holi powders.

Anil lives in this long extended family home with Surendar's family. His own father died years ago and his mother is mentally ill, if not also slightly mentally retarded. She had given birth to eight or nine children and all of them died during their first five years of childhood, except Anil. When he was 6 months old, Surendar's family informally adopted him, deliberately to save him from the same fate as his brothers and sisters. His mother occupies two rooms in the same house, but she is frequently aloof, seldom eating or socializing with Anil or other members of the household.

Santoshi, a young teen, rounds the corner carrying a small steel-lidded milk container. Noticing the handful of lemon yellow powder in Surendar's hand, she grins and playfully warns him, "Don't you dare!" Simultaneously she brings her free arm up in front of her face. Surendar is more judicious this time and tosses the powder directly onto her Punjabi suit, wiping the remaining residue in his hand gently across her cheek. Giggling, she runs off.

Anil returns with his stash of powders. Tall and lanky at 17, he's no match for the even taller and muscular Surendar, but catching Surendar still facing Santoshi, he grabs a handful of lime green powder and dumps it on Surendar's head and, reaching around with his arm, smears more powder on the side of Surendar's neck and face. Surendar whips around and they both frantically reach into their bags for more. Bharti, Surendar's sister, and her two mothers, Saguna Devi and Jamuna Devi, having heard the commotion, emerge from the house armed with their own powders and join in the battle.

Holi expands out into other courtyards. Powder flies. Chortles and screams fill the air. People run helter-skelter. A few have water balloons and water pistols, a modern twist to Krishna's water fights with the gopis (milk maids). By the end of the sorties, the bright greens, reds and yellows have blended into browns and blacks on bodies and clothes. Most people go back to their daily routines coated in powder and paste, washing only their hands and face. Around noon, after the game of Holi dies off, they take bucket baths and change their clothes. Only a few die-hard men continue to celebrate, wandering around the village in groups, looking for other male compatriots to play Holi and drink whiskey.

Holi has been cancelled in Chandpur this year for all of the Thakur clan and part of the Rana clan. Two people from the Thakur clan and one from the Rana clan have died in the intervening months since the last large festival, so it is deemed inappropriate to celebrate a holiday. Those who will celebrate are a handful of members of the Rana clan who figure they're sufficiently distantly related to the Rana woman who died, the Harijan caste folks and an assortment of people who live in Chandpur bazaar but are not considered part of the village (an electrician and plumber who service all the lines out in our area and several teachers that teach in nearby schools). Because my house is surrounded on all sides by Thakurs, I expect Holi to be a quiet affair this year. I'm dead wrong. Roving bands of men drinking whiskey apparently don't come under the no-celebration-of-the-first-major-holiday-after-a-death rule.

A group of seven or eight Thakur and Rana men pound on my door about ten o'clock in the morning, demanding to play Holi and drink whiskey. I don't open up. There are other people sitting inside my house encouraging me not to. An hour or two later I hear a ruckus outside in the courtyard. I walk out onto my deck and, looking down, I spy one of the men who had come by earlier, Parvendar. He's gone berserk.

Parvendar is the Garhwali version of Dr. Jekyll and Mr. Hyde. When he's sober, he's a mild mannered retired army man who barely says a word, let alone speak badly to someone. When he drinks, he turns into a lunatic, ranting and raving about anything and everything in uncontrollable anger. He lives close enough to me that I can sometimes hear him hollering at night, but not close enough that I see most of his antics. I hear about them through the rumor-mill. He goes to people houses and threatens to beat them up or break down their door. He chopped one of his own doors to pieces with an axe while trying to get at his oldest son. He tried to set a truck on fire because he was mad at the owner. During a wedding in Chandpur recently, he physically dragged his teenage daughter home for no apparent reason and she was so upset about the incident, she tried to eat poison. He threw bricks into the middle of the road, blocking traffic in both directions. He poured kerosene on his wife and threatened to set her on fire. He smacked his sister-in-law in the head because he didn't like what she was saying. The list goes on.

So here is Parvendar, drunk again and in one of his uncontrollable moods. At 5'8" and 160 pounds, Parvendar is large compared to many rural Garhwalis. His face is beet-red, veins are bulging from his neck and he's screaming the very same sentences over and over again: "I am going kill a Thakur today. For sure I'm going to kill a Thakur today. I'm going to split him wide open from his groin up to his neck and pull out his innards. Blood is going to flow. I am going to kill a Thakur today."

He angrily spits out his words in huffs and puffs, as if he's the big bad wolf trying to blow down the little pig's house. Whenever he comes to the part, 'split him wide open,' he points with his thumb to illustrate the cut line from the groin to the neck and then follows it up with a visual 'pulling someone's guts out' scene.

While Parvendar rants, he stares menacingly at the three men seated in front of him. The men have been sitting in the courtyard listening to a cricket match between Pakistan and India on the radio. Out of the blue, Parvendar just showed up and, without any apparent provocation, launched into his tirade.

One 72-year old man sitting there has historically been Parvendar's adversary, so he gets up right away and goes inside his house—no doubt locking the door behind himself. The other two men, a father and his son, completely ignore Parvendar, as if he is not even there.

The father is 60 years old, crippled and recuperating from an operation. He had unwittingly swallowed a piece of wire, presumably while eating. His doctor estimated it had been in his stomach for fifteen years. He himself figures he must have eaten it a few days before his visit to the doctor for stomach pain. Treatment consisted of cutting his stomach open and leaving it exposed for four months to drain. His entrails could be seen whenever his bandages were taken off. He became so thin his eyes sunk way back in their sockets and his facial skin darkened. He lied in a bed set up on his veranda all day and all night for three months. Everybody thought he was going to die, prompting every single man and woman in Chandpur to come to sit with him at one time or another, some coming daily or every few days. He was too weak to talk or even to keep his eyes open for very long, obliging his visitors to socialize amongst themselves.

Although his health has significantly improved and his stomach was eventually stitched closed, Ragvir Singh is still convalescing when Parvendar shows up.

To defuse the situation, I decide to talk to Ramesh, the son. At 30 years old he has the physic of a small 15 year old. I assume if I start a conversation with Ramesh, Parvendar will naturally become quiet for a moment while Ramesh and I talk. I further hope that being quiet for a moment will help Parvendar calm down.

I had heard Ramesh arrived in Chandpur two days ago, however, I hadn't seen him yet so I feign surprise and shout out, "Ramesh, you've arrived!"

He can't hear me over Parvendar's ranting and the radio broadcast, so I amplify my voice a couple of decibels and shout again, "Ramesh! Ramesh! Look up!"

When I finally catch his attention, he gazes upward. I repeat myself, "You've arrived! How long are you going to stay?"

"I'll stay for one or two more days, then I have to go back."

His father glances up, brings his prayer-shaped hands up in front of his face and says, "Namaskar!" After which both father and son quickly return to their manikin-like stance, staring down at the ground.

Parvendar doesn't stop his ranting for a minute, not even for a split second when the recognition of a new voice or another person on the scene should have elicited a startle response of some kind; a skip in the rhythm of his speech or a slight movement of his head. He just keeps reciting his same kill-a-Thakur-today slogan.

I try again to interrupt his diatribe. "What are you guys listening too?"

"The big cricket match between Pakistan and India. They're playing together in India for the first time in five or six years!" Ramesh responds enthusiastically, like a typical Indian cricket fan.

Parvendar rages on. I change tactics and, turning toward Parvendar, I call out his name. He doesn't respond, so I repeat his name several times, pausing in-between to give him a chance to react. "Parvendar!...Parvendar!...Parvendar!"

He ignores me completely, continuing to recite his mantra, which by now he must have repeated at least twenty times. I go downstairs where JDF's Director and JDF's Office Manager's brother are sitting and apprise them of the events outside, ending with a plea, "You need to say something. Kaakaa has been run off into his house and Parvendar's still out there terrorizing Chachaji."

Birendar advises, "No, just leave him alone. You know how he gets. He won't listen to anyone. He just goes bonkers."

Followed by Jashpal's refusal, "If I go out there, I'll fight with him, so I'm not going out."

"Well, someone has to do something!" I contend.

In the back of my mind I'm thinking, 'He's intimidating your guy's uncle for Christ's sake! You should do something!' It's a thought that leads me to contemplate how they're my uncles too. It's a feeling of closeness not typical of my personality, but rather a reflection of circumstances here, although I'm not sure if it's inherent in the nature of a small community, culturally induced because of the high respect Garhwalis place on elders or from the Garhwali habit, and thus mine, of not referring to people by their given name. An interaction takes on a whole different feel when you call a neighbor, a fellow villager or even a complete stranger 'respected uncle', 'respected aunt' or 'respected mother'.

"He's been like this for years. Just ignore him," Birendar cautions again.

Birendar is well aware of Parvendar's behavior, everyone is, but Birendar is in the army and has just arrived home, not even a week ago, after a six-month absence, I figure he doesn't know Parvendar's incidents have escalated from monthly events to weekly occurrences, from threats to bodily contact, so I tell him, "The fact is, Birendar, his behavior has been getting worse lately. In the past month there's been two village meetings and he's come and disrupted both with his madness."

Knowing villager's tendency not to get involved, I pick up my large umbrella and head out the door. It's not raining. I'm taking it as a protective weapon in case Parvendar gets physical. Birendar and Jashpal reluctantly follow me for fear of what Parvendar or I might do.

Walking toward Parvendar, I call out his name several times. There's no response. Then Jashpal hollers out, "Parvendar! Parvendar brother! Hey, be quiet for a moment."

Parvendar abruptly stops ranting. It's bizarre to say the least. For twenty minutes he's fumed, barely pausing to breathe, let alone respond to what's going on around him, as if his mind is completely shut off from the rest of the world. Now he instantaneously shuts up in response to Jashpal's plea. It's an eerie silence. Parvendar glares at Jashpal and then starts to repeat his warped message for the umpteenth time, "I'm going to kill a Thakur today...." It's the same old message, but Parvendar is now clearly cognizant of the people around him, in particular Jashpal.

Just then Parvendar's mother strolls by on the trail, hauling cow dung on her head. Despite hearing Parvendar shout his threat to kill a Thakur, she never glances in our direction. Parvendar's biological mother died when he was a small boy. This woman is Parvendar's mother's younger sister. She was given to Parvendar's father over forty years ago as a replacement bride and surrogate mother to Parvendar. She raised him and his two siblings, as well as mothered two more children with Parvendar's father.

Following behind her is the convalescing man's youngest son, a 25 year old, who intentionally keeps his head poised in the opposite direction as well, as if there is something fascinating happening in the empty fields.

Jashpal tries to calm Parvendar down suggesting, "Hey it's Holi. Let's all get along."

Parvendar stops his mantra and trips over quickly spoken words, "Director, Perfector. Who are you? Nothing. Nobody. Who do you think you are to tell me what to do?"

"Listen Parvendar. Go home and sleep it off." Jashpal counsels. At that point Jashpal notices Rana clan members gathered in their courtyards, watching the events unfold from a distance. In-fighting of clan members is disliked, but equally disliked is another clan or caste member from your village watching or finding out about the in-fighting. Jashpal lowers his voice, "Parvendar brother. Ranas are watching everything. Let go of whatever you're angry about. Go home."

Parvendar stands up and moves toward Jashpal, who's become the perfect target for his rage. I step in between them with my umbrella held defensively across my chest.

Parvendar taunts Jashpal, "You think you're such a big shot. What are you going to do about it? Huh? Huh?" Parvendar is like a little kid trying to act tough, but he seemingly doesn't know what to say to appear tough. He finally hacks a 'lugee' and spits it down in front of Jashpal's feet, which is consequently at my feet too.

Spitting at someone's feet is rare and an ultimate insult. It's also the last straw for Jashpal. His nice guy approach turns an about face, "I've helped you out. Gave you a job. Loaned you 10,000 Rs. to expand your business...,10,000 Rs. that you've never returned. And this is how you repay me? By spitting at my feet?"

Parvendar starts jumping up and down like boxers do in a ring just before a fight, except he holds his arms straight down at his sides, as if he's trying to restrain himself or is thinking twice about a brawl. Jashpal is about the same size and strength as Parvendar, so if they get physical, Parvendar is just as likely to get pounded as Jashpal. Jashpal is ornery too. He's from Chandpur village, but he was raised mostly in Delhi, making him an atypical Garhwali. Even his appearance is different. He's taller, stockier, and sports a shaved head. The latter he declares makes him look like a "tough guy," whom he likens to be either a gangster or a Black Cat (nickname for a member of India's terrorist response team). What really sets him apart from his Garhwali roots, however, is his personality: He's sophisticated, assertive, opinionated and self-assured. He doesn't take slack from nobody, including me. These characteristics make him a good Director—he gets things done—and, despite his slightly aggressive character, he is conversely personable, confidant and friendly, which endears him to people instantly.

The other quandary for Parvendar is if he hits Jashpal, he knows me well enough to know I'll jump into the fray, not to mention that I'm standing in-between the two and, if he hits me, even if by accident, he knows people will go berserk, especially the local authorities.

Parvendar suddenly flips off one of his rubber thongs, grabs it and winds his arm back, as if he's going to throw it, but instead stops mid-air and screams, "You want your ten thousand rupees? I'll get it right now. I'll get my wife's wedding necklace right now and give it to you. You want your ten thousand rupees? I'll get it."

Jashpal baits Parvendar, "Yes, I want my 10,000 Rs. Give it to me. Yes, go get the necklace and give it to me." He and everyone else know Parvendar is flat broke and sold off his wife's gold wedding jewelry years ago.

Parvendar storms off.

We go back into my house and discuss the situation. Every time I hear about one of Parvendar's antics, especially assaults against his family, I want to do something to stop him. The problem is most of what I know is hearsay or I hear about the incidences long afterwards. Also, his behavior always borders on the unacceptable. He hasn't hurt anyone seriously yet and today he's threatening to kill someone, not actually trying to kill someone. Most problematic is the people Parvendar harasses adamantly refuse to take any action against him. They're afraid of retribution from Parvendar, both physical assault and being cursed by an evil spell. But it's more than just fear of Parvendar. Garhwalis also believe people should get along with their neighbor no matter what they do and they have a remarkable ability to tolerate people's aberrant behavior, as well as forgive their transgressions.

Nevertheless, the incidents are now weekly, more violent and directed at Parvendar's family and his own clan, the Thakurs. Although he's merely threatening to kill someone, we decide his behavior has gotten completely out of control over the past several months. I'm afraid he's gone off to drink more whiskey, which escalates his tirades. Jashpal is the first to suggest we should have Parvendar arrested, but I'm the one who pushes us into action. We drive to the Patwari's place because we don't have a phone to call him, he doesn't have a phone, the Patwari doesn't own a vehicle and, because it's Holi, there are no commercial jeeps or buses plying the roads for him to get here, anyway. Three Thakur clansmen, including Parvendar's younger brother, accompany us.

While on our way there, we're reminded of why jeeps and buses don't travel on Holi. At the entrance to Mausi bazaar, a dozen men have stationed themselves in the middle of the road and refuse to allow our vehicle to pass until we give them money. Like the young boys who start forming roving bands ten days before Holi, during the two days of Holi the older boys and men form their own bands. A few are genuine musicians who wear creative costumes and play melodic Garhwali music. One such troupe came through Chandpur last year. Three of its members were dressed as Rama, Sita and a jester and they performed short skits based on the Hindu Epic, Ramayana. Their band played well and was even accompanied by a flute. Another band of professional musicians from a more remote area played great Garhwali tunes and wore blankets wrapped around their bodies, like their elders still wear today, proudly announcing on their flag they're from Thapalisain. These bands add character and fun to the roving band tradition. The rest of the bands, however, form solely to drink whiskey. They may carry a drum and a plate of sindhor, but that is the extent of their formalities. Most are drunk and insolent. These guys are no exception. Fed up with bullies, I refuse to pay and climb out of my car, physically clearing the men out of my way. More than just a little bit shocked at my bravado, they let us pass without incident.

We already know Chandpur's Patwari is on vacation so we intentionally go to another Patwari's office. At his office we find one Kangun (boss of 10 Patwaris), three Patwaris and two assistants. One of the assistants is Chandpur's Patwari's assistant. He's well aware of Parvendar's behavior, so as we enlighten the others about Parvendar, he fills in the gaps and verifies our assertions.

The Mausi Patwari in his down-home, country manner tells us, "Hey, we don't mind going out there to get him, but we don't want you chickening out in the end and changing your mind about having him arrested."

"No chance of that happening on my part" I offer. "Put him in jail and throw away the key. I'm sick and tired of his antics and I think they've become dangerous."

Jashpal too assures him he won't retract his statement and sits down to put it in writing. After he's written the complaint, we both sign it and hand it to the Kangun. He, the three Patwaris and the two assistants pile into my car, making us a total of eleven, and we head toward Chandpur, a twenty-minute car drive away. We park the car on the road above Parvendar's house. Seeing the team of Patwaris, a huge crowd of local men and boys immediately gathers around. The Mausi Patwari goes over to Parvendar's front door, which is open but has a homemade curtain strung across the threshold, and calls him out of his house. Obviously surprised, he quickly pulls back the curtain and the Patwari explains to him that we have filed a complaint against him and, "We've come to take you to Mausi."

A now composed Parvendar portrays events in a very different light, "You've got the story wrong. It's them [Jashpal and I]! They threatened to beat me up."

The Patwari tells him he should have filed a complaint about us, saying, "Instead, they've filed a complaint against you, so we're forced to arrest you."

Parvendar refuses to go. The Bidoli Patwari states calmly, "You have to go whether you like it or not, so there's no reason to hassle about it. Get your sandals on and get into the car."

In the meantime the remaining team of Patwaris casually mingle with the crowd, appearing to be in no hurry to haul Parvendar off. Jashpal points out Parvendar's wife to the Mausi Patwari. He ambles over to her; asks her questions and explains what's going on. She confirms Parvendar harasses the family after drinking and does not make a plea for him not to be arrested. No one says anything in Parvendar's defense, except his number one drinking buddy, who quickly shut ups when Jashpal threatens to have him arrested as well (He'd recently stolen money from JDF).

The Kangun orders Parvendar, "Get into the car. We haven't got all day."

"No! I'm not getting into their car!" He protests.

The Kangun mocks him, "Yeah, it's too bad we have to use their car, but it's the only one on the road so get in." Although he didn't raise it suggestively, in the Kangun's right hand is a wooden billy-club whose striking end is carved with dozens of small rounded spikes.

Parvendar doesn't budge.

The Mausi Patwari returns from talking to Parvendar's wife. He must have given a signal of some kind to the others because they all simultaneously corral around Parvendar, insisting with their body posture he get into the car. He climbs in with a huff. The Patwaris had brought a pair of rusted iron handcuffs, the old-fashioned kind that are tightened with a screw, but they don't bother to put them on Parvendar, instead they leave them lying on my dashboard.

The ride back to the Patwari's office is uneventful. One Patwari points out a new elementary school on the hillside across the river and informs us it cost 300,000 Rs. to build. We all guffaw, knowing the amount is outrageous and that it means someone or several people put a whole lot of extra money into their pockets.

Just as we pull onto the side of the road to park below the Mausi Patwari office, Parvendar protests, "I'm not going here. Take me to Pauri. I'm going to the Pauri jail!"

The Mausi Patwari replies, "You don't worry about a thing. After we're finished with you here, we'll send you to Pauri to get your medical."

The meaning of 'medical' is a reference to Patwari justice. Rather than file charges, lock someone up or send them through the judicial system, Patwari's beat people up and then send them home. Colloquially it's known as, 'giving someone a medical', an allusion to their objectionable behavior getting straightened out, fixed, physically taken care, cured.

When Parvendar gets out of the car, instead of walking toward the path leading to the Patwari's office, he heads toward a bend in the road. The other men follow him. I think he's about to run and they're getting ready to chase after him. Instead, they all unzip their pants and urinate on the side of the road.

When they're finished, we climb the steep cement and rock stairway to the Patwari and Kangun's office and home. The old accommodations are dismal. So many rocks and chunks of mud have sloughed off the walls over the years that the decrepit building looks like it's been hit with several rounds of mortar fire. A 5 ft X 7 ft room in the corner with a separate entrance serves as the Patwari's office. Inside is a beat-up table stacked with piles of papers and two rickety chairs. We pass it by and head to another entrance. The low door requires us to stoop down to enter. The ceiling isn't much higher, forcing some of us to hunch over. Inside are several small empty enclosures, hardly large enough to be called rooms. If there was originally a floor, it's long gone, only dirt remains. There's no electricity and it either has no windows or none are open, making the place dark, except for the late afternoon sunlight streaming in through the open door into the hallway. The back of the hallway becomes Parvendar's interrogation room, where officials order him to sit down on the dirt floor.

They ask me to relate to them and to Parvendar what Parvendar has done to wind up in their custody. Looking directly at Parvendar I ramble off a list of things I know to his face, including today's incident. I then let the Patwaris know that what I'd just told them is probably the tip of the ice-burg because I don't know everything that goes on in Chandpur, especially what goes on in the privacy of Parvendar's home.

The Patwaris, Kangun and the assistants take turns asking Parvendar questions, launching into the first and only psychological discourse I've heard in Pauri Garhwal.

"Why do you do these things?"

"What's the problem?"

"Are you stressed?"

"Is someone harassing you?"

"What would make you do these things?"

"Why do you drink if you can't control your behavior?"

Parvendar doesn't say a thing.

The Bidoli Patwari turns to me and poses the question, "You're not going to change your mind about charging him are you?"

I reckon this is his way of asking, 'Are you going to ask us to be soft on him when we start hitting him in a few minutes?' I had already explained to the Patwaris, during our car ride to Chandpur, that I want Parvendar to be prosecuted through the court system, not via Patwari justice, but it is now obvious they're going to ignore my wishes and handle the situation the way they always handle these kinds of situations. Fed up with Parvendar terrorizing people and tired of walking by his house searching for his wife to make sure that she's okay, I turn and walk outside without saying a word.

I stroll around to the backside of the building where a new Patwari office and home is being constructed. All over Pauri Garhwal, they've been building these spiffy Patwari offices-cum-homes, many of which are already up and running. The location of this one is one of the best spots in Mausi: It's set high above and to the far left of the bazaar, so it's quiet; it sits on an outcrop overlooking the confluence of two valleys, offering great views of forested mountains and the river valley below; and there's a continual breeze, which is refreshing during Mausi's unbearably hot summers. I walk around and check out the layout, even though I already know it: There's an office and combined sleeping room and kitchen upstairs and a jail and bathroom downstairs.

Afterwards, I plop down on a rock, enjoy the view and reflect on how the afternoon transpired; wondering if the Garhwali strategy to ignore aberrant behavior might have been a better solution. It is not so much a soliloquy of regret, as an acknowledgement of cultural and personal differences. Just one of seemingly thousands of situations I find myself in that, although inherent in living in general, are enormously heightened experiences when living in a different culture, requiring constant and conscious decision-making about what to do or not to do, whether to speak out or not to speak out about certain matters, frequently necessitating boundaries to be drawn (mine or theirs) and, in more provocative situations, forcing me to choose which battles to fight or not to fight in order to take care of my personal needs, placate cultural beliefs (Garhwali and American) or for the betterment of society—the latter, despite being illusive and debatable aspirations, are nevertheless bigger than self aims.

A half-hour after I disappear, the Kangun calls me into his dreary office. We drink tea and talk about the weather. Long after sunset, a man appears in the doorway. I can barely make out his silhouette and prayer-shaped hands raised to his chin. I have no idea it's Parvendar until he has left. The Mausi Patwari enters and explains to me that Parvendar has written a letter in which he stated he would never bother his family or any other of Chandpur villagers again. If he does, he will be fined 10,000 Rs. and thrown in jail. He also informs me Parvendar has been let go.

When we arrive back in Chandpur, I ask one of the men with us to go to Parvendar's house and explain to his wife what has happened and to let her know Parvendar is probably walking home right now. Two days later she and Parvendar storm dramatically through the village, announcing to everyone they are heading to Kachyaa's temple to put a curse on Jashpal and I. They hire a Baaman to bolster the power of their curse, meeting with him regularly and openly for everyone to see. Three of his four teenage children now turn their face the other way whenever I walk by. The fourth teen, the oldest son and the one who has had to repeatedly physically fight his father to protect his mother and siblings, barely used to acknowledge me before his father was hauled off by the Patwari. Now he makes a point of offering me prayer-shaped hands and a heartfelt 'Namaskar' whenever we meet.

>*Parvendar's behavior was unbelievably impeccable for the next five months—not even one outburst. Seven months later, however, he got into a fistfight with a man from the Rana clan. Twelve months later, it was his only fracas.

Bhudeshwar Mahadev Mela, despite bearing the name of the Shiv temple adjacent to the fairgrounds, is a secular fair designed to showcase Garhwali culture. It also gives people living in far-flung rural areas an opportunity to come to a large bazaar to buy goods and see friends and relatives. I have never gone before, but this year the organizing committee sent me an invitation and JDF's office manager, Lakshman, is imploring me, on almost a daily basis, to go with him to the fair. He thinks that because I'm a foreigner I'm imbued with enough prestige and power to persuade his hero, a popular singer schedule to perform at the fair, to let Lakshman sing with his band. Although I am fairly certain I will not be able persuade him to allow Lakshman to sing, I decide to go anyway, as a favor to Lakshman. And since both Mausi and the fair have a reputation of being strolling grounds for young people, I invite three neighbor girls to go with us: Kaneeka, Meetu and Lakshmi Devi.

I no sooner pull my car out of the garage to drive to Mausi, when Lakshman slips into his role as a Garhwali male, commenting on and determining the actions of the females. First, he orders the girls to get into the car even though they can see for themselves that it's time to get into the car. Once they sit down, he changes their seating arrangement. Next, he insists they reopen and slam their doors shut again to make sure they are closed tight. He follows the demonstration with explicit instructions not to roll down their windows, explaining that the car has a machine in it, an "AC," which keeps the car cool. Finally, he tells them they should have invited more girls: "Three girls are not enough!"

This all happens before I start driving. The girls do everything he tells them and do not appear miffed in the least. I'm annoyed but remain silent. While driving through Chandpur bazaar he orders me to honk my horn to let everyone walking in the middle of the road know I'm coming up behind them. I reply, "Are you going to dictate to the girls and I what to do and how to do it the entire trip?"

The girls audibly gasp. Lakshman merely says, "No" and keeps to his word the rest of the day.

In his mid-twenties, Lakshman is intelligent, ambitious and a loyal employee of JDF. The latter is the reason I'm going with him to the fair to support his dream of singing on stage. When other JDF employees were caught misappropriating JDF funds, Lakshman was one of the few who did not and had even helped gather information about the others, earning him my respect, but henceforth branding him a traitor by some of the other workers, their families and fellow villagers, a difficult position for him to be in, but an interesting predicament, particularly in light of his grandfather's history as a traitor.

Five generations of the Thakur clan had lived in Chandpur as remote and poor farmers, tilling small, rocky fields and raising livestock in a harsh climate. Barely eeking out an existence, villagers necessarily supplemented their meager diet by eating dozens of wild plants and fruits. There were no stores, no roads, no towns and no income generating work, giving them no way to lift themselves out of poverty.

Between 80 and 90 years ago, the hardy Thakur boys began migrating down onto the plains to find jobs, including Lakshman's grandfather, Kundan Singh, who left at the age of 14. He wound up in the British army fighting against the Japanese in Burma during World

War II. He was captured by the Japanese and languished in a prisoner of war camp until he and all of his Indian comrades were released at the behest of a famous Indian Independence Movement Leader, Subhash Chandra Bose, a contemporary of Mahatma Gandhi. Unlike Gandhi, however, he believed in violence as a way to gain Indian Independence. He promised the Japanese that the released Indian prisoners would fight against the British instead of for them, a move which would not only help the Japanese, but as Bose hoped, would help India gain freedom from England.

The newly resurrected army became known as the Indian National Army (INA) and fought the British in Burma, eventually making its way across the border into India. Then suddenly the Japanese surrendered to Allied Forces, leaving the INA powerless and compelling it to abort its mission. The INA disbanded and its soldiers, now sought after by the British as traitors, snuck back to their homes.

It took Kundan Singh over two years to walk from Burma to Pauri Garhwal, a roughly 1500-mile journey up and down one mountain range after another. The young boy returned a battle-scarred man; hobbling around Chandpur like the hunchback of Notre Dame with shoulder-length hair, fingers gnarled almost beyond use and a bullet riddled body.

Only later, long after Indian Independence in 1947, Kundan Singh was designated a 'Freedom Fighter', earning him enormous respect and inspiring an inordinate number of the next generation of Garhwali men to join the army. Years later his heroic efforts earned him a monthly check from the Indian government and other benefits, such as free passage on all government buses and trains for the rest of his life and reservations for his descendants in jobs and education—not in posts but in calculating their qualifications.

I drive exceptionally slow during our twenty-minute ride to Mausi to prevent the girls from becoming sick. Nevertheless, I'm surprised no one does, particularly Meetu. At nine-years old she has ridden in a car only once in her lifetime (nine-years old by Indian standards, where age is determined by the birthday a person is working towards, rather than by how many birthdays have passed, which is how age is calculated in America).

I ask Lakshmi Devi, "How do you like being married?"

Recently married into another village, she is back in Chandpur visiting her family for a couple of weeks. She is unsure of what I mean, so I rephrase the question, "How do you like your mother-in-law? Does she speak to you in a nice way?"

Lakshmi Devi scrunches up her face. It's a response I gauge to reflect how she views all mother-in-laws—the banes of daughter-in-laws everywhere—as opposed to her mother-in-law specifically.

"How do you like living in your new village?"

"What's there to say?"

"Well, if I lived in one place my entire life and then suddenly changed locations and left all the people I love behind, I'd feel sad and lonely.

"Yes, I cried at first. But I have to live there, so I stopped crying and make the most of my life in Duggada.

"What do you think about your husband?"

"What's there to think?"

"Do you like him?"

"Thus far he's okay." She responds.

"Does he talk to you in a nice way?

She shrugs.

"Does he work and bring his money home?"

"Yes."

"Where does he work?"

"He works in Chandigarh."

"What does he do?"

"He works in Chandigarh."

"Yes, but what kind of work does he do in Chandigarh? Does he work in a restaurant? A factory? A school?

"I don't know."

"Does he work for a private company or for the government?"

"I don't know."

"Have you asked him what kind of work he does?"

"No. And he hasn't told me."

During the day, Mausi is a thriving hub of activity; congested with people, cows, dogs, commercial jeeps and buses. It's a cluster of 80-something small businesses and push-carts, catering to villager's everyday needs: Food rations, kitchenware, photo shops, jewelers, locally made wood furniture, iron products and STD phone booths. The latter belong to an antiquated phone system that often does not work and is purposely shut down whenever it rains because "water causes exposed copper wires to spark and catch on fire."

Mausi bazaar was made popular further afield by a famous Garhwali love song, aptly named 'Mausi Bazaar', about a boy falling in love at first sight with a girl wandering in the bazaar, inspiring Mausi bazaar to be a favorite strolling place for young people. Knowing its reputation, as we drive along the one and only street, I ask the girls if they want to get out, roam the bazaar and meet Lakshman and I on the fair grounds later. They do. I give them money to eat rasgulla (a sweet) and drink soda pop, knowing they will indulge in eating and drinking these treats so few times in their life that they will be able to recount every single event.

As they walk off, I experience a pang of concern or maybe it's fondness. Kaneeka, bright-eyed and alert, takes in the bazaar with flitting eyes, glancing around repeatedly, soaking it all in or possibly even searching for someone she knows. Meetu, with her chin cocked downward, appears to be hiding behind her long lashes; a striking contrast from the self-assured and ultra responsible girl at home who runs errands for everyone on our courtyard older than her: Fetching water from the spring or lentils from the market, relaying messages between people, watching over her younger sisters. Lakshmi Devi, 22, the pillar of confidence and stalwart, trudges across the street like a man, a characteristic she shares with her mother and that I often hear early in the morning reverberating off their mud floors, through our attached walls. She's not manly, however. Her long hair is neatly plaited in a braid and her sea green salwar-kameez (baggy pant & long baggy shirt) and long scarf in varying shades of white, sea green and spruce are flowing and feminine as she moves through the crowd.

Lakshman and I drive beyond the bazaar, park on the side of the road and then walk down a long hill to the fairground. The venue is a large flat field located at the confluence of two valleys, bordered by a river. Enough grass sprigs poke up here and there to give the field a green hue from a distance, but up close it appears to be composed of dirt and rocks. The entrance smells like a bakery and is crowded with food venders selling warm jalebis (sweet made from white flour, water, and red food coloring dropped into oil in such a way that the end product looks like 3-D pretzels, which are then saturated in sugar water), freshly made saltines and other finger foods. To our far left, alongside the river, twenty or so people are sitting on the ground, displaying an odd assortment of wares laid out on tarps: Plastic children's toys, women's glass bangles, incense, photos of gods and goddesses. The right side of the field is interspersed with tall Mango, Tun (toon ciliata) and Banyan trees, ending abruptly at the base of a steep cliff a hundred feet below where my car is parked.

The cultural program is being held straight ahead, at the far end of the field. A red, yellow and green striped tent has been set up over a rectangular cement platform, with the front wall rolled up and tied to the roof to form a stage. Immediately behind it is another tent for performers to dress in and out of costumes. Two long blue tarps have been strung out from the stage to demarcate the formal seating area, shading onlookers from the harsh sun, diverging farther and farther apart and tied to roughly hewn tree poles planted in the ground, leaving a sun-drenched aisle in-between.

As Lakshman and I stroll over to the seating area, members of the organizing committee approach and in typical warm Garhwali hospitality welcome us with prayer-shaped hands and a chorus of "Namaskar." They sit us down underneath one of the tarps where two rows of plastic chairs have been set up in front for honored guests. Everyone else sits on the bare ground, although very few people have arrived yet. Lakshman's younger brother, who has been hired to videotape the whole affair, comes over to say 'hi', albeit not literally, and informs his brother, Narendar Singh Bisht and his band will not be performing today. They will be replaced by another band from Pauri. I ask Lakshman if he still wants to sing. He says, "No," with no perceivable disappointment.

A girl in her late teens or early twenties is singing a contemporary Garhwali song, accompanied by a synthesizer, dhol (large hand played drum), tubla (hand played floor drum) and a flute—the same band that will accompany all of the local performances. Her exquisite voice is masked by a fuzzy sound system and a microphone that has already gone dead a couple of times because people keep tripping over the wire, pulling the cord out of the generator socket.

When the song finishes, the announcer invites the local state representative, Madan Prasad Konkriyal, onstage to perform puja, formally opening the program. Konkriyal would not normally have come for such a small function but coincidently his cousin's son died two days earlier, so Konkriyal attended the funeral, held not far from Mausi. This is Konkriyal's first foray into local politics and after three years as this area's state representative, no one has anything good to say about him. Villager's primary complaint is he has done nothing to develop the area or improve employment since he took office. Part of the problem may be he's out of touch with the hill people themselves. Konkriyal is Garhwali but he was raised on the plains in Mumbai (Bombay) and now lives in Dehra Dun on the plains, rather than in the mountains where his constituency lives.

The plains versus the mountains is a sensitive issue. The Himalaya and its people are geographically and culturally unique from the people living on the plains of India, with diverse needs, but theirs needs have been historically deferred and subjugated to the more populated and accessible plains. When India became independent from Britain, the regions in the middle of the Himalaya known as Tehri Garhwal, Pauri Garhwal, Chamoli and Uttarkashi were placed into the huge plain's state of Uttar Pradesh and from that day forth ignored. While the rest of India moved forward economically and technologically, building infrastructure (roads, waste disposal systems, reliable power, etc.), factories and markets, development in this part of the Himalaya has been seriously limited or whatever development has occurred frequently does not benefit the local people.

The one and only project in our area, the Veer Chandra Singh Horticultural College, Barsar, illustrates this point. Although it's still in construction stage, it's up and running. The school, however, despite being in the heart of rural Pauri Garhwal, 12 kilometers from my house, does not have a single Garhwali student. When I asked the Vice Chancellor of the college why there are no Garhwali students, he subtly denied culpability by stating, "All administration decisions are made from Pant Nagar University on the plains," which is where the students are recruited as well. A completely separate functional electrical system was constructed for the school of which no one in our area benefits. Construction laborers on the project are all Nepalese. The teachers and administrators are from the plains. The Garhwali consolation prize is two contracts, one to run a teashop and the other a ration's store on the University grounds, and a handful of fourth-class positions (i.e. guards, clerical staff, etc.).

From the time of India's Independence, there's been an ongoing movement by the 'hill people', as they call themselves, to have a separate hill state. It gained momentum in the early nineties with massive protests and police retaliations, resulting in several deaths, a climax that heralded in the state of Uttaranchal on November 9, 2000. The original intention was to give hill people fair representation in government and to undue the decades of neglect and lack of development here, but ironically, because of the lack of infrastructure in this part of the Himalaya, the Central Government (national government) felt Uttaranchal could not survive economically, so it carved four large cities from the plains within the new state's boundaries: Rishikesh, Udham Singh Nagar, Haridwar and Dehra Dun, assigning the latter as the Capital. Money is filtering into Uttaranchal from the Central Government to develop the new hill state, resulting in tremendous development, but again, paradoxically, it is all happening down on the plains in these cities. Minimal funds are trickling into the heavily traveled mountain pilgrimage routes for much needed development, but otherwise there is virtually nothing happening where we live, besides Barsar.

The hill people periodically protest to have the capital moved to Gairsain, in the heart of the Himalaya, to give local people control of their destiny and to motivate bureaucrats to improve conditions in the Himalaya by forcing them to live under the same primitive conditions as everyone else does. Their cries are muffled by bureaucratic babble.

Puja consists of Konkriyal lighting incense, a fair organizer applying turmeric paste to the foreheads of a handful of people on stage and Konkriyal offering prayer-shaped hands to the audience as he walks off stage. Afterwards, local politicians and I are formally welcomed up on stage and colorful tinsel necklaces are placed around our necks. I raise prayer-shaped hands to the audience, utterly embarrassed to be treated with such grand hospitality, and all but slink back to my chair.

When the girls arrive, I pick up our coffee table (a tall wooden bench on which Lakshman and I have been served tea, biscuits and never empty glasses of water), intending to convert it into a seat for the girls to sit on, alongside us. While in mid-air, however, people snatch up the space left behind before I can set the bench back down again. I am an honored guest with my own personal plastic chair, but that does not separate me from the hordes of people gathered around. Every inch of ground around me is taken up by a body, transforming my legs into backrests and my feet into stools. With some finagling and a little more push and shove than is politically correct in the West, I manage to set the bench down, enabling the girls to sit up high to watch the show.

The song and dance programs resume. One by one, local children and young people come on stage to sing and dance traditional Garhwali style. Garhwali songs are folk songs recounting daily exploits or romantic notions, using dance theatrics to depict the stories. Onstage now, a young shepherd holding a stick pretends to be herding goats, his head bobbing up and down and his upper body slowly swaying from side to side, while confessing his infatuation to a girl who's holding a sickle in her hand, pretending to cut grass, pausing periodically to bring her pointer finger up to her chin thoughtfully, while batting her eyes and coyly turning her face away from the boy.

In between acts the announcer tells jokes; an antidote about the politician from the plains who was suppose to put development money into Pauri Garhwal but inadvertently put it into his pocket instead and the drunk who couldn't find his trail home. The announcer's main objective, however, is to plead for money from the audience to defray the cost of putting the fair on, which he does at every break, after every couple of acts. To show his appreciation, he reads the name of every person who donates during the acts preceding the intermission and the exact amount of each donation.

Suddenly a stiff wind whips up. Dust flies everywhere. The poles holding up the overhead canapés sway violently, threatening to collapse on top of the audience. Event organizers come to our rescue, physically holding the poles upright for the half-hour or so it takes the wind, an almost daily afternoon occurrence during the summer, to die down.

Politicians are called up one by one to give speeches. They boast how much money they've donated to today's program and what they've done for the community as a whole since being in office. When Konkrlyal mentions his accomplishments—still trying to get a farmers market going and building highway 121—I wince, knowing the market was recently cancelled and highway 121 is a one lane, decrepit road.

Another hour passes. The 21 acts come to an end. Now it's time for the main event, the replacement band from Pauri. It consists of two female singers, a male singer, a flute, four drums, a synthesizer and a harmonium. They spend fifteen minutes setting up their own mike system, separate microphones for each person and instrument, and testing out their quality. The local program was well done and well rehearsed but now it looks like we are in for an even more professional treat.

They have just started singing their first song when Meetu slumps over onto my shoulder. Garhwali children fall asleep anywhere and everywhere, oblivious to noise or bright lights, without making a peep and without warning signs like crankiness (after the 'terrible twos') or yawning, so I assume Meetu has fallen asleep. I briefly grapple with her body, pulling her around onto my lap, and then turn my attention back to the performance.

Lakshmi Devi and Kaneeka begin whispering loudly. Finally Lakshmi Devi taps me on my shoulder. I jump to the conclusion the two of them are worried Meetu is too heavy for me to hold, so instead of giving her a chance to speak, I volunteer, "It's okay, she can sleep here."

"Madam. She's not sleeping."

"She's not sleeping? What makes you think that?"

"She's been hit by the wind!"

"What? What makes you think she's been possessed by a ghost?"

"She's unconscious."

Brushing back Meetu's thick matt of black hair, I look into her face. She looks asleep but I shake her just to be sure. There is no response. I shake her again, this time more vigorously, to wake her up. She still doesn't respond. I shake her again and call out her name. When there is no response this time, I lift her up and, picking my way through the bodies sprawled along the ground, carry her away from the crowd. On the trail running alongside the tent, I jiggle Meetu and try to make her stand up; holding her under her arms, letting her legs hang down, her feet unwillingly touching the dirt. I call out her name repeatedly.

"She needs water" I shout. "Where's the water spigot?"

"It's behind the stage by the Shiv temple."

I rush along the trail toward the temple with Meetu in my arms. Lakshmi Devi reaches from behind me and tugs at my arm, urgently requesting, "Don't take her to the water spigot."

"Why?"

"It could be dangerous."

"What? She needs water!" I don't understand what Lakshmi Devi is alluding to but the expression of alarm on her face stops me in my tracks. "Why don't you want me to take her to get water?" I ask, but then don't give her time to answer. I order Lakshman to go find a container and bring back water. A woman passing by hears my plea, takes a bottle of water out of her plastic bag and begins splashing water on Meetu's face.

"Let's get her to drink," I suggest. Lakshmi Devi asks for the bottle and while I hold Meetu, she tries to pour water into Meetu's mouth. It merely trickles across her lips. The girls then jointly pry Meetu's clamped jaw open with their fingers, creating a slit large enough to dribble water into. The water immediately gurgles back out and when the girls let go, Meetu's teeth snap shut.

I shake Meetu again. There are still no signs of consciousness. I'm not sure what to do. I've never seen anyone passed out for such a long time. I assess our options. It's past 2:00 pm, so nearby Mausi hospital is already closed. If we drive to Pauri, the hospital there closes at 3:00 pm so by the time we arrive, it too will be closed. There are plenty of resident doctors in the bazaar, all Quacks with no medical training and I fear that because they too are Garhwalis, they will treat Meetu as if she's possessed by a ghost.

Ghosts are not figments of the imagination. They're real people, essentially caught between life and death and most propelled into limbo because they either died in pain or suddenly, interrupting their normal process of reincarnation. Despite this common origin, however, ghosts are multifarious, manifesting themselves in different ways. Unseen ghosts take three main forms. One is an unconscious person, like Meetu. Absolutely everybody who is unconscious is possessed by a ghost. Newborns, young people in general, and people with adverse horoscopes are particularly susceptible to these kinds of possessions. As Lakshmi Devi expressed to me, "Meetu's been possessed by a ghost because she hasn't had a special puja done this month yet and she should have because she has a weak horoscope!"

Another form of unseen ghosts is unexplained phenomenon at night such as strange sightings and noises. When I asked a Garhwali to explain this kind of ghost to me, he told me the following story:

> "Before the road was built in this area, a group of Nepalese came to Chandpur to cut logs for the government in the nearby forests. They would float the logs down river to Musagali, where there was a road for trucks to transport them further afield. The Nepalese made a makeshift tent from sheets of plastic and sticks near the river, in what appeared to them to be an abandoned field. When darkness fell, they heard agonizing screams and scary howls and their tent was pelted with rocks. Someone even physically grabbed the plastic and shook it violently. The Nepalese assumed local villagers were playing pranks on them but whenever they stepped outside of their tent, they never saw anyone and the noises immediately ceased. Conversely, whenever they went back inside, the screams and rattling of their tent started up again. The next day they performed puja to get rid of the menace. The next night, however, the same thing happened, and the next night. On the fourth day, a wandering naked Sadhu showed up in Chandpur. The Nepalese told him what was happening at night and asked him to

help. The Sadhu waited with them in their camp until nightfall. They built a fire and the Sadhu heated up the two-foot long fire tongs that he carries with him everywhere. When the night grew pitch black, the Sadhu picked up the glowing red-hot tongs from the fire and began fighting invisible children's ghosts. Unbeknownst to the Nepalese, the field where their tent was pitched was a graveyard where children below the age of ten are buried in unmarked graves. The Nepalese watched on, traces of light trailing in the pitch black like sparklers, until the battled ended and the glowing tongs turned cold. The religious mendicant instructed the Nepalese to go across the river the following day to a Narsingh temple set in the cliffs, do puja and offer rot. The next day the Nepalese went to the Narsingh temple, performed puja, offered rot to Narsingh and ate the remaining bread as blessed food. The ghosts never haunted them again."

A more recent example of this kind of ghost is from a neighbor of mine. Two years ago he was coming home late at night on the trail that passes by the village spring when a ghost began pelting rocks at him from the hillside above. He described the ghost as trying to scare him and added, "He was successful." Although there are sinister ghost types who try to harm people, ghosts are feared primarily because of their tendency to taunt people.

A third common manifestation of an invisible ghost is ghost possession, often by a dead relative, albeit not always, and it often becomes apparent during puja, albeit not always. During one family puja, a young woman started crying. She had become possessed by her dead mother. Her mother's ghost described the cancer that had killed her, the pain she had experienced in her stomach and the difficulty she had breathing just before her death. She then asked about her son—a main preoccupation during her lifetime was her only son's future. She pleaded to know how her son was doing and cried while expressing her concern about his managing in the world without her. The Baaman presiding over the worship ceremony performed puja and comforted the dead woman's spirit, acknowledging her tragic death and reassuring her that her son was fine. He told her, "You don't have to worry about him any more. He is a grown man who can take care of himself." And then he encouraged her to continue on the process of reincarnation, "It's time for you to move on to the place where dead people go." The daughter came into her own senses again and the dead woman has never possessed her daughter or anyone else again.

Ghosts that can be seen are usually seen at night, as either a cluster of glowing lights in the distance or they look human. The former come on nights when there is no moon. Two of my male neighbors saw them one night last year while walking on the road, making their way home from a nearby village. They spied the glowing forms in a forest ravine known to house ghosts. The lighted forms kept disappearing and reappearing: Initially they saw five ghosts, a moment later two disappeared, another minute passed and they multiplied to seven. Being afraid of ghosts, one of them told me they didn't stop to watch any longer, but instead bolted for home.

The people I know who have seen human-like ghosts were on their way home late at night as well. In all of these situations, when they first saw the ghosts they assumed the ghosts were humans so they tried to talk with them. When the ghost's did not respond, they realized they were ghosts. Although these ghosts made no attempt to taunt, scare or harm any of the informants, they all describe their encounters as "eerie."

There is one more visible ghost called a shaid. People insist he exists, but no one I know has ever seen one. He is tall and wears white clothes. His modus operandi is to approach a person from behind and bum a cigarette or bedi from them. Afterwards, he lures the person to a precariously high place where he tries to trick him or her into falling.

Being from a society in which science is revered, I can't help but assume Meetu is either dehydrated, suffering from heat stroke or from some other medical abnormality. The girls bolster my suspicions with a cursory account of what had transpired just before Meetu fell onto my shoulder. Meetu had been complaining about being thirsty before and during the performance. Two of the girls finally walked Meetu to the water faucet located behind the stage, adjacent to the Shiv temple. Meetu passed out as soon as they arrived, before she had an opportunity to drink any water. The girls revived Meetu by shaking her, but then quickly ushered her away from the faucet, refusing to let her return to have a drink because it's located next to the Shiv temple, which they perceived to be surrounded by ghosts waiting to possess Meetu again.

Shiv temples are found throughout Pauri Garhwal, most along a river in close approximation to cremation grounds because Shiv is one of the main guardians of death. Ghosts live in and around the cremation grounds and thus around the nearby Shiv temples. This month, the first month of the Hindu calendar (last half of March and the first half of April) is deemed a particularly opportune time for ghost possession because during this month ghosts intentionally seek people to possess.

I decide our best option is to go to a medical store in Mausi bazaar, buy a box of glucose, mix it in water and somehow force Meetu to drink it. Lakshman and the girls take turns hauling Meetu up the long hill. At least ten minutes have gone by and Meetu is still unconscious, with no signs of awakening. At the top of the hill, I run off to get my car.

When I return four minutes later Meetu is, miraculously, semi-conscious. Lakshmi Devi informs me they woke Meetu up by putting a one-rupee coin in-between her teeth, which, upon questioning, I find out is standard first aid for someone possessed by a ghost. I look closer at Meetu. She is still obviously quite dazed and wobbly and her eyes are barely able to focus. Examining her closely, I am suddenly taken aback, literally jerking my head down and back simultaneously. Meetu's naturally blackish-brown eyes are surrounded by yellowish-green highlights. She looks possessed!

The pharmacy is a half-kilometer away from where I picked up Lakshman and the girls. We buy glucose, mix more of the powder than we probably should into the water and force Meetu to drink a couple of pints. Propped up on the car seat between Lakshmi Devi and Kaneeka, Meetu appears increasingly normal by the minute. With encouragement, she even gives us a smile.

By the time we arrive back in Chandpur, Meetu is able to walk on her own but she's still not quite herself: She totters listlessly, is quieter than usual and her eyes remain a bit odd looking. As we walk through the bazaar and down the trail toward our houses, Kaneeka and Lakshmi Devi announce to everyone we pass that a ghost possessed Meetu at the fair. They even disclose the ghost possession to people they might not normally strike up a conversation with, such as older males. It's hard to tell if they're compelled to tell fellow villagers, are upset by what had happened or are boasting news that everyone will find fascinating, albeit disturbing. The news spreads swiftly.

There is no doubt in anyone's mind that Meetu had been possessed by a ghost and that the key to Meetu becoming conscious again was the one-rupee coin treatment administered by my companions. Nonetheless, villagers do not totally dismiss my intervention, readily talking about how I fed Meetu glucose and how her condition improved and later, when I give Meetu's father the remaining glucose and suggest Meetu drink glucose in her water until the box runs out, he graciously thanks me for helping her.

>*Uttaranchal's name was changed to Uttarakhand in 2007. The new name is not only significant because of its use in ancient religious texts; it came to symbolize the hill people's struggle for self-determination, making the name change a triumph for local political groups.

"Our roof fell in. We can't sleep at night. The rain comes in and soaks us. I'm a widow with six children. I have no source of income. I go from village to village doing odd jobs. I barely make any money. People give me rations like rice or flour instead. My husband died two years ago. Things were fine when he was alive. We weren't rich but we got by. Since he died, we've had nothin' but trouble. Now I'm pregnant. We don't have food to eat. My children go to bed hungry. I'm sick. We sleep and eat in a place this big...." She motions with her finger, indicating the size and length of my veranda (4 ft x 10 ft), on which she is standing outside my front door.

I take advantage of the five-second pause in her rambling, quickly hold up my hand like a stop sign and direct her to "Hold on!"

I ask, "What's your name?"

"Anita Devi."

"Which village are you from?"

"Dikholi."

"What specifically do you want from JDF? Why have you come here?"

She starts rattling off what sounds like a potentially long list, "Give me food. Our roof needs to be fixed. Give me work. We..." Again I hold up my hand and instruct her to "Hold on!"

Walking away from the door, I grab my workbook off the table and when I come back, jot down abbreviated details of what Anita Devi has just told me: Anita Devi, Dikholi, widow, six kids, roof fallen in—get repair estimate. Looking up from my book, I briefly explain JDF's procedure: "One of our employees will come to your house within the next two weeks to assess your situation. They'll verify and clarify your circumstances and then we'll decide if and what to do next."

Upon reflection, I decide she might not fully understand my explanation, so I break it down into more concrete terms. "A JDF worker will come to your house. He or she will talk to you and talk to your neighbors. He will check to see if you are poor or not. He will go inside your house and look around. He will look at your roof. If there is a mason around, he will ask the mason to look at your roof, to tell us what needs to be done to fix it and how much it will cost. The worker will come back and tell us what he has learned. After that we will decide if we can help you." Again rethinking my last statement I elaborate, "We cannot give you food, work or fix your roof until the JDF worker has come to talk with you. If he says you are poor, at that time JDF staff will talk about whether we can help you or not and how we can help you. The worker will then come to your house a second time to let you know if we can help you and how we can help you."

Anita Devi appears indigent. Her sari is worn thin and the petticoat hanging slightly down below her sari is more than just a little tattered. Everything about her is tiny: Her hands, her head, her frame. At the most, she's 5 feet tall and doesn't weigh more than 80 pounds. My first impression is she has never had enough food to eat her entire life, resulting in her body failing to develop normally and preventing even a morsel of fat from accumulating. Her voice is the only big thing about her. It isn't particularly loud, but it's unremitting and her Donald Duck-like lisp coupled with Garhwali, which is spoken from the back of the throat and nose, make every other word coming out of her mouth plosive. The statement her children go to bed hungry is heart rendering, although she may be exaggerating the truth in order to get us to help her. The part about being pregnant is baffling. If her husband died two years ago, how can she be pregnant? Moreover, how can a baby be hiding in that flat stomach? She is probably a widow. There are so many widows and abandoned women in Pauri Garhwal, they could match the number found in war zones—that, or I happen to meet them all by virtue of the work JDF does.

"What's your husband's name?"
"He's dead."
"I know. What was his name?"
"Bhigar."
"What was his caste?"
"Harijan."
"But was his name Bhigar Lal, Bhigar Ram, or Bhigar Kumar?"
"Bhigar Lal."

Whenever women used to give me their husband's first name only, which they still often do, I would ask, "What's his last name?" "What's his full name?" or "What's his family name?" These questions not only didn't solicit the right answer, no one had a clue as to what I was talking about. Finally, by watching other JDF employees interview people, I learned that if I asked women their husband's caste, they either tell me his caste or sub-caste, which is also his last name, or they'll give me an answer close enough to the right answer that the husband's last name can be quickly deduced.

To do an on-sight assessment of a woman, first we have to find out where she lives in a village. A husband's name, even a dead one, is an important way to find her. There are no addresses in villages and finding a woman using her name alone poses several obstacles.

When I first moved to Pauri Garhwal, I was determined to liberate my sisters from male domination. Even their dependence on their husband or father's name for their identity was my battleground. When women came to JDF asking for help, I refused to write their husband's name, especially the dreaded 'wife of'. My plan was wrought with problems, however, as I soon found out. I sent a JDF employee, Bhagawati, to Sundergoan to look for a woman named Lakshmi Devi, whose husband's name I had purposely not written down. Bhagawati found four Lakshmi Devis in the village. Initially all four denied having filed an application with JDF, meaning the Lakshmi Devi we were looking for wasn't even amongst them. Even so, after the four Lakshmi Devis found out Bhagawati had come to talk to a 'Lakshmi Devi' about starting a new business, all four changed their minds and professed to being the Lakshmi Devi who wanted help from JDF to open a business.

After marriage, every Garhwali women's last name becomes 'Devi', meaning goddess. Subsequently all women in any given village have the exact same last name and several have the same first name. Their names are never followed by a family name. Anita Devi would never be referred to as Anita Lal, not casually nor in legal documents. As a child, she was legally known as Kumari (unmarried goddess) Anita, daughter of Rajbir Lal, village Phaldwari. After marriage, her legal name became Anita Devi, wife of Bhigar Lal, village Dikholi. Now that her husband has died, her legal name is Anita Devi, wife of the late Bhigar Lal, village Dikholi. Consequently, many people refer to Anita Devi as Bhigar Lal's wife.

Another problem of searching for a woman under her own name is people might not know her by her name or, even if they know her name, they say it so seldom that they have to think about it for a while before they can remember what it is. One reason for this anomaly is in Pauri Garhwal people do not say a person's name out of respect for the person. It is considered bad manners or bad luck to speak many people's names. The general rule of thumb is you never say the name of someone older than you, especially in the first person. Depending on a person's relative age and sex to the speaker, all elders are addressed in the first person as: Respected grandfather, respected grandmother, respected uncle, respected aunt, respected mother, respected father, respected big sister or sister, or respected brother or brother. These titles are used regardless of whether the person is a true relative, a fellow villager or a complete stranger. If a relative is younger, their name can usually be spoken, however, even that rule does not always apply. A man would never call his younger sister-in-law by her name. In my case, whether people are older or younger than I am, they stubbornly refuse to call me by my name. Hundreds, maybe even thousands, of people know 'Madam', but only one or two know my name is Vicki.

  A man never says his wife's name, not to her or anyone else. A woman never says her husband's name, not to him or anyone else. The only exception is in formal situations when saying the spouse's name is necessary, such as when I asked Anita Devi her husband's name. Yet, even in these situations a woman will often hem and haw before she will actually say her husband's name. More often than not her first response will be "You mean my gharwala's (the house one's) name?" or she'll use one of the children's' names, customarily the oldest boy's name, as a frame of reference, "You mean Manu's father?" She rarely says 'my husband' in the third person, although I sometimes hear husbands saying, 'my wife'. Husbands also use the term 'gharwala', generally not using the grammatically correct feminine reference 'gharwali' when referring to wives and they too often refer to their wives using the oldest boy's name, 'Manu's mother'. As a result, many people in Dikholi refer to Anita Devi as 'Manu's mother'.

I decide to check out Anita Devi's situation myself. By the time I arrive at ten in the morning in Dikholi, a village located on the mountain across the river from Chandpur, Anita Devi has already left to another village to mend someone's clothes. Her mother, three of her four brother-in-laws and two of their wives greet me. Without delay, they begin searching for a chair. I assure them I don't need a chair to sit on and even tell them I don't want a chair to sit on, but they ignore me and run off to find one anyway. Indians are often described as treating guests like gods. This is particularly true of Garhwalis. They do everything possible to make me feel honored. Besides actually calling me an honored guest, they go out of their way to make sure I am comfortable. Many rural people do not own chairs, but my hosts will invariably borrow a chair from someone in the village who has one or if they cannot find one, they give me a blanket or burlap bag to sit on. Furthermore, because serving tea is essential, even the poorest of poor hosts, who often do not have tea leaves, milk and/or sugar in their own homes, will go to fellow villagers houses, entreating them to donate the ingredients, which they frequently do because they too don't want the 'honored' guest's visit to their village to be tainted by not receiving a cup of tea.

Anita Devi's seven-year old son heads off to a village over the hill to bring Anita Devi back home. While we wait for her return, her family, several nearby villagers who've gathered in their courtyard to find out why I'm here and I chat.

I scrutinize the outside of Anita Devi's family's home during lulls in our conversation. The design is like most traditional mud and rock houses in our area, a two-story house with a long body, however, this one has at least ten rooms (five on the first floor and five on the second floor) as opposed to the standard eight rooms, information easily ascertained because mud and rock houses usually do not have inner stairways connecting floors or inner doors connecting rooms, so rooms necessarily have outside doors, and they're almost always front-facing.

The first floor is squat, as if the foundation has sunk a foot or two into the ground, but low first-floor ceilings are in fact a salient feature of all two-story mud and rock houses, making it impossible for an average height person to stand up straight. Needless to say, first-floor doors are short as well, 5 ft tall by 2-½ ft wide. They are two planks of wood that swing independently inward on old-fashioned hinges. The latter are rounded pegs carved into the top and bottom corner of each door panel and that fit into holes cut into the corners of the door frame (single boards below and above the door), nearest the wall. The wooden pegs then swivel back and forth in the holes when the door is opened and closed, albeit they generally have to be jiggled and lifted to move, wood scraping against wood.

The second floor doors function in the same manner, however, they're standard size, as are second floor ceilings. The wood rafters either slant to the front of the house or, like Anita Devi's, pitch horizontally into a v-shape, running down the center of the roof. Heavy pieces of slate are layered on top.

A remarkable characteristic of Anita Devi's house is the extra-large open veranda on the second floor. If villagers are not sitting in their courtyards during their free time, they spend it on their verandas, seldom sitting inside their houses, except during afternoon siesta and after dark. This veranda is ten feet long and seven feet deep and accessed by a set of narrow, grossly warped, mud and rock stairs. Placed along the front edge of the veranda, every meter or so, are huge wooden beams to support the heavy slate roof overhead. These wood beams are bare and rotting, but on most homes they're painted sky blue and on a few of the older houses scattered throughout Pauri

Garhwal, the beams and trim around the verandas are ornately carved with geometric and swirling designs, elephants and lotus flowers.

Another noticeable attribute are the first floor ceiling planks, which protrude a foot out from the house, creating a pitiful, sagging line across the entire length of the front wall, giving the house a lopsided appearance—a prominent feature of even the best constructed traditional homes.

Seven glassless windows are visible in the front of the house; three 1-foot square shuttered windows on the bottom floor and four slightly larger shuttered ones on the top floor. Five cubbyholes built into the front façade and spaced at regular intervals across the center of the first floor, appear to be the perfect place to burn a candle, but are in fact empty.

Overall, the exterior of Anita Devi's extended family's home is decayed. Thousands of mud-crusted fractures cover the wall, which is rare because women generally apply fresh coats of mud to their walls about once a year and every couple of weeks to floors and fireplaces. A couple of long, wide cracks cut deep into the front wall, making it appear as if it will split apart at any moment, suggesting other walls are in similar condition. There's no hint of the house having ever seen a coat of white distemper on its upper façade or sky blue paint on its wood doors, shutters or trim. Instead, the upper and lower walls are scarred black from fireplace smoke billowing out the doors and windows, which is rare. Usually only first floor rooms are used as kitchens and storage spaces, the second-floor rooms being reserved as bedroom cum sitting areas.

After half an hour, Anita Devi has still not arrived. I ask her mother-in-law for permission to go inside Anita Devi's place. It turns out to be the room at the far left of the house on the second-story, accessed by a private stairway. Immediately inside is the room Anita

Devi described to me as the size of my veranda. It seems even smaller. Along the nearest wall there's a disheveled pile of clothes and black, frayed rags taking up a quarter of the space and along the far wall, there's a mud and rock fireplace, pots and pans and a stack of sticks taking up another fourth of the room. The remaining area is where Anita Devi and her children sit and sleep. The soot-blackened walls are bare and cracked and although the ceiling is still intact, the blackened rafters appear rotten and bits of mud from overhead have fallen onto the floor. There is no furniture, extra food grains, bedding--except for the black rags, and like most Garhwali homes, there are no luxuries like piped water, electricity or bathrooms.

Anita Devi's mother-in-law informs me, "Even this limited space is cut in half when it rains. The wind drives the rain through the open door, soaking the floor and forcing them to huddle in the middle of the room." She is referring to the doorless entry separating this room from an adjacent room in back. The entire roof of that room has collapsed and is now lying on the floor, exposing the room to the sky, allowing rain to enter it and the room Anita Devi and her children occupy.

Although this is the worst condition I've ever seen of a house with people still living in it, it's not surprising and not that far beyond the condition of many other homes. Many traditional rock and mud houses are old and have roofs that are ready to or have already fallen in. Wood beams decay from termites, that ravage the wood in a matter of months, and the untreated pine shrinks during the winter and swells during the summer, jarring adjoining mud and rocks, allowing rain to seep in, eventually becoming rivulets during the monsoons, washing away more mud, shifting more rocks and keeping the wood soaked. Houses become so saturated that it's difficult for people to find a dry place to sit, sleep or store their wares. The rotted wood, the perpetually wet mud and delicate Phyllitic Schist rock walls all slowly crumble, weakening support for the heavy slate rocks overhead, becoming accidents waiting to happen. The number of people who have told me they lie awake at night, worrying that their roof may collapse is more than I ever want to remember.

Upon returning outside, Anita Devi's brother-in-laws beseech me to check their roofs. I ask if their roofs have collapsed. They admit they haven't, so I tell them that if JDF fixes any roofs, we will fix only collapsed roofs. On the one hand, I said it purely to stem the tide of requests. Once word spreads to other villages that we are thinking about fixing someone's roof, we'll be inundated with nothing less than fifty people wanting their roofs fixed. On the other hand, I believe her brother-in-laws can repair their own roof and tell them so: "You guys can repair the roof yourselves! Or, better yet, build a new house. Three of you are not working, right? You have plenty of time to do it. One of you is a house mason. He has all of the know-how. Another owns his own mules, so he can transport building supplies for free. Rocks and dirt are free...if you dig them out of your own fields. You can reuse the old slate. You know how to cut down trees to build the roof frame. All you have to do is hire someone to cut it into boards. Why not?"

They ho-hum and reluctantly shake their heads 'yes'.

I set out to find Anita Devi in Sakayana, a village on the other side of the ridge. We meet on the trail, half way in between. She is gnawing on a short piece of sugar cane, part of her payment for the sewing job she has just completed. I explain to Anita Devi that I have seen her house and talked with neighbors, verifying her poor status. I agree with her that the remaining half of the collapsed roof is dangerous for her and her children to live under, but then go on to explain how fixing the roof is not possible, "To fix only part of a roof on an old house like this is possibly more dangerous than to leave it like it is. Once men get up on the roof and start tearing it apart, more of the roof can cave in. Even if during construction other parts of the roof where your brother-in-laws and their families live don't cave in, they could later, making JDF liable. And given time the rest of the roof will surely collapse. If we fix the entire roof, the expense would be tremendous for JDF's budget. Not to mention it would be ridiculous to fix the roof when the walls are about to fall down."

Unperturbed, Anita Devi replies, "Don't fix the roof than. Build me a new house instead."

My first response is "JDF can't afford to build a house for someone!" I don't have a chance to verbalize it though as Anita Devi talks non-stop. She informs me that she owns a field near the river, next door to the Shiv temple. Her husband had started to build a house on the property years ago, but when he died construction stopped. She rambles on about several other unrelated topics, eventually divulging how she became pregnant. She said one evening while sitting in her room with her children, her drunken brother-in-law barged in and raped her in front of them.

She is either incredibly clever or it's just pure dumb-luck. Upon hearing about the rape, the proposal to build her a house, which I'd thought was absurd only a few minutes before, suddenly becomes sensible. If we build her a house by the temple, she and her children will be safe from the collapsing roof and from her brother-in-law. The Mai (the woman mendicant who takes care of temple) and the Baba (a male Sadhu) who live in the building attached to the Shiv temple can keep an eye on her.

When we arrive back at Dikholi, I ask Anita Devi to point out which brother-in-law had raped her. I stride over to him and ask him about it in front of a crowd of people, including his wife. With a grin on his face, he cocks his head, raises his eyebrows, shoulders and palms upward and blathers, "Shucks, yeah I was drunk."

Irritated by his demeanor, I warn him not to do it again and threaten to bring the Patwari with me if he does.

It's presumptuous of me to use the Patwari's name, but the Patwari himself had given me the idea not even two weeks earlier. He and I had been talking about another matter when he unexpectedly revealed, "I talked to the Pipli woman's husband."

I didn't even know that he knew JDF had taken the Pipli woman and her mother-in-law to the hospital a month earlier. The Patwari then described what he meant by his overemphasized 'talked': "I summoned him to my office, slapped him around and locked him in jail overnight. The next morning when I let him go I told him, "If you ever beat your wife or mother again, I'm going to tell Madam!"

At the time, I was astounded the Patwari would use me in his threat and, even more so, that he deemed me to be a scarier adversary than himself. However now, on the spur of the moment, I decide if he can use my name in his threats, I can use his name in my threat to Anita Devi's brother-in-law. The brother-in-law and I both know the Patwari will not prosecute him, but I am counting on the prospect of a jailhouse thrashing to keep him from raping Anita Devi again.

Anita Devi's situation proves to be a conundrum for JDF. Everyone concurs Anita Devi and her six, soon to be seven, children live in a hazardous situation, however, we can't decide what to do about it. JDF's Director and I are totally against fixing the roof because of the aforementioned reasons I had quoted to Anita Devi. I am leaning toward building her a one-room house, but it's an up hill battle all the way. The Director is against building a house because it would be too expensive: "JDF can't afford to spend that much money on one person!"

Then comes the Mai's objection. When Anita Devi mentions her husband had started constructing a house near the Shiv temple before he died, I visualize a foundation and a couple of partially built walls, so I send a JDF employee to the site to check it out, knowing a half-built house will offset costs and hopefully change the Director's mind. There ends up being virtually nothing on the field, other than a handful of rocks strewn on the ground. After the worker looks at the field, she naturally goes to the nearby temple to pray and subsequently talks with the caretakers at the Shiv temple. When the Mai finds out JDF might build a house for Anita Devi on adjacent land, she vehemently protests. She has always refused to let Harijan caste people enter the temple because she believes they will pollute it. Now she asserts Anita Devi and her children, Harijans, will pollute the temple just by living near it. To reinforce her position, she threatens not to share the piped water next to the temple with Anita Devi and her family, which means they would have to drink polluted river water or haul water from an unreasonably long way away.

The caste system has been outlawed in India since British rule. The Indian government maintains this official stance and has instigated laws to curb the practice, such as government job and education reservations. Regardless, the caste system is very much alive, especially in rural India. In simplistic terms, it is a system of social organization and labor delineation. The social organization is based on the notion people have varying levels of purity. How pure a person is or which category one belongs to is determined by one's family heritage. There are technically four major classifications but there is actually a fifth category inherent in the way the system is set up: Brahmins (teachers and priests), Kshatriyas (warriors and administrators), Vaishyas (tradesmen and agricultural workers), Shudras (artisans and service providers), and Dalits (menial laborers), formerly known as 'outcastes'. Brahmins are deemed most pure, followed by Kshatriyas, and then Vaishyas. Shudras are impure and Dalits are so impure they are deemed to be outside the caste system. Within these five classifications are thousands of minor sub-castes. Sub-caste names were developed based on the specific job a family was doing when the system was developed. For example, a goldsmith's sub-caste (and consequently his last name) became Sonar from the word for gold, sona. Subsequent generations of the Sonar family were born into their family surname, into their job (they became only goldsmiths), and into their social status. Whether it's a fundamental part of Hinduism or a misinterpretation of it, the caste system became a rigid classification system designed to keep the purer castes from being contaminated by lower castes, as well as to keep purer castes from engaging in polluting activities, the vilest being the handling of dead bodies or scavenging through garbage.

Although the caste system has gradually become more flexible, especially in cities and in the job market, caste groups still live divergent social lives and caste still dictates a few specific job opportunities. In Pauri Garhwal, there are three castes of Garhwali Hindus: Brahmin, Kshatriya and Dalit. Colloquially they're known as Pandit, Rajput and Harijan, respectively.

One hallmark of the divide between the three groups can be seen in the placement of homes in villages in which multiple castes live. Pandit caste homes are generally located at the top of a village, Rajput caste homes in the middle and Harijan caste homes are located at the bottom of a village. Even if a village is spread out or has an atypical arrangement, village homes are invariably clustered according to caste. To look at most villages, however, houses appear to run contiguous with one another, regardless of caste. Regardless, Harijans are considered to live 'outside' every village in which multiple castes live, an invisible line difficult to see but readily discerned in conversations with Pandits and Rajputs. References about one's village do not include the Harijan caste. There are both Rajputs and Harijans living in Chandpur. Nonetheless, 'our village this' and 'our village that' means 'the Rajput caste people this' and 'the Rajput caste people that.' A village feast means a feast for Rajputs. A village meeting means a meeting of Rajputs. A village wide puja ceremony means a worship ceremony for Rajputs. The village temple is for Rajputs. This attitude is not unique to Chandpur. I have asked numerous upper caste people from a variety of villages how many people live in their village. They invariably count Pandits and Rajputs and omit counting Harijans because they consider them to be living outside the village in an area called Harijan Basti.

Another distinction between castes is job opportunities, albeit to a much lesser degree these days. There remain two main distinctions. One is Garhwali Pandits are the only people allowed to become priests. This distinction is strictly adhered to even today—the only exception is that in the two or three famous temples in which Rajput families have been the caretakers for many generations, they are deemed capable of performing puja in those temples. The second is Garhwali Harijans have traditionally made tools, pots & pans and baskets, as well as played drums in local festivities. This is still true today. Rarely do Rajputs or Pandits do these jobs or any jobs they associate with the Dalit caste on the plains (i.c. Sweepers, leather workers and so forth).

Change of occupations in modern times does not change one's caste status. Rajputs were traditionally warriors and court administrators in small kingdoms centuries ago, but have become primarily farmers, soldiers, fourth-class office clerks, shopkeepers, teachers, drivers and restaurant employees. Pandits and Harijans have also spread out into these job markets. Nevertheless, Rajputs remain Rajputs, Pandits Pandits and Harijans Harijans.

A prominent feature of the caste system is its rules for social interaction amongst the different groups. A broad common rule is no inter-caste marriages. In rural India this is a hard and fast rule. The division extends into sub-caste status as well. Only certain sub-castes can marry certain other sub-castes. The two Rajput clans in Chandpur are from different sub-castes that also represent different status levels, so they can never intermarry. The same goes for the two distinct Harijan clans in Chandpur.

The only other major difference between Rajputs and Pandits in Pauri Garhwal is Pandits cannot eat rice cooked by Rajputs. Otherwise, the relationship between these two castes is compatible and symbiotic. They are friends with one another. They eat together. They sleep in one another's homes. They have binding religious relationships. They can share facilities such as cremation spots and they worship in each other's temples. Even so, there is a subtle line separating the two castes. A Pandit-Rajput relationship rarely has the quality and depth of a Pandit-Pandit or Rajput-Rajput relationship.

All other major social distinctions involve the Harijan caste. Harijan means 'Children of god'. The name was made popular by Mahatma Gandhi to replace derogatory labels such as 'untouchables'. Rajputs and Pandits social relationships with Harijans are virtually the same. Neither can eat food cooked or served by Harijans. They cannot drink tea or water given to them by Harijans. They cannot sleep in a Harijan person's house. Harijans cannot go inside a Rajput or Pandit's house. If by chance Harijans do go into an upper caste house (which I've never seen happen), for absolutely sure they cannot go into a Rajput or Pandit's kitchen. In Chandpur, Harijans are not allowed to go into the main Shiv temple nor any of the other temples in Chandpur used by Rajputs (at odds with this practice is Rajputs use the rock pile in Harijan Basti known as Kachyaa's temple to caste spells). Baamans may perform some Harijan's religious rites, but they do not perform their Devi/Devta puja. Harijans are not allowed to burn bodies at Rajput or Pandit cremation sites and vice versa. Harijans are generally not invited to Rajput and Pandit functions. If they come on their own accord or pass by, they must stand at a distance, and if a function is being held inside, they stand outside the door. Harijans can dance at some weddings, Holi and Diwali along with Rajputs and Pandits. They might even be fed food at a wedding, but they have to wait until all of the upper caste people have eaten before they can eat. If non-disposable dishes are used, Harijans must wash their dishes afterward and then set them upside down in a conspicuous place. For most other village feasts, Harijans are not fed. Although Harijans get their water from the village spring, they are not allowed to touch the spigot, and if there are Rajputs waiting in line, Harijans sometimes wait until all of the Rajputs have filled their containers before filling their own. Harijans touching a Rajput or Pandit or vice versa is frowned upon. As a result, dissimilar castes often step to the side of a trail when passing one another. It is especially taboo if a Harijan touches a Rajput or Pandit while they are carrying a liquid. Accidental touching in this circumstance is cause for a ruckus among the castes and a Rajput or Pandit who has been touched is required to take a bath right away. During any Rajput or Pandit event in which sweets are distributed to fellow villagers, they are not distributed in Harijan Basti, although a Harijan is given some if they happen to be standing near Rajputs and Pandits who are being given the treats and it would be an obvious rude omission not to give the Harijan person one too. Harijans often refer to adult male and female Rajputs and Pandits as grandfather and grandmother to their face as a sign of respect. Rajputs and Pandits do not refer to Harijans in the same manner. No one has ever said Harijan children cannot attend the private school in Chandpur, however, out of thirty students not one is Harijan. Conversely, all of the children in the government school are Harijan except three.

When JDF decided to remodel toilets in Chandpur, caste became an issue. Ten years earlier, the village Pradhan had built seven small cement and rock rooms (five bathrooms and two showers) and a separate sewage tank with government money. There were no holes in the bathroom floors or pipes connecting the toilets to the tank because the builder had run out of money before the project was finished, so human waste had nowhere to go. Less than a year later villagers abandoned the toilets because filth had piled up on the floors. Ten years later JDF remodeled them. We cleared brush overgrowth, cleaned the rooms, fixed the doors, painted the buildings inside and out, installed plumbing from the village spring, laid pipes to the waste tank and installed Indian pots (flat, porcelain bases with a hole and footrests on which people stand and squat to go to the bathroom). The project was a complete success until we found out Harijans refused to use them. They alleged the Rajputs would not allow them to use the toilets and would taunt them if they did. Although the Rajputs never actually verbalized that Harijans couldn't use the toilets, we assumed the allegation was probably correct, so JDF built separate toilets and a shower in Harijan Basti. Villagers have segregated every toilet/shower complex we've built in other villages as well.

Although all three castes talk civilly to one another and Rajputs and Pandits serve tea to Harijans outside their houses, close friendships between Rajputs and Pandits and their Harijan neighbors are restricted. Within a village the only acceptable bonds are the historically binding contract between Harijan musicians, metallurgist and basket makers and the Rajput or Pandit families they do work for, indenture to storekeepers and political alliances. Conversely, on several occasions, in cities, away from fellow villagers, I have witnessed people of diverse castes readily ignoring caste rules, even people who I had thought, until that moment, were staunch bigots.

Several JDF staff wind up being against building a house for Anita Devi. Some workers proclaim we shouldn't help Anita Devi because "She's a bad character," "She's a liar" and "She wasn't raped, she's having an affair!" Others do not directly attack Anita Devi, but assert things like "Ghosts live around the temple so it would be too perilous for Anita Devi and her children to live there." Still others just drag their feet when given jobs associated with Anita Devi's house. One worker in particular is supposed to bring the Patwari to Dikholi to get land documents drawn up in Anita Devi's name. The land Anita Devi wants to build the house on has been handed down through male heirs so despite being her husband's share of the family land, it's in her brother-in-laws' names, not in Anita Devi's. Although it is highly unorthodox to have the land put in her name, I know this Patwari well and am certain he would be willing to do it. The JDF employee, however, has been to the Chipalghat Patwari's office several times—or at least says he goes—but each time he makes an excuse as to why the Patwari can't go to Dikholi to map out the land and get Anita Devi's brother-in-laws' signatures.

Maybe Anita Devi really has an unpleasant personality, but I surmise there are probably other factors influencing people's reluctance to build her a house. Maybe jealousy—many of their homes are in disrepair. Perhaps it is a caste issue. I propose it probably has more to do with the tendency to align behind leaders and go along with group consensus. In this case, to align behind JDF's Director and the temple caretaker who are opposed to building the house, although for different reasons. Whatever their reluctance stems from, I feel like I'm trying to pick up a mountain and move it by myself.

I try to reason with JDF workers during a morning meeting, "Okay, maybe I'm wrong about Anita Devi. Maybe she's a liar, of bad character and wasn't raped. But these things are all irrelevant. She and her children live in a dangerous situation. We should do something to help them be safe, no matter who they are. Fixing the roof is not practical. There is no place to rent. Building a house is our only option."

Then one day Anita Devi shows me where her other three fields are. One is near her old place in Harijan Basti. It is perfect in terms of being near her community and a water source. It would appease the temple caretaker, who is arousing the sympathies of villagers and creating a big row about building a Harijan house near the temple. The proximity of the land to Anita Devi's brother-in-law isn't much different than her old house, but by this time the workers have all but brainwashed me into believing Anita Devi is voluntarily having sex with her brother-in-law. The Director reluctantly acquiesces. The new plan takes hold. A different man is sent to summon the Patwari, who completes the necessary land documents within two days. We build Anita Devi and her children a one-room house. It's nothing to brag about, but it's safe, dry and their own.

*Three months after Anita Devi moved into her new house, the roof of her old house collapsed, killing one of her sister-in-laws.

They're a motley crew. Boys with shirttails partially tucked in and zippers unabashedly open. Salwar-kameezes darned with Frankenstein stitches. Hair once secured in ponytails sticking out in disarray. Buttons either not buttoned or missing. Snot flowing freely from noses. Running helter-skelter and kicking up dirt as they play, the children's only redeeming features are their effervescent laughter and polite manners. Upon seeing me they immediately stop their shenanigans, huddle around and, clasping their hands in prayer, respectfully intone, "Pranam Madam!"

It's midday at Chandpur's government elementary school and not a single adult is in sight. When I ask the children where their teachers are, a fifth-grade boy named Neru—the only boy whose appearance is presentable—reports that the Madam didn't show up for school today and the Master left awhile ago to eat lunch in the bazaar.

Prompting me to ask, "Well, where's the cook?"

After a moment of silence, Ganeshi timidly speaks up, "She left to her mother's village a couple of days ago."

"Whose cooking lunch for you today then?"

"No one."

"You didn't eat lunch today?"

Several children shake their head 'no', as if they haven't, prompting Neru to set things straight by clarifying that some of the children had gone home to eat.

To pass time until the teacher returns, I appeal to the girls to teach me the game they were playing when I arrived. They initially respond with giggles and shy smiles. Then a couple of children prod Nina and Meena to show me, well aware that they are the most brazen girls of the bunch. Without further prompting, Nina and Meena spring from the crowd, merrily grasp one another's hands and, leaning back as far as they can, begin spinning dizzily around and around, chanting a favored nursery rhyme:

> "Boy, oh boys!
> Yes sir yes.
>
> What is eaten?
> Round balls of ghee (clarified butter).
>
> What is slept in?
> In a red bed.
>
> Where is Bhabhi (older brother's wife)?
> She's in her native village.
>
> When will she come?
> She'll come now.
>
> What will she bring?
> She'll bring a comb.
>
> Lice will play in the comb
> And we'll dress up in sari's and sandals!"

The two girls don't stop there. Still spinning dizzily, they repeat their chant, obviously taking great delight in both the game and from being on center stage.

Shortly thereafter, the Master arrives with a friend. I ask permission to stay to see what he teaches the children and to check out the school's condition. My second reason elicits a plea from the Master for JDF to rebuild the wall between the school grounds and the trail, primarily to make the old one higher and add a small gate. He explains, "The children are distracted by cows and goats wandering into the schoolyard and by people passing by on the trail on their way to the fields."

At the Master's command, the dust-caked children sit themselves down on five dust-caked burlap runners laid out on the school grounds, each runner representing a specific grade level. They plop their school bags down beside them in the silt.

He then orders them to take out today's assignments and work on them. The children dutifully take them out, along with their pencil stubs and small, tattered notebooks called copies. There are no schoolbooks. The mature fourth and fifth grade students begin to work on their assignments as directed. The remaining children play in their seats, some glancing around with vacant eyes, as if they either don't understand what the teacher wants them to do or don't understand their assignments.

The Master and his friend begin to ply me with questions, "Which country are you from? Where is your family? What is America like? Which do you like better, America or Pauri Garhwal?"

I answer their questions, one after the other. After about fifteen minutes, I start thinking our conversation has drug on way too long and wonder when the Master is going to teach the children. Immediately after answering his questions, I turn my head and stare at the children, trying to make it apparent I want to watch them, not talk.

The teacher doesn't get my hint or ignores it. "What kind of work does your NGO do?"

217

"We cement village pathways, set-up garbage cans in bazaars, and buy supplies for new businesses."

I remind the Master outright that I've come to see what he teaches the children. In response, he pulls out a mango-colored slip of paper on which today's fifth grade assignments are printed and proceeds to explain how the government has developed a standard curriculum for all government schools, which is issued on these pieces of paper. Every day students are given one of these grade-appropriate assignment papers and teachers are responsible to teach each class all of their lessons. Written on this particular paper are seven assignments, including a math problem requiring the children to figure out how many neighbors a person can sell milk to in one day if her water buffalo gives 4 Kg of milk a day and she sells it to her neighbors in 1/4 Kg portions.

"Do you think you'll be able to build our wall?"

"I don't know. You will have to ask JDF's Director. He makes those decisions."

The Master continues to ask questions about JDF's work, America and I. After giving him brief responses to each of them, I try to divert his attention back to the classroom by posing questions about the children and school. "Why aren't the children wearing their school uniforms nowadays?"

He offhandedly proposes, "They're probably being washed today."

"All 25 uniforms are dirty today? How is that possible?"

"School clothes are washed on Saturdays because then they can dry on Sunday too, if necessary. Besides, you know how these parents are. They don't care. They send their children to school wearing anything."

The irony of his blasé attitude about the children not wearing their school dress is during the first month of the school year this

Master and the Madam were regularly smacking the children around who didn't come to school wearing a uniform. A practice at most schools at the beginning of every school year, it eventually gets the requisite items bought, but it also leads to more than a few dropouts at any and every grade level. This year the government issued a change in school dress color for all government schools, forcing every child to buy a new white and cocoa-colored uniform. JDF was inundated with requests from parents to buy them, as well as to buy their children's shoes, bags and copies. We bought several of these children's uniforms at the behest of their parents and then a month after school started, the school's Madam personally requested we buy uniforms for the remaining seven students who did not have them, which we did.

"Is the Director here in Chandpur?"

"No. He's in Delhi right now. He'll return in a week."

My patience wanes. "Why didn't the other teacher come to school today?

"I don't know. There's no phone for her to call."

And because he didn't get any of my hints, I ask him directly, "What are you going to teach the children today?"

He ignores my question and asks if JDF has done any projects around Khirsu, where his village is located.

"Not yet."

An hour has passed and the Master not only hasn't taught the children anything, he continues to completely disregard them, not even to maintain order. Instead, his friend, a teacher from a nearby village, orders the children to be quiet and do their work a couple of times. They quiet down for a minute or two and then return to snickering in their seats. In my repeated attempts to redirect our conversation to the school and the children, I end up grilling the teacher, intentionally and unintentionally, "Why is the school yard littered with hundreds of little pieces of paper?" You don't use the burn barrel we set up for you?

"They [the children] just throw their papers anywhere."

"Why are there only 25 students today?"

"It's Saturday. Less children come to school on Saturdays."

"The school roster says there's 51 students enrolled in school. Twenty-six children are absent? Over half the class?"

He presses his lips together and nods affirmatively.

Sometimes I know when someone is feeding me a bunch of malarkey. This is one of those times. The Master is trying to tell me 26 children are absent on the same day. It's an absurd assertion: It's not like the plague is going around . . . and it isn't plowing or harvest season either. Garhwalis take these kinds of untruths at face value, often treating them as truths. It's a cultural tendency I have yet to fully comprehend.

I refrain from saying anything more on the subject, but to keep a check on my sanity, I decide to check out my suspicions. During the two months following my visit to the government school, I have the number of students at the school surreptitiously counted on three different occasions. There were 25, 32 and 28 students present during those counts.

The discrepancy between roster numbers and actual attendance is because the numbers have been fudged. Showing 51 students enrolled in school probably earned the school its special two-teacher status, making the teachers' workloads more manageable and their absences and early departures less apparent. In this case, someone is likely putting money and food into his or her pockets as well.

To make sure parents send their children to school and to keep children in school, the Indian government sets up a number of incentive programs. For elementary school children the old incentive was 3 Kg of uncooked rice, which was distributed to each student at the end of every month to bring home. This program was scrapped last year and a new school lunch program instigated. An initial five thousand rupees ($111) was given to each rural government school to build a kitchen on its premises. It bought Chandpur a four-foot square mud and rock structure with a mud and rock fireplace, a tin roof and no floor or door. A Chandpur woman, Urmila Devi, crawls into it and cooks rice and lentils for the children every day for a nominal fee.

One hundred grams of rice and one rupee (to purchase lentils and spices) is allocated to the school per child per meal. School roster numbers determine how much rice and money are allotted each month to each school. When they claim there are 51 students and the most we have counted thus far is 32, it means the school receives extra money and food supplies every month. For 32 students the school would have received 3200 grams of rice a day, just over 3 Kg, and 32 rupees for lentils and spices. For 51-students the school receives 5100 grams of rice a day, over 5 kilos, and 51 rupees. Extrapolated into monthly figures (based on 22 days—a six day school week minus four days a month for government holidays) the school would have received 70.4 Kg of rice and 704 Rs. to buy lentils and spices for 32 students, but instead, for 51 students, the school receives 112.2 Kg of rice and 1,122 Rs. to buy lentils and spices. This means that every month the school receives an extra 41.8 Kg of rice and 418 Rs., enough rice to feed a family of six every month and more than enough money to buy the same family a month's supply of milk. The likelihood the students consume the extra rice and money is nil, meaning someone or possibly all three (the cook and two teachers) are putting the additional food and money into their pockets.

There was a time when I would have thought a leap from a discrepancy in student enrollment numbers to embezzlement without proof was far-fetched, if not just plain ludicrous. That time has long passed. In Pauri Garhwal, corruption is not measured in whether you do it or not, it's measured in whether you 'eat a normal amount of money' or 'gorge yourself'. Pilfering 10% to 15% of the total money or resources available, whether it be the government's, your boss's or anyone else's is considered respectable behavior. Taking 20% or more of the total money or resources available is thought of as excessive. Being excessive, however, does not stop people from doing it. The food scam program above would be classified as excessive, as someone is garnering over 37% of the total amount allocated to the school.

Government officials demanding money to do their job is the other major source of corruption. A government official demanding 50 to 500 rupees to do his job like filing your application in a government office, fixing a broken water line or any of a thousand other tasks is not just common behavior, it's the way it is. Government employees are paid extra money to do the job they are also paid by the government to do or the job doesn't get done.

The fortifying and heightening of the elementary school's wall that the teacher requested JDF do is eventually done with government money allocated to Chandpur for infrastructure projects (as opposed to money from the education department). Chandpur's Pradhan is in charge of the undertaking. The budget is 100,000 Rs. The Pradhan pays the government Engineer responsible for approving the school wall project, 20% of the 100,000 Rs. budget. The Engineer pockets 20,000 Rs. to okay a project he is supposed to inspect anyway as part of his job. He doesn't do anything extra. He just signs a piece of paper. He most likely didn't even look at the site nor will he come back later to check the wall. I know for a fact that the Pradhan and Engineer did not discuss the wall's construction plans.

To not pay would mean the wall wouldn't be built because the Engineer would either not approve the project or would stall approving it for years to come—until the Pradhan wised up and paid him the bribe—and all future Chandpur development projects handled by that particular Pradhan would be in jeopardy if the development officials believed they would not be compensated under the table.

If the Pradhan had a government connection, a friend, whose position was higher than the Engineer's was, he might have been able to get the Engineer to approve the project as a favor, without having to pay a bribe. Otherwise, no one, not even the Engineer's bosses, other government officials or police will do anything to stop the Engineer from demanding a bribe. In this case, all of the people responsible in our area for allocating rural development funds and monitoring them, all higher up the echelon than the Engineer, knew he received the 20,000 Rs. kickback: The Block Pramukh (District Chief) knew, the A.D.O (Assistant Development Officer) knew, the B.D.O (Block Development Officer) knew and the Panchayat Mantri (Village Development Council Secretary) knew. They did absolutely nothing about it. One of the reasons is they too perceive receiving money under the table as acceptable behavior—albeit should be done with discretion. Another reason is they too skim money off the top of development funds. One contractor told me he pays the B.D.O., A.D.O. and Panchayat Mantri, collectively, a 12% kickback off the top of any money he receives for any government projects he's awarded. Another told me he pays 15%.

Giving the Engineer 20,000 rupees is excessive even by Garhwali standards, so it's not clear if the kickback is only for the Engineer or whether he will share it with the B.D.O., A.D.O. & Panchayat Mantri. I believe the Pradhan was sincere when he told me he paid off only the Engineer but the Pradhan is new to politics and naïve, so he may not know if the money was split with the aforementioned officials. Either way, for his own trouble of having to falsify his records to explain the missing 20,000 Rs., the Pradhan pockets 5000 Rs. of the construction money for himself.

In a famous speech a former Indian Prime Minister, Rajiv Gandhi, acknowledged bureaucracy and corruption were so out of hand that out of every rupee (100 paise) the Indian Government allots to rural development, only 15 paise actually make it to the village. He was astute, but I wonder if he factored in how much money is taken out of the 15 paise once it gets to the village?

I blatantly attack the practice but my antics don't appear to change anyone's acceptance of it. Matter of fact, my actions just seem to make things worse, impeding JDF's ability to do good work. Conversely, Indians accept bribes, kickbacks, extortion and 'miscellaneous fees' as a normal part of their system. They approach the bureaucratic monster with humor, as exemplified in the hilarious TV parody, 'Office Office'. And rather than fight it, they use it to their advantage, transforming the daunting into the un-daunting: Paying off traffic tickets and for other crimes up front and under the table, skirting and expediting complicated government formalities with simple financial transactions and fixing genuine mistakes by readily extending favors to the appropriate officials.

Nina, the same young girl who performed the dizzying children's rhyme, approaches the Master and asks him a question about her math assignment. He responds by posing fundamental questions about the problem to her, none of which she's able to answer. Instead of explaining to her how to solve the problem, step-by-step, he quickly tells her the answer and sends her back to her seat. With bewilderment written all over her face, she sits down on her mat and seeks help from the girl sitting in front of her.

At 1:30 pm the Master abruptly dismisses grades 1- 3, an hour and a half before school ends (school hours are 10 am to 3 pm during the winter and 7:00 am to 12:00 pm during the summer). He did not teach these children a single thing while I was there.

On a freestanding blackboard the teacher then draws a diagram of a river, clouds, raindrops and a tree with accentuated leaves and roots. He briefly explains to the remaining children how rainwater is absorbed into roots to quench a plant's thirst and how river water evaporates into the sky to make clouds and eventually rain, as part of the fifth grade assignment for today. He calls the two and only fourth grade students up to his table and corrects one girl's assignment. Then, within ten minutes of dismissing the younger children, he dismisses the older children.

Turning towards me, the Master explains that he's leaving school early in order to arrive at his native village before dark. He lives in Chandpur bazaar during the week but he goes home to be with his family every Saturday afternoon and returns to Chandpur Monday mornings via a series of commercial jeeps. This is the reason for his friend's presence as well. Their native villages are near one another, so they come and go together every weekend. The Master's friend either abandoned his students even earlier in the morning or had never even opened school today.

The Master hands his keys to the mature fifth grade boy, Neru, and instructs him to lock up the school and hold onto the keys until Monday morning. I ask permission to peek inside the school, before it's locked. The Master sticks around to give me the grand tour.

Almost all of the government elementary schools are made in the same rectangular shape, divided into one classroom, a small storage room, a teacher's office and an outside veranda. Older buildings like this one (built 23 years ago) are made from rock and cement and the newer ones from brick and cement. All have tin roofs.

This school is in great shape on the outside. The veranda has a perfectly flat, intact floor, suggesting it has recently been repaired and the walls have recently been touched up with cement plaster and painted beige with brick red and green stripes painted horizontally through the middle of the building. Inside the school, the situation is grim. Besides not having basic amenities such as electricity, tables & chairs and blackboards, the walls are crumbling and the floor is severely rutted. It's as if an excavation team has come in and unearthed the entire floor with picks. It's outrageous but not surprising. The phenomenon is common. It results from mixing a paucity of fourth-rate cement to an overabundance of dirt-contaminated sand dug out from nearby riverbeds. New floors and paths immediately disintegrate into sand. In less than a year they can be completely destroyed and within five years a newly built structure can appear to be a hundred years old.

The government school's shortcomings are intensified by a visit I make to the only private elementary school for miles around, Shanti Mandir School. It was set up in Chandpur by parents twelve years earlier because they were frustrated with government schools and wanted to give children a better education.

At the private school, before school even starts, the children are getting organized. One of the school's proprietors has opened the classroom doors a half hour early, enabling children to set their school bags on their assigned seats as soon as they arrive. The boy assigned to open windows and back doors does so as soon as he enters the room. Two other boys drop off their school bags, pick up a 5-liter metal bucket and a long stick from the classroom, and head off to a water pump in the bazaar. They fill the bucket with water, and then, threading the stick through the bucket handle, sling the ends of the sticks over their shoulders and haul the water back up the road to the school. The bucket is placed on a stool outside near the front door, along with an empty pint-size container, for students who need a drink of water or to wash their hands during the day.

When the teacher arrives promptly at 10 am, the children leap into three lines. Girls stand in one line, boys in another and a mixture of both in the leftover third line. Without being instructed, each child stretches his or her right arm out in front to create the appropriate standing distance between one another. Every single child is dressed in a white uniform: Boys in white pants and shirts with red ties, blue sweaters, red socks and black shoes and girls in white shirts, white jumpers or skirts, blue sweaters and, because it's winter, they're also wearing a mismatched assortment of whitish-colored pants underneath, obviously not an official part of their uniform but practical for this time of year. Long hair is pulled neatly back into pigtails with red ribbons. A scrap piece of cloth is pinned to the front of every child's sweater to blow his/her nose on. Every Saturday children wear white clothes rather than their normal two-toned blue ones because, as the teacher tells me, "It makes them pay strict attention to what they're doing in order to stay clean."

The teacher's assistant, a recent high school graduate, arrives with her 2-½ year old cousin. She positions her cousin in front of the line. The little girl, whose face is completely hidden by a white floppy hat, stands at attention, not daring to move even an inch and appearing as if she might topple over at any moment from rigidity. Although elementary schools are meant for children class one through five, village children around this little girl's age often start following their brothers, sisters and other school children to school. They are even encouraged to attend government schools under a program called Anganbari.

A village woman is paid to gather village children age three to five and take them to the local government school where she teaches them how to sit still, be quiet, how to hold a pencil and supposedly how to write, although I know the Chandpur woman who runs the program does not know how to read or write. As an incentive to attend, the children receive free gram flour and wheat flour every month, in varying amounts as each school is given exactly three 5 Kg bags of gram flour and six 5 Kg bags of wheat flour every month nomatter how many children participate in the program. Which days these preschool children attend school or how long they stay depends in part on the motivation of the village woman responsible for supervising them, as well as her seasonal fieldwork.

The two oldest girls are called to the head of the lines to lead the group in prayer and song. Upon command, the children close their eyes. The two girls chant in unison, one line of the song at a time and then pause, allowing the other children to repeat what they've just sung. They sing three prayers. The first praises all those who teach children, likening them to mothers and fathers, saluting them as special friends who help, when times are bad or when there's no one else, acknowledging that it's because of their kindness that children blossom as they grow. The second prayer asserts god lives in everyone; in the Muslim and the disciples of Rama, Raghunath, Jesus Christ and Guru (Sikhism) alike. In the third prayer, the children appeal for god's grace in order to live religiously righteous lives, help those less fortunate than themselves, treat people with respect, sacrifice themselves for their country and be successful in life. The children then open their eyes and sing the Indian national anthem, Jana Gana Mana.

Afterwards the students file, obediently and quietly, into school, which is actually not a school at all but two small adjoining rooms in the basement of a cement house owned by one of the proprietors. The building is not that old but because of the aforementioned shoddy craftsmanship and poor quality materials, it appears to be ancient. The walls are moldy and crumbling. The floor has disintegrated or maybe was never applied. Tarps, rusted iron rods and beat-up wooden planks supporting the ceiling are exposed. Both rooms are 10 feet by 12 feet and crammed with plain wooden benches, functioning as both tables and chairs for the children. The back room houses grades one and two, where the teacher's assistant is teaching, since the other teacher has not as yet shown up.

The front room houses the third through fifth grade students. They immediately delve into their assignments, working diligently. Their teacher is a young Garhwali man from a nearby village. He's clean-shaven, from which I infer he's not married since many Garhwali men grow moustaches after marriage. He's short and rail thin, erroneously making him look frail when he's most likely strong as an ox. He's wearing a western style shirt and stained polyester slacks. In a soft-spoken, but nevertheless commanding voice, he speaks in Hindi, with a smattering of Garhwali inadvertently thrown in, methodically ordering one class after the other up to his table; correcting yesterday's homework, teaching new concepts and giving out new class assignments. He's thorough in his explanations and makes the children think for them, questioning them continuously until they get it right. He's gracious to me, but he doesn't spend any time dilly-dallying or talking. He's all business.

Meetu raises her hand for permission to go to the bathroom. Since there's no walking space between benches, she walks on top of the benches, climbing over her fellow classmates to get outside. She squats alongside the road. When she returns, she dips the tin cup into the water bucket and, tilting her head back, holds the cup directly over her mouth and pours water in, simultaneously careful not to touch the container to her lips and not careful. She's guzzled water in this manner her entire life, so the water falls into her mouth like a judiciously arranged waterfall, without spilling a single drop on her face or down her chin. She climbs back over the other students and studiously returns to her schoolwork.

Third grade students take turns working out math problems on a black board set up in front of the class. One boy makes several calculation errors, prompting the teacher to reach up and smack him hard across the face. The boy doesn't budge. After the 'terrible twos', at age three or four, Garhwali children's behavior starts diverging from American children in a variety of different ways, including their ability to tolerate pain. More than one child has come to my door with a dangling broken arm and no tears in his eyes. Children stoically accept punishment as well. A slap on the face or being walloped on the hand with a stick are perceived as a necessary part of a teacher's job. No one makes a big deal out of it, least of all the child.

I might have dismissed some of the government school's irregularities, like the Master talking to me rather than teaching the children, attributing it to his excitement at being able to visit with a foreigner, but coupled with the school's numerous other shortcomings and the fact villager's have been telling me about these very same inadequacies for years, the situation is far too disconcerting for me to ignore.

Seeing how well the private school is run and how much children can learn, I am hopeful the government school can become just as good. A few days after my visit, I describe the school's weaknesses to Ganesh, a JDF employee, and then send him to talk with the teachers about improving the school and to offer JDF's help. The preliminary discussion is meant to open a dialogue for further discussions but whatever my good intentions, the message is either garbled along the way or the teachers just plain don't like my message that the school needs improvement.

The Master and Madam adamantly maintain that nothing needs to be changed at the school. Every time Ganesh tells them one of my concerns, the Master buddies-up to Ganesh and, with a wink of the eye, explains, "You know Madam [a.k.a. the foreigner], she obviously doesn't understand what I said."

The statement is not so much a reference to my comprehending his Hindi or not, as it is to a difference in cultures. I understood exactly what the teacher said and I saw exactly what the conditions were. My opinion differs from him, so he interprets this to mean that I didn't understand his explanations for things being the way they were. He assumes that if I understood what he said, I would think the same way that he does.

The Master thinks I didn't understand that school uniforms are generally washed on Saturday because then they can hang dry all day on Sunday too, if need be. I understood what he said and even concede to the possibility that all 25 children's school dress were being washed on that particular Saturday. However, I know the children haven't been wearing their uniforms to school lately. I've noticed for over a month that whenever I meet the children on the trail on their way to or from school, more often than not they're not wearing their uniforms. This is what had inspired me to finally check out the school in the first place—that and the fact I could hear the children screaming and playing in the school grounds for inordinate amounts of time during the day. The teacher thinks I didn't understand the children's uniforms were being washed on the day of my visit—implying in his statement to me and stating directly to Ganesh that the children wear their uniforms every other day, which is just not true. The irony is I don't even care about school dress. For me It's merely become a metaphor for the level of attention shown to the children.

The Master also thinks that if I understood the Madam couldn't call to explain her absence, it means her absence could be legitimate. I understood what he said, but I disagree. True, there's no phone to call and inform the Master why she didn't show up. The problem is no excuse is going to be excusable to me. This Madam is notorious for not showing up to school. Before this male teacher was assigned here a year ago to help her, the school was often closed for days at a time because she just didn't show up.

In numerous situations like this, I explain over and over again until I'm red in the face and shouting at people that I understand what they're saying. I even repeat what they're saying to illustrate my understanding, but to no avail. The fact that I disagree with them equates with 'I don't understand what they're saying'. I even explain to them that it's not a misunderstanding of what they've said that's the problem, it's just that I disagree with what they've said. I usually try to fortify my position with numerous examples, such as recounting how many times I've seen the children not wearing their uniforms or how many times the Madam has not shown up to school, but my logical arguments rarely clarify anything.

I feel compelled to try to improve the children's situation at school. Addressing the matter with the teachers, however, now takes on overwhelming proportions. If I go to the school to discuss some of my ideas and they tell me the only problem is that I don't understand what they're saying, I envision myself getting caught up in the same old repartee, explaining over and over again that I understand, I just disagree. It's a conversation I need to bypass in order to focus on the real issue, the school's condition, but I can't; stymied by a cultural difference that boggles my mind, even today, rendering me ineffective.

I decide instead to talk with village elders assigned to oversee the school, hoping they will be able to help. Upon explaining to two of the elders the current school conditions, their response is, "All government schools are like this!" The elders totally agree on the inadequacies of the school and that there shouldn't be inadequacies, but they refuse to talk with the teachers about these matters. I suggest to them that it's their job as members of the school committee to intervene to help improve the school. They tell me it's not their job to make recommendations to the teachers about how to do their job, only to assist them when asked to.

I then go to see the man who oversees all of the government elementary schools in our area at the Block Research Center (BRC). I'd inadvertently met him a year earlier at the Mausi Block government offices and in parting he'd offered his services, "If there's ever a problem in one of our schools, feel free to come talk with me. My office is in Kotli-Mausi." His statement was fortuitous and is an invitation to talk to him about Chandpur's government school.

I start out by sharing with him positive things about the school: The cost of education is reasonable (three to four rupees a month), the outside of the building is in great shape, the school is conveniently located near the epicenter of Chandpur (schools are built on land donated by villagers and villagers tend to donate far-flung, unwanted fields), and the Master speaks both Garhwali and Hindi to the children, a necessity since children speak Garhwali in their homes and around the village, making it essential to know both in order to facilitate children's understanding of material being taught, as well as to teach them formal Hindi.

Then I tell him my concerns: Disheveled children, sitting in silt, an absent Madam, not a single uniform, no lunch, the Master leaving early and coming late every week-end, the pitted floor, litter everywhere, no discipline and no learning. I omit my school lunch corruption theory, opting instead to merely point out the discrepancy between enrollment numbers and the number of students actually present. Within two days the BRC man shows up in Chandpur. A day later the children are all wearing their uniforms and sitting quietly on the school veranda, studying.

> *JDF paid a steep price for my meddling. The following year when JDF needed the BRC to verify work it had done in various elementary schools, it took 1½ years for them to write the letter and even then it was inadequate and unflattering. A woman had replaced the BRC man and I assume she's a friend of the Chandpur teachers because her uncooperative attitude and obvious distain for me was far too acrid for someone merely fishing for a bribe.

The goddess Durga was made from the collective power of all the gods to destroy evil that they could not vanquish themselves. Afterwards, an illustrious battle ensued between Durga, the water buffalo demon Mahishasura, demon brothers Shumbha and Nishumbha, demon generals Chanda and Munda, Dhumarolochana and Raktabija. To help her fight, Durga pulled the goddess Kali out of her angst. Kali chopped off demon heads and drank their blood before it touched the ground to prevent more demons arising from the droplets.

Kali is invariably depicted in this fierce warrior stance. A garland of skulls hangs around her neck. Her red tongue protrudes and blood drips from her mouth. Her black hair is long, hanging down beyond her waist, and extraordinarily bushy. She wears a belt of dismembered arms and hands. Beneath her feet lies a conquered Shiv. In three of her hands, she holds a sickle, a freshly chopped head and blood. Her fourth hand is raised, flat palm turned outward, giving her blessing to all and alluding to her true nature. Despite her ferocious appearance, Kali is Mataji, respected mother, and the Great Goddess. She's the vital energy of the universe. Without her god is rendered impotent: He's the ocean, but she's the waves. She appears in different forms in different lifetimes and has thousands of different names: Parvati, Durga, Gauri Devi, Saraswati, Vaishno Devi, Lakshmi, Shakti, Uma, Jankari, Mahadevi, Surkanda Devi, Jwalpa Devi and so on. As the goddess living in heaven, she commands the world. As mother earth, she reflects everything in nature. As divine mother, she's compassionate, giving unconditional love, knowledge, success, fortune, creativity and boons. She's the quintessential protector of mankind, slaying evil in all of its forms, especially unfavorable human qualities and adverse human conditions, such as arrogance and poverty.

"Dibakhal Kali Devi is one of Durga's nine incarnations. She saved mankind and the gods. If you pray to her, many of your problems are solved. She's our great goddess! Long live mother Kali!" Pradeep proclaims in response to my query about who is Dibakhal Kali, his face beaming with pride, as if he's talking about the prowess of his own mother.

"But who is Dibakhal Kali? Why does this Kali have 'Dibakhal' in her name?"

Obviously delighted I'd asked, Pradeep enthusiastically chronicles Dibakhal Kali's history:

"A long time ago, just before the Gorkha soldiers from Nepal invaded Pauri Garhwal, a group of children had brought their cows and goats to graze on the hilltop above Dibakhal village. While playing, they dug a deep hole in the dirt. Some say a gold chain was dropped inside the hole and the children challenged each other to see who could get it first. Whether there was or not, a little girl around eight or nine years old was the first to crawl into the hole. The rest of the children covered her with dirt. When they tried to dig her out again they couldn't. They ran back to the village and told the girl's family what had happened. By the time her family reached the site where she'd been buried alive, she was dead. That night the girl came to her mother in a dream. She told her mother not to worry about her. She had become Kali. Her only request was to be worshipped once a year at her burial site by offering blood.

From then onward, Kali came regularly to Dibakhal and the surrounding villages to protect villagers. When the Gorkhas invaded, they set up a camp on the hill where the girl was buried. Kali howled and screamed at night near their campsite, trying to scare them out of Pauri Garhwal. Whenever the Gorkhas tried to steal chickens from villagers in the middle of the night, Dibakhal Kali thwarted their efforts by rousing villagers from their sleep with her cries, causing the Gorkhas to run back to their camp, empty-handed. Eventually the Gorkhas found out the little girl had been buried where their camp was set up. Being of similar religious temperament to Garhwalis, the Gorkhas did puja rituals to stop Kali's harassment. Even after praying, however, Kali continued to haunt them, so the Gorkhas dug up the girl's body, turned it upside down and reburied it. No one ever heard from Dibakhal Kali again."

"So Garhwalis revere Dibakhal Kali because she protected them from the Gorkhas?"

Shaking his head he groans, as if I've missed the whole point of his story, "No, no, no. She watches over people in all kinds of ways, warning them when bad things are about to happen. There's one old man...uh...I forget which village he's from, but it's near Dibakhal. He'd been plowing his fields all day when dusk fell. He had only one small plot left to plow, so he debated whether to continue plowing in the dark or come back the next day to plow in daylight. Dibakhal Kali appeared and advised him to go home, reminding him he was tired and warning him that working in the dark was dangerous. Then she left. Although the man knew Kali Ma [mother Kali] was right, he decided it would be ridiculous to come back tomorrow, hauling the oxen and lugging the heavy wooden plow all for such a small amount of work. He continued plowing. Suddenly he slipped and the plow blade cut through his leg. In pain and bleeding profusely, he dragged himself back home. That night while lying in bed, Dibakhal Kali visited him again. She asked the man why he ignored her advice and continued working in the dark? He pleaded stupidity and confessed there is never a reason to ignore the advice of god. Kali left without saying another word. The next morning when the man awoke, he noticed there was no pain in his leg. He took off his bandage and discovered his leg had completely healed. Dibakhal Kali believed he sincerely regretted not listening to her, therefore she cured him."

After a long pause I pose the question, "Could the story of Dibakhal Kali be just that, a story? Many people in the world believe these kinds of tales are myths and metaphors."

Shock and bewilderment spring across Pradeep's face—the identical expression another Garhwali man had on his face a month or two earlier when I asked him the exact same question about the Hindu epic the Mahabharat. Pradeep recovers from the momentary jolt, smiles broadly and confidently states, "No! It really happened Madam. It's all true! Dibakhal Kali really protects villagers around Dibakhal. The old man who got hurt by the plow is still alive. You can talk with him yourself."

I quickly do some calculations in my head. If the Gorkhas arrived in Garhwal in 1803 and left in 1815 and no one has heard from Dibakhal Kali since then, this means the man talked with her at least

180 years ago. I doubt he's still living. Alternatively, if he's still living, Pradeep's earlier assertion that no one has heard from Kali since the little girl was turned over in her grave is erroneous. I don't bother to point this detail out to Pradeep. He can probably give me a rational explanation, but I don't need one. Facts take on a different quality in Pauri Garhwal. Those vital pieces of concrete information based on the scientific method and rational analysis, the cornerstones of the modern world's consensus reality, amenable to change only through time and advancements in technology and not capable of conflicting with one another unless someone or something is wrong, are rendered impotent in the face of god and custom, which reign supreme.

Pradeep strictly adheres to traditional beliefs even though he has more knowledge about outside worldviews than many of his peers. His father died when he was a boy, so a distant uncle on his mother's side took it upon himself to send Pradeep to private schools, giving him a good education and a teaching degree. He's been unable to find a job as a teacher, so in the meantime he works for our foundation. I'm glad he does. He has a likeable disposition: He smiles readily, is extremely polite and likes to talk and share information, making him a natural teacher. He's handsome with his milk chocolate skin and uncharacteristic square face, and he always dresses in slacks and shirts with collars, as if in his warm welcoming way he's waiting for the modern world to show up.

"What is Dibakhal Kali Fair all about?"
"Every year on this day thousands of Garhwalis make a pilgrimage to the hilltop above Dibakhal village where the girl was buried and pray to Kali."
"What's special about this particular day? Is it her birthday or was this the day the little girl was buried alive?"

Pradeep turns to the two men, Mahesh and Vikram, who are sitting in the car with us on route to Dibakhal Kalinga Mela, his eyes pleading for them to answer the question. All three confess they have no idea why the fair is held on this day, but assure me that no matter what the reason, it's a propitious day to talk with and pray to Kali.

As we drive, the men talk amongst themselves. Vikram reports there was an article in yesterday's newspaper about a Garhwali soldier who'd died in Jammu and Kashmir. Mahesh and Pradeep respond with concern; asking his name, which village he was from, how it happened. This is followed by a discussion about a new pahari (person from the mountains) cricket player; Mahendra Singh Dhoni, including details about what he's doing and how he scored in the last game. Notably, they never mention the other players who are much bigger cricket stars. When I ask how cricket player from the Himalaya managed to be recognized at the national level, they divulge that he never actually lived in the mountains. He'd been raised on the plains.

They begin to reminisce about JDF's employee trip to Lansdowne. Vikram declares it's a shame I didn't visit the Garhwal Rifles Regimen's museum (Darwan Singh Sangrahalaya), while we were there and proceeds to gush about the numerous Garhwali heroes saluted in various displays. He then brings up Veer Chandra Singh Garhwali's name. Being a freedom fighter, Chandra Singh is not contained in the museum, but he's nonetheless the most famous and favorite local hero, so even though everyone, including myself, knows Chandra Singh's story by heart, Vikram recounts it to us anyway:

> "In the early 1940's when the Indian army was still under British rule, the Royal Garhwal Regiment was stationed in Lahore. One day a group of Indians, who were originally Muslim tribals from Afghanistan, staged a peaceful protest against the British. The

British didn't like it, so one of the British officers ordered a Garhwali soldier named Chandra Singh to shoot the protesters. Chandra Singh refused. He contended they were unarmed and stated, "I'm in the army to protect Indians not to shoot them." He was thrown in jail for insubordination. After India's Independence in 1947, he was released and hailed as a hero. Later 'Veer', meaning brave, was added to the front of his name, and 'Garhwali' was added to the end of his name, denoting his ethnic origins, as well as his regimen."

Garhwali identity is important to Garhwali men. This extends to their identity as mountain people in general. They tell me people from the plains view them as backward and subsequently inferior, so they do not always advertise their ethnicity in the big cities, but amongst themselves their Garhwali identity, especially their sense of connectedness to one another, is passionate and visible in a variety of everyday interactions.

One day several JDF employees and I were eating at a restaurant together outside of Pauri Garhwal. We were all talking in Hindi, but my companions have Garhwali accents and inevitably throw Garhwali words into any conversation and, since the dialect changes every 50 kilometers or so, they have very specific pronunciations. Not to mention, Garhwali's often say 'bal' at the end (or sometimes at the beginning) of every Hindi sentence regarding something someone else said or did. The waiter immediately recognized their language habits and struck up a conversation with us. He was from a village less than 14 kilometers from Chandpur. Together the men began to weave a web of familial relationships. A man from our group, Dinesh, asked the waiter if he knew, Birendar Singh Bisht. The waiter exclaimed, "He's my Brother!" Dinesh returned his excitement, "His wife is my sister!" Everyone smiled and nodded affirmatively at the familial connection. After some discussion the waiter's brother turned out to be a man from his village who is of his same generation and caste but from a different clan and Dinesh's sister turned out to be a second cousin on his mother's side who he's probably seen less than a dozen times in his lifetime. This knowledge, however, did not diminish their sense of close kinship whatsoever.

Another man from our group discovered his sister's husband's cousin's wife's aunt is married to the waiter's uncle. The conversation went on for another ten minutes as they made other familial connections, uncovering the names of mutual friends and acquaintances as well. They finally got around to stating their last names. When the waiter declared himself a 'Rana', two Rana clansmen sitting at our table, proudly announced they too are 'Ranas'.

We travel the back way to Dibakhal, the closest access route from Chandpur. After parking alongside the road, we wade across the river and begin the hour-long, gradual uphill climb. The sun is shining and the temperature pleasantly cool. A well-defined trail winds mostly through scrub brush, providing open vistas of the surrounding area. Hundreds of people are walking ahead of us and hundreds more behind. The fair crowd consists of men and women of all ages, although notably few children. Also sharing the trail with us are dozens of goats, most of whose coats are dusted with red powder or necks adorned with red-netted scarves, and a dozen or so water buffalo.

Roughly a fourth or fifth of the people who attend the fair bring he-goats or water buffalo to offer Kali as part of their prayers. Bringing a goat is significant, but bringing a water buffalo is even more significant, prompting village-wide pujas to send water buffalo and their handlers off to Dibakhal with fanfare and proper religious blessings.

Sibu's family was the only family from Chandpur bringing a water buffalo to the fair this year. Last night his family held a village-wide puja ceremony. A Baaman conducted Devi/Devta puja, inviting gods and goddesses, in particular but not exclusively, Kali. Several people became possessed by gods and began to dance to the frenzied beating of drums. Later in the program, Sibu brought his water buffalo into the courtyard, tethered with ropes that Sibu and his extended family had made earlier in the day from dried grass and Bhyunl tree bark. The Baaman administered more puja rituals and applied sindhor and rice to the water buffalo's forehead. Sibu painted its horns red and then tied a small red-netted scarf around one horn. His brothers and cousins liberally applied mustard oil over the water buffalo's back as an offering to Kali. Sibu and his male siblings then paraded the water buffalo through the village for everyone to see. At around 11:00 pm a procession of thirty odd men, women and children danced its way up to the road, as far as the edge of Chandpur bazaar. From there, seven Rana clansmen, two drummers, two goats and one water buffalo walked off into the dark, heading toward Dibhikhal.

Half way up the mountain a lone water buffalo is lying in the middle of the trail. Exhausted, he's unable to climb any further. It happens all the time when newly purchased water buffalos are moved from one village to another. Unlike water buffalo on the plains, most mountain water buffalo spend their lives sedentary, tied up in a yard or in a shed, seldom roaming free. Women cut, carry and deliver food and water to their doorstep. Thus, they're physically not used to walking, let alone traveling long distances or scaling mountains. Once they lie down, they generally refuse to get up again for a day or two. There's some concern a leopard might attack it during the night, but it's not a major worry since leopards rarely attack water buffalo. Nonetheless, owners periodically check on their recumbent beasts to make sure they're okay, bring water for them to drink and coax them to rise, usually to no avail. Only time and rest seem to get water buffalo back on their feet.

We cross over a mountain ridge. From there the constant din of drums grows louder and louder as we approach the hilltop. Our trail eventually meets the end of a one-lane dirt road where we join a sea of people, some of whom have arrived in buses and jeeps coming from the other direction. It's the unofficial and unmarked entrance to the fairgrounds, a series of small plateaus connected by numerous pathways on top of a mountain. Although the land falls within the perimeters of Dibakhal village, the village is located on the other side of the hill, far away from the fairgrounds and completely out of sight.

Hordes of people make it impossible for us to proceed on the main trail to the first plateau, so instead we make our way up the hillside on unrefined trails barely etched into the dirt, our feet clinging to tufts of grass sticking up here and there. At the top, venders selling everything from cheap jewelry to fourth rate ice cream on a stick have spread out their wares on every available strip of flatland.

We slide down a wet narrow slope and wind up in front of a crumbling temple. It was built to commemorate the spot where a local villager had seen Dibakhal Kali sitting one day. The temple has no façade, making it look like a small one room cement cave. In the far back are barely visible idols cloaked in darkness. Alongside them are piles upon piles of items donated to Kali by worshippers: Plastic bags filled with coconuts, incense, rice and red chunnis (long scarves). Standing in front of the donated items are three Baamans. As the throng of worshippers passes in front of the temple, the Baamans prod us along, allowing ten second glimpses of the idols, while hastily applying tilak to our foreheads and dropping miniature white golf-balls that taste like sugar into our hands.

The trail to the adjoining hilltop is wide, flat and split in two, giving opposing directions of traffic their own lanes, but running parallel and so close to one another that we can hear every word spoken by the people passing us by.

"Englezi!" A young girl whispers excitedly to her friends. They stop and stare, seemingly examining every inch of my body.

"Engrezi." A man states as fact to his companion, as if he's all-knowing and his companion is not.

"Englezi?" The woman questions. She's not really sure what I am, but having heard of such things, she imagines that I must be one of them. Upon her saying, 'Engrezi', the old woman accompanying her glances up from the trail. Her eyes flash open and her mouth drops. She's so stunned by the sight of me her whole body cringes backward and, making a quick side step, she rushes away without glancing back.

"Engrezi," a teen announces to everyone nearby, followed by, "She lives in Chandpur."

"Englezi!" The glint in the young man's eyes and his gaping smile express his genuine delight at having the opportunity to see such an anomaly.

It's like listening to a song whose only words are 'Englishman', but whose melody changes every time someone different says it. I'm not English, but according to Garhwalis there are only three kinds of people in the world: Garhwali or pahari, deshi (people who live on the plains of India), and Englezi.

The Engrezi song is interrupted by a water buffalo approaching from the rear. He bolts forward, scattering both directions of pedestrian traffic up and down the hillside. The water buffalo's handlers yank at ropes tied around his muzzle, chest and stomach, trying to hold him back. One man clutches his tail. Another man darts from side to side in front of the water buffalo, flailing a stick.

Goats, being small and sure-footed, come and go on the trail, easily moving through and around us unnoticed. Water buffalo are a different story. Not only does their size make it difficult to share the trail with them, but also many of them are newly purchased just for the occasion and therefore not used to playing follow-the-leader with their new owners, typically being downright disorderly most of the time, either barging out of control or refusing to budge. We watch this tug and pull comedy all the way to the main fairground: Sometimes the handlers tug and pull the water buffalo and sometimes the water buffalo tugs and pulls the handlers.

The main venue is a semi-grassy plateau about the size of a football field. Pomp and circumstance surround two water buffalo that have just arrived on the field with an entourage of 20 to 25 villagers. While their drummers and a bagpiper play a spirited Garhwali tune, the group half-dances and half-saunters across center field. Noticeably, a few people in their group are possessed by gods; hopping like pogo sticks or twirling like dervishes, with that duel utterly exhausted and exhilarated glow to their faces and hair and bodies glimmering with mustard oil. The front of the procession abruptly breaks into a run, hooting and hollering. The rest of the group, water buffalo and all, frolic after them. When they reach the end of the field, the group turns and runs back, joyous and exuberant.

"That one is huge!" I remark.

"Yeah. Malund villagers always bring huge water buffalo. They live near the jungle so their water buffalo roam free and have lots of fodder to graze on. The girl who was buried alive was engaged to a boy from Malund at the time of her death. In honor of her in-laws that never were, water buffalo from Malund always enter the temple first. The girl was from Chopara. Water buffalo from her village enter the temple last, formally ending the fair."

"What about everyone else? Do they just scramble to get into the temple?"

"All of the other water buffalo are placed in line according to the number their owners secure from the lower temple when they arrive at the fairgrounds."

On the other side of the field is the main Dibakhal Kali temple. Although most people worship in both temples, this one is deemed more powerful because it's built over the spot where the little girl is buried. It's approximately 20 square feet in size and gives the impression it's only partially constructed because there's no roof and the walls are of varying heights. Two cement and brick walls are five feet high and six inches wide. They're crammed with male spectators sitting and standing on every square inch. A third wall is not a wall at all. It's a makeshift cattle fence made from 2-inch diameter, iron water pipes. On either side, four-foot wide gaps function as separate entrances and exits for goats, water buffalo and their handlers. The main temple entrance for worshippers without animals is located on the fourth wall, an eight-foot high cement wall whitewashed robins-egg blue. Standing in front of the temple are two Baamans from Goda village's Godiyal clan. They frantically apply red paste and a pinch of uncooked rice to disciple's foreheads. In return, disciples bring their prayer-shaped hands up near their chins as a sign of respect and drop rupee coins into the Baamans' tin plates.

A dozen brass bells of varying sizes hang in the doorway, some adorned in miniature red-netted scarves with gold fringe. Ringing the bells as we enter, the crowd pushes my friends and I through the door. I glimpse around expecting to see an idol of Kali or an altar, but there's absolutely nothing inside the temple, except the wall-to-wall crowd standing on the floor and on the walls overhead. While I search around for the significance of the temple, I slip a couple of times. The first time I think nothing of it. The second time I peer down at the floor to see what I keep slipping on. It's hard to see below the multitude of waists and legs crushed together and what I finally do see is difficult for me to conceive, so I turn to Mahesh and ask for conformation, "Is the floor covered in blood?"

He answers nonchalantly, "Yes Madam. This is where they sacrifice the animals. They sacrifice goats until 1:30 pm and at 2:00 pm they begin sacrificing water buffalo." Glancing at his watch he adds, "It's 2:15 pm. they'll begin sacrificing water buffalo soon. Two is an auspicious time." Pointing to the far corner of the temple, Mahesh adds, "Over there is the hole where the blood drains down into the girl's grave."

I push and shove my way over to the square foot sloping indentation in the floor. In the middle is a three-inch diameter hole running several feet into the ground. Suddenly a murmur ripples through the crowd. The water buffalo sacrifices are about to begin. I make my way back to my friends. We decide it'll be too hectic when the water buffalo come into the temple, so we go back outside to watch. I stand on my tippy-toes to peer over one of the five-foot high sidewalls and stick my head between the pant legs of two men who are standing on the wall, literally holding their pant material apart with my hands. They both glance down to see what's going on, but neither one says a word to me nor do they show any signs of being annoyed at my lack of manners.

Down below a water buffalo wrenches his way through the gate, tussling with his handlers the entire time. He's enormous. It takes five men to hold him in place and even then, whenever the water buffalo is determined to move a leg, his head or some other body part, the men are powerless to stop him. They quickly extend his neck away from his body. Two men standing on either side of the water buffalo lift their hockey stick-shaped butcher knives into the air and slam them down onto the water buffalo's neck, one right after other. Six or seven whacks later the water buffalo's huge head falls to the floor. The crowd cheers, whoops and whistles in jubilation. He's immediately dragged out of the temple, using the ropes still wrapped around his body and head. Simultaneously, another water buffalo and his entourage cram their way in.

We leave the wall and start walking toward another plateau. We pass by the handlers pushing the huge beast over a precipice. Surprised, I ask, "Do you just chuck the dead water buffalo over the cliff?" A question I pose with such casualness, it prompts me to ask myself, "'When did I cross the line between being a person who thinks animal sacrifice is barbaric to one gallivanting around as if nothing is dying? How?" Questions I mull over privately, but for which I have no answers.

"We throw the water buffalo over the cliff, but the government has already contracted with people to come after the fair to butcher them. The contractor cuts up and hauls the meat away to sell and tans the skins to make leather goods."

"I've never seen or heard of anyone eating water buffalo meat in India."

"Rajputs and Brahmins don't eat water buffalo, but Harijan and Muslims do."

"They eat a whole lot!" Vikram opines, raising his eyebrows and cocking his head to emphasize his point.

"That's a strange paradox. Every year government officials make public announcements against animal sacrifice, yet they regulate the distribution of sacrificed water buffalo and financially benefit from it as well?"

"Yeah. They say we shouldn't sacrifice animals, but if they're Garhwali, you'll see that very same official sacrificing his own animals.

Did you see Konkriyal's car? He's here today. On several occasions he's made public proclamations against animal sacrifice, but last year he sacrificed his own water buffalo. Our belief runs deep."

Walking around the back of the temple, we scramble up an embankment, winding up on the upper most field, which sits three feet higher than the main grounds. Six or seven venders are selling tea, rice and dal, samosas and jalebis. We drink tea and watch the activities in the field below.

Women who've already prayed at the temples congregate together on the field, most sitting on the bare ground talking and waiting for their men folk. A few young men are strolling around checking out the unmarried girls who are also strolling around checking out the young men. Most of the other men and teenage boys are engaged in the animal sacrifices, either killing or watching.

Attendance at Dibakhal Kalinga Mela is estimated to be well over 5,000 people every year, but it doesn't appear that crowded. The various plateaus and trails naturally divide people into smaller groups and many worshippers come in the wee hours of the morning to pray and leave before all of the hubbub starts.

One hundred or more male water buffalo and their chaperones are lined up below us, waiting to enter the temple. Mahesh observes, "There's been noticeably less water buffalo the last couple of years."

"Yeah, and those buffalo are smaller in size than usual." Vikram concurs.

"What do you think that means?" I ask.

Pradeep offers his opinion, "There are less water buffalo Madam because there's nothing big going on. If another war with Pakistan starts up, then people will feel the need to sacrifice a water buffalo to save their sons or husbands from being killed." And then adds, "Or if there's an earthquake......or an election."

The other men nod in agreement.

A teacher who boards in Chandpur and teaches at the intercollege happens upon us. He stops to chat for a couple of minutes. In the course of our conversation he informs us, "1683 goats and 117 water buffalo were sacrificed at Dibakhal last year."

Right below us a man pulls on a rope tied around a goat's head and another man grips the goat's tail with his hands. Together they stretch the goat lengthwise, consequently spreading his legs apart, as if he's about to be frisked. Two men standing on either side of the goat chop its head off with three quick strikes of their butcher knives. The men pick up the goat's body, stuff it into a burlap bag and then toss the head inside. One man slings the bag up onto his shoulder. They stroll across the field toward the exit, their giant knives and bag dripping blood.

"Why was that goat sacrificed on the field? I thought they killed them in the temple."

"Goat sacrifices have been halted in the temple for the rest of the day."

"It doesn't matter for the goats, anyway," Pradeep chimes in. "People sacrifice them almost anywhere on the hill."

Mahesh conjectures, "Madam, some people prefer to sacrifice their goats outside the temple. If they sacrifice it inside, they're required to give a leg piece and the head to the Baamans (Brahmins, especially priests, are often vegetarians but not in the Himalaya, where they eat lamb and chicken). They're choice pieces. People don't want to give them away."

"But what about offering the animal's blood to the little girl? If they do it over there, the blood doesn't drip down into her grave."

Mahesh replies again, "Madam, it doesn't matter. They're here on the field and sacrificing a goat in Kali's honor. That's enough. It's blessed. In their village, they'll roast the meat over an open fire and then divide it among fellow villagers as prasad.

I loathe the name 'Madam', but I like the way Mahesh says it. Most people say Madam accenting the first syllable and not the second. Mahesh accents the first syllable and then holds the accent through the second syllable, causing his voice to rise slightly and always giving the impression he has something important to tell me. He's one of my favorite Garhwalis and a bit of a walking contradiction. He's always willing to do whatever someone asks him to do without any apparent feelings or thoughts about not wanting to do it, as if he doesn't have a mind or will of his own. His squat physique, unmanageable hair and squinting facial features give him an almost comical appearance, especially when he laughs, playing into the buffoon image. In reality, he's the exact opposite. He's a deep thinker, which has fostered numerous admirable qualities in him: Integrity, insight and empathy to name a few.

"I don't understand. The sacrifices are perfunctory and seem completely devoid of religious experience. Explain to me why you sacrifice animals? What's the reason?"

"We've always done it."

"Our ancestors did it, so we do it too."

"Yeah, but why? There must be a reason your ancestors sacrificed animals?"

The question is followed by a long pause and apparent consternation.

Eventually someone offers, "The gods will be angry if we don't sacrifice animals to them."

Pradeep clarifies, "We must sacrifice a goat every three years or for sure something will go wrong in our lives."

"What will go wrong?"

"Madam, anything can happen. Someone will get sick or die. There'll be conflict with our neighbors or in our families. We won't get the job we're waiting for or we'll lose our job."

"We'll experience a run of bad luck."

"You sacrifice goats to Narsingh and Bhaironath for these reasons. You sacrifice to Dibakhal Kali for the same reason?"

"We sacrifice animals to Kali because she wants us to."

"No matter what your problem is, you can ask Kali for help. If you worship her, she'll watch over you. Many couples come to the fair to request a male child. During the Kargil conflict, people prayed their sons and husbands would return home safely from battle. People pray for anything."

"We don't just sacrifice animals when we want something from Kali, we also sacrifice animals to thank her for giving us what we wished for. If we don't, she'll get angry." Vikram emphasizes his last statement by raising his eyebrows and cocking his head to the side in his stereotypical manner. To non-Indians the gesture can be confusing. Indians wobble their heads back and forth when they agree with something being said or to flat out answer a question with 'yes' without actually saying 'yes'. It looks like they're shaking their head 'no'. Vikram's cocked head is a shortened version of the wobble with the exact same meaning. Vikram does it a lot. Garhwalis sometimes do it, but rarely compared to their plain's counterparts who cock and wobble at the slightest opportunity.

"Why do some people bring goats and some bring water buffalo?

"Bhaironath likes us to sacrifice goats and Kali water buffalo."

"Then why do some people sacrifice goats to Kali if she likes water buffalo?"

"If a person's problem or demand is big or they're extremely happy their prayers have been answered, they'll sacrifice a water buffalo, but only if they have the money. Male water buffalo are expensive, 10,000 to 15,000 rupees [$222 to $333]. Only the very rich or desperate can afford this much money. All others bring goats."

A crow lands nearby and starts rummaging through a plastic bag lying on the ground. Another crow lands nearby and begins hopping sideways around the first one, cawing obnoxiously, as if he's trying to shoo him away in order to feast on the plastic bag himself.

With a silly grin on his face Pradeep quips, "Madam, you're going to have guests tomorrow!"

"What?" The statement catches me off guard.

"You're going to have guests tomorrow. Garhwalis believe if a crow comes near you and starts cawing it means guests are going to show up."

"Oh! That reminds me. Last week on Monday... or Tuesday around sunrise, jackals came into Chandpur. They howled and howled for no apparent reason." Turning to Vikram and Mahesh I ask, "Did you hear them?"

Both nod their heads affirmatively. I turn back to Pradeep, who lives in Banekh, to continue telling him the story; "I heard them howling and then noticed that the rest of the village had gone stark quiet, so I went out on my deck to see what was going on. Several jackals had gathered in a field across the river, below my house. While watching them I spied Suru out in front of his house, spitting repeatedly. I assumed he'd swallowed something that he shouldn't have, like a fly. Then he put his hand in his mouth. Again, I thought he was reaching into his mouth to remove whatever it was he shouldn't have eaten or maybe that something was actually stuck in his throat. Then he jammed his other hand in his mouth. I couldn't for the life of me imagine what he was doing. When he removed his hands from his mouth, he noticed me. I asked him what's up [a gesture asked with raised eyebrows and chin and by lifting a partially opened, upward-facing palm into the air and shaking it back and forth for a second]. He told me howling jackals are a bad omen and the only way to stop their howling is to spit seven times and then stick your hands as far as back in your mouth as you can. I was thinking, 'what a bunch of hogwash,' when the jackals suddenly stopped howling!"

Pradeep exclaims, "See Madam! It really works! You should try it sometime."

We head back to the trail leading to the river and our car. Scores of vultures hover in the sky above. It seems like we've walked a long way, away from the hilltop, but we have in fact looped around the mountain and are now several hundred feet directly below the main fairground. A loud commotion overhead captures our attention. Looking up we see a huge, dark-gray, blubbery mass tumble down the steep mountainside, crashing through the brush and bouncing high into the air. It lands in a ravine not far from where we are standing. A second one comes crashing down, then a third and a fourth.

Saguna Devi and Jamuna Devi are both in their late sixties, yet they're anything but fuddy-duddy old ladies. They're always up to something interesting: Growing a garden of sunflowers or fuchsia-colored roses, nurturing newborn goats at home or shaving sheep and using the wool to make bedding. Today, basking in the sunlight drenching their courtyard and chatting with seemingly every person who passes by, they're making rope; both standing at opposite ends of a handful of dried hemp, braiding the fibers from the middle out, twisting and turning in opposite directions, stooping over to grab more strands of the bleached out bark from a pile nearby, weaving them in, extending each rope out to about four feet, long enough to tie up one of their goats or sheep up at night.

They make rope out of almost any hardy fiber. When I was building my house, the empty gunnysacks in which cement had arrived kept disappearing. It didn't matter to me. I wasn't planning to reuse them, but I was curious as to where they had gone, even though I never asked. Later in the year, I inadvertently found out. Over a period of two days, during the deep of winter when women had no fieldwork to do, Jamuna Devi, Saguna Devi and a dozen other women and girls gathered on multiple courtyards throughout the village to unravel dozens of the canary yellow, plastic sacks and rethread them into rope. Instead of two people, however, there were four women threading simultaneously, standing at right angles of one another, making one-inch thick ropes.

Jamuna Devi and Saguna Devi are the wives of one man, or were. Their husband died last summer. Jamuna Devi was Amar Singh's first wife. After giving birth to four daughters, Amar Singh decided to take in another wife to give him a better chance of having a son. In the interim, Saguna Devi married a Chandpur man at the age of 14, although she didn't actually come to live with him in Chandpur until she was 17. He died a short time later, leaving Saguna Devi a widow with one son and, without a male wage earner, destined to live in poverty. Living in the same village, Saguna Devi and Amar Singh knew one another's predicaments and since their needs were compatible, she became his second wife.

Polygamy is common. In our village, there are at least six polygamist threesomes, invariably two women and one man. The reasons cited for this practice are: The need for a male child, the need for a male wage earner and the need for an extra female to do the copious house and farm work. No one has ever suggested physical attraction or sex play a role in the decision to take on or be a second wife. As a Westerner instilled with romantic ideals, it's difficult for me to imagine that it doesn't, but I must admit it appears to be an ancillary motive most of the time.

Between them they have seven children, including the son Amar Singh wanted from Saguna Devi, and eight grandchildren. They dote on the one grandchild who lives in Chandpur as if she's the most precious thing in the whole wide world. She was almost never seen during her first six months of life, as per convention, but now that she's almost a year old, once or twice a day Jamuna Devi wanders around the village with her granddaughter in her arms, helping her to interact with other villagers. They hang out on my veranda in the shade during the afternoons, visiting with whoever happens by. Jamuna Devi explained one day, "We like to sit on your veranda because it's made of cement: The baby can crawl around and there's no mud for her to pick up and put in her mouth."

Older women in Pauri Garhwal either become less constricted by cultural norms as they grow older or cultural norms for them are less constrictive. Jamuna Devi smokes a tobacco-filled hookah (1 ½ foot tall free-standing pipe in which smoke is filtered through water) and Saguna Devi smokes bedis. Although they usually smoke in the confines of their kitchen, smoking-parties spontaneously break out in their courtyard on a bi-weekly basis, in which several elderly women gather to smoke and talk. When marijuana is in season, they smoke it as casually as tobacco. Even though it grows wild here, Jamuna Devi and Saguna Devi grow an annual crop of their own. Few people smoke marijuana other than the elderly, but almost everybody in the village harvests the seeds of the wild plants, roast them and eat them as a snack. During high season, an empty pant pocket or an un-knotted, end corner of a sari is rare.

Jamuna Devi and Saguna Devi have extensive knowledge of local wild plants. When they were young, indigenous plants made up a significant portion of their diets. They still eat them occasionally. They know how to make traditional medicines from local plants as well and do so when the occasion arises: They cure skin rashes brought about by allergic reaction by grinding the Khabbaa plant with cow's butter and feeding it to the sufferer; alleviate the effects of poisonous snakebites with Dumakhaaphal seeds and salt; cure sore throats by grinding Khabbaa roots into cow's cream; treat dysentery with a drink made from ground Sajji, Kirmali Pahari root, Anise seeds and Javaan mixed with hot water and strained through a cloth; heal cuts by rubbing Lalphul or Budnyaan plants between their hands, extracting the juice and adding cow's urine, which they then apply to the wound; stop bleeding by wringing juice from the Almora plant, dribbling it directly onto flowing blood; and, for cows that have eaten poisonous leaves, causing their stomach to swell and their appetite to wane, they feed them a mixture of ground Jaree or Sajji roots, ghee and strained tea water.

There are several homeopaths like them spread throughout villages in the region. They're the first line of medical defense in Pauri Garhwal, popular because they are easily accessible, culturally appropriate and affordable, most treating only a few specific illnesses for which they've become well known.

Up over the hill from Chandpur, in Kalou, is a woman famous for treating eye ailments. The bulk of her patients either have something stuck in their eye or something, usually wood chips, have flown up and hit the eye. She extracts objects by running the edge of her shawl along the patient's eyelid. She pulled a five inch piece of fuzz out of my neighbor's eye and then prescribed eye drops made from black tea, cooled and strained, which Sharti Devi had to put in her eye several times a day for several weeks before the discomfort went away.

To sooth eyes and reduce inflammation from flying wood chips, Giveni and Fyulari plants are minced and mixed with breast milk, if available, water if not. The liquid is then strained through a cloth and put directly into the eye, like eye drops. If a patient doesn't want to put the medicine into his eye, he can take the three middle fingers of the same hand as the ailing eye, dip them into the mixture and then, reaching as far as he can over the shoulder opposite the ailing eye, apply the medicine to his back instead.

Up around the bend, in Kui, there's a Ved, a person trained in traditional Ayurvedic medicine, who cures jaundice by blowing a homemade powder concoction into patient's noses a few times a week until the jaundice symptoms completely go away. He also restricts his patients' diets to no animal products (milk, eggs, meat) and minimal salt and spices for six months or longer. Shiva, a neighbor who was bed ridden with symptoms of extreme stomach pain, nausea, no appetite, weakness and yellow eyes, was cured within three months and swears by the treatment.

In a village down the road and around the corner is a Jhaard-Taard, a colloquial term for people who use herbs and incantations to cure ailments. One of her specialties is 'spider's urine disease', a common skin disease caused by contact with spider's urine. It looks like Herpes Zoster but after itching and subsequent infection it looks like Gangrene. The treatment is well known for its efficacy: One fly, the Bhimoldo plant and pipe tobacco residue ground together and applied to the infected skin. Mantras are then whispered into a vulture's feather, while waving it in front of the afflicted person. The secrets handed down from elders are intended to put the practitioner in touch with god to facilitate healing. A neighbor boy, Biru, was cured using this traditional method.

The next in line on the medical defensive are Quacks. They're uneducated men who run small medical stores in bazaars, dispensing allopathic medicines as if they're pharmacists and diagnosing and treating illnesses as if they're doctors. A Chandpur boy, Suru, broke his arm and was taken to a Quack for treatment. The Quack cut off a piece of his elbow and placed his arm alternately in a sling and a plaster cast. Three months later Suru's arm was frozen in place, as if it was in a sling, and still in pain. At the behest of his parents, JDF brought him to Pauri's district hospital multiple times. The government doctor readjusted his arm, applied plaster and afterwards made rigorous attempts to exercise the arm, all the while muttering about the Quack's incompetence. It took more than another year for Suru's arm to heal. Even so, it remains slightly crooked and does not fully extend.

Despite their sometimes overzealous treatments, Quacks play a role that would otherwise not be served in rural areas. They give shot regimens prescribed by doctors, readily make house calls to give pain medication to ease a dying patient's suffering, extract abscessed teeth, clean wounds with iodine products and apply sterile bandages.

My neighbor, Shanti Devi, was making tea one morning. While removing the boiling hot pot from her fireplace, a little tea spilled on her, causing her to falter and spill the entire pot of tea on her hand, hip and thigh. It appeared to be an accident but, according to Shanti Devi, it was not an accident at all but an assault on her by her husband's first wife, who is dead and who is the source of all of the other serious accidents Shanti Devi has endured since being married ten years ago.

The hot tea burned through Shanti Devi's skin and muscle down to the bone. She immediately wrapped a dirt-stained cloth around her hand and leg and for two days lay in pain, barely able to move. Finally her husband requested JDF take her to the hospital, which we did. The doctor cleaned her wounds, wrapped them in sterile bandages, gave her injections to ward off infection and gave her pain medication. He told Shanti Devi she needed to have her bandages changed every other day. Shanti Devi refused to make the four-hour round trip car ride to the hospital because, as she explained, "I'll throw up riding in a car...I don't have money to pay for transportation back and forth...getting jostled in a crowded jeep will cause me more pain...I have work to do at home...."

JDF paid a local Quack to clean her wounds with an antibiotic ointment and wrap them in clean bandages every couple of days for six weeks.

When an illness is prolonged, a Soothsayer is consulted, usually simultaneously with treatment of symptoms by a Quack. It is presupposed that the cause of long-term suffering is god is displeased with the sufferer or that someone has given the sufferer the evil eye. Soothsayers prescribe rituals to please god or ward off evil spells, depending on how they perceive the situation. Cures vary widely, but always include puja ceremonies and generally include restricted food intake, wearing talismans, goat or chicken sacrifice, making amends in relationships, or tantra-mantra rituals.

A common tantra-mantra ritual for curing illness, either by passing it onto another person or sending it back from where it came, can often be seen smoldering in the middle of village trails; a pile of burning pinewood coals from a home fire, on top of which rock salt, dried red chilies and urad dal (black lentils) burn slowly. This same burning pile, if placed at crossroads of trails, is specifically to keep the evil source of an illness (bad vibes, a curse, a ghost, god' wrath, etc.) from coming onto a particular path.

When all else fails, rural Garhwalis either go without further medical care or go to a government hospital, usually reluctantly because inherent in the trip are innumerable hurdles, snags and unknowns.

We pull into an empty parking lot and Mahavir announces, "Here's the hospital."

I glance around in disbelief. On the lot is a dilapidated two-story building. Huge portions of cement plaster had crumbled off the outside walls. Where the walls are intact, green and black mold mask a barely perceivable faded pink distemper. All fifty or so of the building's small glass window panes are broken, many with not even one shard left inside the frame.

I blurt out, "This can't be the hospital!"

"Yes, I think this is the hospital, Madam."

"Well, it may have been a hospital at one time, but they've obviously condemned the place. Look! There's a padlock hung on the door."

"The hospital closes everyday at 2:00 pm. It's now three."

"But how can a hospital close at 2:00 pm? Where are the patients? They can't be locked inside!"

"There must not be any in-patients," he suggests in a matter of fact manner.

We step out of the car and walk around the building, searching for an open door. When we don't find one, we pound on the front door. No one responds. As we pull away in the car, I am certain this hospital is no longer in use and has moved elsewhere. Mahavir insists otherwise but I assume he doesn't really know since he's been living on the plains for most of the past 10 years. To avoid being rude, I express my opinion less emphatically, "Let's go down to the block offices and ask if this is still the hospital. If it's not, they'll probably know where the hospital has moved to."

The block offices that house rural development officials appear to be deserted too. We eventually find a man wandering around on the grounds, however, who confirms the building next door is indeed the hospital and "No, it hasn't closed down."

I don't need medical treatment. Our foundation heard there is going to be an eye camp held at the hospital during the following two days, so we've arranged to bring 36 people to the camp. I just want to reconfirm the camp will be held, find out how to get to the hospital and get other details about the camp beforehand.

The next day when we show up with patients, the decrepit building is crammed full of people. There's no reception in the foyer. To find out what to do and where to go, we ask patients waiting in long lines that wind back and forth down the hallways. They steer us to a room on the first floor. Immediately inside is a man sitting on a plastic chair behind a folding card table. One by one our patients file up to the table. He writes down their names in a register and hands them a 3-inch square piece of blank paper on which he has written the person's name and age. Later, the doctor will write prescriptions, referrals or other instructions on it. We then pay the hospital entry fee of two rupees (4 cents) for each patient.

Those who need eyeglasses are sent into the next room. An Optometrist is sitting on one of only two chairs. An eye chart hangs on the far wall and a brown boxy suitcase, seemingly circa 1950's Americana, lies open on a wooden desk, exposing a multitude of round lenses filed neatly inside. It looks like a rectangular version of a slide projector tray filled with slides. The doctor asks his first patient if she has trouble seeing rocks and sticks when she's cleaning rice and dal of debris or if she has trouble seeing people and animals far off in the fields. She has trouble seeing animals and people in the fields. He pulls out a lense from the case and holds it up in front of the woman's eye. In dim lighting, she strains to see the chart with Devanagari script letters, eventually informing the Optometrist she can't read whether her eyesight is good or not. He tells her it doesn't matter: "Just decide if the letters are clear or fuzzy." According to her answers, he narrows down the possibilities, one by one. It's time consuming.

Patients with cataracts or other blinding ailments are directed to the eye doctor. He's conducting exams in the same room as the registration table, in the corner farthest from the door. His examination equipment consists of a flashlight and a narrow, chest-high metal table that requires patients to place their hands on the table, hop up and then use their arm strength to pull their bodies all the way up on top of it. There's no chair or stool to facilitate patients' climb and, because all of the cataract patients are elderly, many of them have difficulty hoisting themselves up.

The doctor barks at a patient to get up on the table. When she starts to climb, he barks again for her to take off her rubber thongs. He then berates the elderly, chubby woman because she can't get herself up onto the table. After several attempts, he threatens not to give her an exam if she doesn't hurry and climb onto the table. I walk over behind the old woman, grab her under her arms and give her boost. It takes a couple of heave-hoes, but she finally manages to get up on the examination table. Once on top, the doctor barks, "Lie down!"

The doctor, the optometrist and an assistant have come from the main district hospital as part of a two-day rural outreach program; the first day is exams and the second day operations. About 150 people have shown up on the first day, maybe more. Many patients are given prescriptions for eye drops, oral medications or eyeglasses. Most of the prescriptions can be filled in the bazaar, a ten-minute walk away, except for eyeglass prescriptions. Anyone who needs glasses will have to go to Pauri, another 1½ hours away, order and pay for the glasses themselves, and then pick them up a week or two later—an expense and multiple trips that probably not even a fourth of the eyeglass patients will follow through with. Many of them have already come from distant villages just to get this far. Some with seemingly insurmountable difficulty.

I meet a blind woman holding onto the walls trying to find her way around the hospital. She had walked several kilometers to get here, all by herself, astonishingly negotiating village trails and roads and necessarily avoiding a cliff that borders a significant portion of her route. She's hoping her sight can be restored. Unfortunately the doctor tells her he can't help her. She joins numerous other patients who are told they need to go to more sophisticated hospitals down on the plains in order to receive treatment. The only operation the doctor can do or is willing to do is for cataracts.

Sixteen people from our group need cataracts operations and are told to come back tomorrow to have them performed. I assume there were at least two, three, maybe even as many as four times that number of cataract patients who showed up today, but they were turned away because there's only one doctor to perform the inordinate number of cataracts operations already scheduled for tomorrow—nineteen!

We're surprised when we show up at the hospital the next morning at ten and find out the cataract patients will need to spend the next two nights in the hospital, maybe three, depending on how quickly their eyes recuperate. The sudden news poses several problems. For one, hospital stays require patients to bring a family member or friend to attend to them like a nurse does in modern societies, but since no one knew they would have to spend the night, only two of the patients we brought are accompanied by a family member.

Another problem is sleeping arrangements. According to the Chief Medical Officer in Pauri, "Mausi hospital is a 32-bed facility" but, in fact, there are only eight beds in the entire hospital; each with 1-inch thick cotton-batting mattresses and a gray wool blanket, no sheets or pillows. The final problem is meals. The hospital has no food service.

Our problems are solved relatively easy.

The three other cataract patients who are not with JDF's group, upon seeing JDF's large group of sixteen patients, ask to be a part of our group. Their status changes without fanfare. We merely write their names and addresses down in our register and have them confirm the information with a signature, which in all three cases turns out to be inked-thumbprints since no one knows how to write. The camaraderie is instant and, as luck would have it, two of the new patients have been accompanied by family members, so those two family members plus our original group's two family members volunteer to stay and look after all of the patients and the doctor deems four caretakers is plenty.

JDF's Director and I dash off to Mausi bazaar to rent mattresses and blankets for the eleven bedless patients and their four caretakers to sleep on the floor, supplies readily found in towns throughout Pauri Garhwal because of the staggering number of weddings in villages and subsequently the just as staggering number of wedding guests that require a place to sleep.

The doctor restricts patients' diets to mush and dried fruits in the morning and minimally spiced curried lentils and rice in the afternoons and evenings, so while in town we buy food supplies for three-days. A nearby teashop owner volunteers to prepare and bring the food to patients, their caretakers and the hospital staff: "If JDF can go through all of the trouble of bringing poor people to get treatment and buy their food, I can pitch in by making their meals for free and delivering them!"

Meanwhile, patients are brought into an empty waiting room where they sit down on the floor. The doctor's helper comes into the room to put drops in the eye of the first person to be operated on. Twenty minutes later he gives another dose of eye drops to the same man and the first dose of drops to the second person to be operated on. Patients are then taken, one at a time, into the adjoining room where their operations are performed. The high metal examining table patients had struggled to get up on yesterday has been moved into the operating room. The registration card table now doubles as a side table with a few instruments on it. A portable light strung from the ceiling is attached to a generator to make electricity for the one bulb, if needed.

Because the Optometrist has gone back to Pauri and the doctor's helper is continuously leaving the operating room to put drops in people's eyes, the doctor requisitions one of JDF's employees, Pradeep, to be his operation assistant. Pradeep, who has no medical experience whatsoever, nonetheless holds people's eyes open, holds the light and does anything else the doctor commands him to do. In between patients I ask him what it's like being a surgery assistant. In his typically enthusiastic way, he describes it as "very interesting" and reports he has no qualms about watching the doctor cut into people's eyes, while simultaneously giving me a sideways, quizzical glance, which I understand to mean, 'What in the world would make you think watching a person's eye get sliced up would make a person queasy?'

The doctor performs 19 operations in a row, one eye for each patient, without pausing for a break or lunch. After each operation, patients with bandaged eyes are led back into the room and plopped down on the floor next to their rubber thongs. When all nineteen operations are finished, the orderly leads everyone to a room at the opposite end of the hospital and randomly assigns patients and caregiver's beds or mattresses on the floor. In the ensuing days a few people report their eye feels like it has grains of sand in it, otherwise there are no complaints and prognosis is good for all of the patients. When they're discharged, each is given a pair of huge, black plastic glasses with flaps, to be worn for the next 30 days to protect their eyes against flying debris and bright lights.

Munga Devi, one of the patients, had come to Chandpur a couple of months before the eye camp. In a husky, no-nonsense tone of voice she had groused, "I need my eyes fixed! Everyone's dead. I live alone so I have to care for myself. But I can't see! Not even to cook! On the way here today I crawled on my hands and knees to get down the mountain. It's steep and I couldn't see the trail!"

Two and a half months after her eye operation, Munga Devi shows up on my doorstep again. Having either missed the instructions or misunderstood them, she's still wearing her black glasses. Beaming, she declares, "I can see!" And then reveals the reason for her visit, "Now I need you to help me get the other eye operated on!"

Captain Sahab, like most Garhwali men who've been in the army, has been indoctrinated into a world run on time—something many rural Garhwalis have a different concept of. He's nothing short of angry because of it. The village meeting is supposed to have started at 12:00 pm, but it's now 12:30 pm and only a handful of people have shown up. Every five minutes he scowls at his watch, threatening to fine anyone who doesn't show up or who shows up late 50 Rs., a hefty penalty that would coerce even the slowest of the slow pokes to hurry to the meeting, if they could hear him. To bolster his threat, he periodically dispatches young men to round people up and spread word of his ire.

People straggle into the courtyard. Three plastic chairs and a wobbly table have been set up in the center for village council members to sit on, although it's hardly enough chairs to accommodate the dozen or so members. A large rug owned by the village has been hauled out of storage and laid across the mud and rock ground for people to sit on. A few women sit down on the rug, only to abandon it a short time later because whenever they glance in Captain Sahab's direction, the focal point of the meeting, the sun shines directly into their eyes. Eventually most of the women wind up sitting on the stairs and second-story veranda of Rajeshwari Devi's house. Clear across the courtyard, kitty-corner from them and near Captain Sahab, the old men are perched atop a two-foot high rock wall that skirts a small section of the square, sitting on their haunches with their backs toward the sun, a few lighting bedis at regular intervals. Behind Captain Sahab, on the second floor veranda of Kaneeka's house, the younger men sit scrunched together yoga-style, late arrivals necessarily spreading onto the stairs, starting at the top and gradually sprawling down the steps and along the wall of the house, in one continuous line.

Captain Sahab, a nickname he acquired before his retirement from the army 24 years ago, formally begins the meeting at 1:00 pm, after 30 or so people have shown up. As Director of Chandpur's village council, it is Captain Sahab's job to keep village business records, to call village meetings occasionally to enable villagers to discuss and vote on important issues and, along with the other council members, help solve any problems that may arise. He welcomes those present and tells them the village coffer contains 27,000 Rs. ($600), qualifying his statement with, "That's if everyone pays up what they owe the village treasury today."

Most of the money, he explains, has come from renting the village wedding supplies (large cooking vats, rugs, tents, etc.) to Chandpur villagers and other nearby villagers, from interest made on loans given to Chandpur villagers and from fines levied against people whose animals have wandered into other people's fields. He elaborates, "There's been some discussion the fine money should not go into the village till, but instead should be reimbursed to the person whose crops were eaten, but we'll probably not have time to talk about that matter today. We have many other things to do. It can be taken up in a later meeting."

Captain Sahab barely finishes his last sentence when my 72-year old neighbor, whom I affectionately call 'the Curmudgeon', becomes agitated on the sidelines. While talking to his friend he intentionally raises his voice periodically to air opinions he wants everyone to hear, "He can't do that!...I didn't disrupt his work!...It's a lie!"

The Curmudgeon is one of only a few people who complains aloud when somebody does something morally or legally wrong, sometimes following up his complaints with formal letters to authorities. Recently he did just that and now he's being threatened to be locked up in jail by Chandpur's Pradhan.

Elected every five years, a village Pradhan is the village's liaison to the government, making him responsible for managing village development projects carried out with government money, as opposed to running village internal business affairs like Captain Sahab does. Chandpur's current headman has been controversial from the very beginning, winning his position only because it was a reservation year, requiring whoever wins to be from the Harijan caste.

A year ago Chandpur was allocated money from the government to cement and extend its limited mud and rock irrigation canal, a project and money managed by the Pradhan. Several villagers had volunteered their time to fix the irrigation canal and a handful of Chandpur's poorest residents were paid to help. The Curmudgeon confronted the Pradhan several months back and accused him of misappropriating funds. He believes the people who volunteered their labor were written down in the Pradhan's ledger as being paid, wages the Curmudgeon asserts the Pradhan pocketed. The allegation is difficult to prove since the Pradhan is refusing to show anyone his village accounting records. The last time he was forced to read his records to Chandpur villagers an uproar ensued. He'd written down that he'd held this meeting and that meeting and that he'd given money to this person or that person, but during the reading every single person he'd written in his records either denied being present at the meeting or denied receiving any funds. In other words, all of the signatures in his accounting book were fake.

Initially the Curmudgeon merely complained to fellow villagers, but when he found out more money had been received by the Pradhan to do more work on the canal but no more work was done, he openly accused the Pradhan of 'eating' all of the newly acquired money and wrote scathing letters about the matter to the government officials responsible for distributing and monitoring development funds.

Now the Pradhan is mad at the Curmudgeon for tattling on him. He has filed a counter-complaint stating the Curmudgeon is disrupting his development work by coming to projects to complain and accuses the Curmudgeon of threatening him with bodily harm. The Curmudgeon did go to the project site and complain, but it's highly unlikely the Curmudgeon threatened to hurt the Pradhan. The Pradhan is a strapping forty-year old and the Curmudgeon is doddering and fragile. He's probably the only elderly person in the entire village who would fall down if the wind blows too hard. No one would think twice about the matter except that in India thesedays, there is a heightened sensitivity to and laws against threatening or committing bodily harm to Harijans. They've historically been abused and subjugated like black Americans were during slavery and are still periodically abused by people from the upper castes, at least according to the newspapers on the plains.

There's no doubt in anyone's mind that the Pradhan embezzled the irrigation funds, that the Curmudgeon didn't threaten the Pradhan with bodily harm and that the Pradhan is merely taking advantage of the current zeitgeist to detract from his own wrongdoing. Everyone also knows it will not be the Pradhan who will be aggrieved for stealing village money, but the Curmudgeon for speaking up. That's why he's fretting. Development officials will make him jump through a lot of hoops; force him to make numerous trips back and forth to Mausi to be formally and informally deposed, require him to write rebuttals that will be tossed in the trash at a later date or any other of an infinite range of tricks they'll have him perform. The exasperating formalities teach people not to complain to or about government officials and is the perfect guise under which officials extort money from people in order to drop real and erroneous cases alike.

Captain Sahab quiets the Curmudgeon by telling him, "Perhaps we can discuss your issue later, but for now we're discussing old business."

There's a moment of silence while Captain Sahab shuffles through his papers. While still thumbing and without looking at the crowd, he casually mentions, "The proposal to build a new village meetinghouse was passed unanimously in the last meeting."

Jashpal Singh Thakur, JDF's Director, jumps up and, addressing Captain Sahab and Balvir Singh, two of the three men who run the private elementary school in Chandpur (the third owner belongs to another village), commences to speak:

> "Who approved changing the site of the village meetinghouse? That hasn't been decided yet. That wasn't a village meeting. You called an impromptu gathering of a handful people in which you did nothing more than tell them what your intention was. What's the point of building a new meetinghouse? We've [the village] just built a brand new building that we haven't even been able to use yet because you guys won't hand over the keys. You want the meetinghouse for your private school. If you want to expand your school, do it! You have money! Students pay you high fees every month for their education. Where is all of that money? If it's gone, you still have land! Build it on top

of one of your big houses or fit it inside one of your many multi-story buildings. To build another meetinghouse makes no sense for us. The government gave Chandpur one lakh (100,000 Rs.) to build the first village meetinghouse. Now you say you have another one lakh to give us to build another meetinghouse. It's two years later. Do you think the same amount of money it took to build a meetinghouse two years ago will be enough money to build one now? Besides, it's not even your money. Do you think that if the government knew, it would approve of paying twice to build us a meetinghouse just so that you can inherit a free school building? [Balvir Singh's wife is Jilla Panchayat and has offered to give 100,000 Rs. from her development funds to build a new meetinghouse] And, I heard you want everyone to volunteer his or her labor to build the new meetinghouse. Why? We already have a village meetinghouse. To say the new one will be closer is ridiculous. The meetinghouse is closer than the bazaar! I think what happened is that all along the three of you built the village meetinghouse right next to your school so that you could later confiscate the building for yourselves. And you should know it's illegal to build a temple on top of a village meetinghouse. Gobind Singh said he'd donate his field for a new meetinghouse on the condition you build a temple on top of it. You can't build a temple on top! Government regulations prohibit a temple from being built within 50 feet of a government building and the meetinghouse is a government building, so he probably won't donate the land to you to build a new meetinghouse anyway." Without pausing, he turns his attention to the rest of the crowd, which has ballooned to about 50 adults, "If anyone here thinks we should build a new meetinghouse, speak up. If you can give me one good reason why we should abandon the building we've just built for the village and give it to these guys for their private school, I will support your decision and drop the matter. But, give me a reason."

It's dead silent for an excruciatingly long two minutes.

Suddenly Balvir Singh's face turns beet red and his eyes grow to the size of baseballs. He leaps out of his seat espousing, "Government Povernment! We're the government here. If we want to build a temple on top of our village meetinghouse we can build a temple!"

And then, in his next breath, in a complete and sudden turnabout, he scornfully blurts out, "You don't want to move the village meetinghouse? We won't! You can have your meetinghouse. You think we care? We don't need your meetinghouse! We'll build the school on our land next to the meetinghouse. See if you'll have access to the village meetinghouse!"

Jashpal doesn't miss the opportunity to capitalize on Balvir Singh's outburst. He addresses Captain Sahab "Okay! It's agreed. We will not build another meetinghouse. It's agreed. Write it down! Write it down right now in the meeting register. Later I don't want you to tell me it was not agreed upon. In addition, when you build your new school, you had better leave a pathway to our meetinghouse. I'm warning you. It's illegal not to!"

Captain Sahab sighs, obviously disappointed and probably as shocked as the rest of us that his partner, rather than justifying the need to build a new meetinghouse, in a fit of anger agreed to hand over the already-built-one to the village. Captain Sahab reluctantly acquiesces, "Okay, okay. A new meetinghouse will not be built." And then assures Jashpal, "I'll write it down in a few minutes. We've got to press on to other business."

Jashpal insists, "Write it down now!"

Raising his hand in stop-sign fashion, Captain Sahab bobs it back and forth, "We'll write it. Hold on. Hold on."

Lakshu steps in, offering to write it down for a now befuddled Captain Sahab. Captain Sahab hands him the record book, visibly relieved.

"The next order of business is hiring a village guard. There's been a lot of discussion about assigning one again because numerous animals are roaming into other people's fields. It will cost us 400 Rs. ($9) a month. Rather than take it out of the village treasury, each family can take turns paying 400 Rs. to the guard each month."

While he peruses his notes again, there's a commotion intensifying among the women. They're talking frantically amongst themselves, upset about something. Finally Dukali Devi speaks up, "Who can come up with 400 Rs. at one time? Everyone should donate a little money each month."

A chorus of women follows her lead, reiterating in loud protests: "Yeah, who can pay that much?" "We should all give a few rupees a month!" and "It's too expensive!" Other women shake their heads vigorously in agreement. The men remain noticeably silent.

Captain Sahab scrambles to quell the growing agitation. "Okay, okay, a few rupees a month." He calculates in his head and after a moment announces, "That would amount to about 10 rupees per family per month. Is that going to work out?"

Dukali Devi exalts, "Yes, that's fair! Ten rupees a month per family is manageable."

The rest of the crowd nods in agreement.

"Is there anyone here who wants to be the guard?"

No one volunteers, probably envisioning the last village guard who worked for a mere three months before quitting. Fellow villagers had continually harangued him, blaming him every time he was unable to prevent animals from sneaking into their fields and eating or damaging their crops.

Finally Jashu suggests, "Someone from Harijan Basti will do it. Maybe Shiv Lal. His financial situation is bad."

Someone else speaks up, "He can't work! His health is no good. I don't think he can manage to wander around the village all day to keep an eye on the fields."

"He can work. He just can't lift anything heavy."

"He needs to pay attention. Cows are eating my crops daily," an old woman contends. "They shouldn't be allowed to eat the grass growing out of my terraced walls either!"

"They went up into my fields the other day and messed up the seeds we just planted!"

"Spring is coming. The monkeys will come back soon. He should bring a dog with him to help scare them away."

"We should have invited Harijans to the meeting so we can get this matter cleared up." Ragvir Singh adds.

"He...." Another woman is about to spout off her opinion when Captain Sahab interjects, "Hold on! Hold on! We can talk about all of that later, after we know who the guard will be."

Jashpal gets back up on his feet, "Whoever does the guard job should also guard the forest. Someone has been cutting trees right and left. There's going to be no more forest left. I heard a tree falling the other day [a loud "ker-thump" had reverberated through the valley]. Who cut that tree a few days ago?"

"The Pradhan cut it. Narendar needs wood for his house. You know he's building a new house."

"Narendar, oh, oh, yeah." Jashpal quickly concedes since Narendar is his close friend, as well as a fellow clan member. "So who else? There have been four trees cut in the last six months. Where is all of the wood going? We're only supposed to cut two trees a year. The Pradhan and the forest officer are in cahoots together!"

Because it is a common scenario, Jashpal does not need to elaborate on his allegation that the Pradhan is cutting down trees, selling them and pocketing the money and, in return for the forest officer's silence about his excessive tree cutting, he's either splitting the profits with the forest officer or buying him bottles of whiskey.

"Also people are buying the wood at cheap village prices and then storing it in their houses to resell later at a profit. This has to stop! The trees should be for poor people to build homes only. Twice a year when villagers cut trees, we should plant trees too. Not Pine trees. The kind of trees that help retain water in the soil, like Oak. Our forests are shrinking! Water is scarce! All of the trees and water are going to disappear if we don't stop indiscriminately cutting trees and don't plant new trees. Our ancestors would not recognize the place. What would Arjun Singh Jhinkwan think if he saw Chandpur's forest today?"

Arjun Singh Jhinkwan was Chandpur's original founder eight generations earlier. He'd come to this area from Chamoli, another district in the Himalaya. No one is sure why but the most likely reasons are he either came here to escape the plague that was ravaging villages in Tehri Garhwal, Chamoli and Uttarkashi at the time (during the early to mid 1600's) or he was sent to nearby Kuransi to be the government administrator there, as that was his caste's job and Kuransi village was the administrative seat for this area.

When Arjun Singh Jhinkwan first arrived, people were skeptical about his caste. They had never heard of 'Jhinkwans'. The caste inhabited a mere 10 to 15 small villages in the Himalaya (then and now) and although his native village is a mere seven-hour car drive away from Chandpur, in those days by foot it was as far away as the moon, making it difficult for people to verify his caste credentials and since caste played and still plays an important role in every villager's relationships and activities, the unfamiliar name was a source of trouble for him.

Traditionally, Jhinkwans and Thakur's both worked in small Raja's courts in Chamoli district as administrators. Jhinkwan was a higher sub-caste than Thakur in the warrior hierarchy, but they were both Rajputs and because Thakur was and is a well-known name throughout Pauri Garhwal, Arjun Singh added 'Thakur' to the end of his name, ending suspicion about his caste and making him Arjun Singh Jhinkwan Thakur.

A marriage was arranged between him and a warrior caste girl from Kuransi. The bride's father gave him some of his far-flung land on which to build a homestead. Over the next several generations the place became known as Chandpur and 'Jhinkwan' slowly lost its place in the legal names of Arjun Singh's descendants, turning the Chandpur Jhinkwans into Thakurs.

Changing the subject, Captain Sahab tries to refocus the group, "Okay folks, there's lots of business to take care of. I want to apologize for the break-up between the Rana and Thakur clans. This will not happen again. I personally will never vote for a split between our two clans again. But as a consequence of the divide, we haven't met for two years. There's a lot of business we have to take care of today. All of you who've had weddings and rented the village wedding supplies, you need to pay up. There have been several loans taken out from the village till too. They also need to be paid. Balvir Singh, Surendar Singh Thakur, Shyam Singh Rana, Magan Singh..."

Several men rush up to the table. Aware beforehand that they were going to have to pay what they owed the village till during today's meeting, about half of the people have the money in hand. After recounting it in front of Captain Sahab, each man hands over his bundle and watches him write it down in the village records. The other half does not have the money, not in their hand nor in the bank.

Ten minutes pass sorting out debts.

"We need to pick new officers. I've been the Director for 4 ½ years. Someone else needs to do the job."

Rajendar uncharacteristically speaks up, "Chachaji! Chachaji!" and having gotten Captain Sahab's attention pleads, "With all do respect to our elders, we need their counsel. They must be part of the board, but currently all village council positions are being held by people 50 years old and older. It's time to appoint young people to the board too. We are capable and what we don't know we can learn from our elders..." His voice trails off.

"Okay, you're idea is well-taken. Who will be Director?"

"Dadhu!" someone offers.

"Yeah, Dadhu!"

"Dadhu. You will be the Director?"

Dadhu nods his head vigorously, his face framed in a big smile, excited to do the job and no doubt confident as well. He gets along with everybody and has a good head on his shoulders for business. He just started a new school supplies store about a year ago. Before that he owned a successful cloth business on the plains of India, in Ghaziabad, but it folded when a sub-contractor stole a truckload of goods and stuck Dadhu with the loss, legal hassles and bills, forcing him to surreptitiously return to Chandpur to start all over again.

Other people nominated appear less enthusiastic than Dadhu, but nonetheless proudly accept the post when their names are called out. Not one person refuses their nomination nor volunteers their services. It's not clear why. I suppose the potential for conflict or envy, especially if someone else wants the position for himself, may be enough to keep even the most eager candidates from offering their own name. Out of 11 positions, 6 are assigned to young men, 3 to women, and 2 to elders.

The next meeting is held a month later. I did not attend. A month later another meeting is postponed until the following week because 98% of the village men have taken off this morning to attend one of the many weddings being held today, a particularly auspicious day, resulting in 14,000 weddings in Delhi alone, according to the newspaper.

This is the second meeting held in the meetinghouse since it was handed over to the village. The composition of the group is strikingly different from the last meeting I attended, with no women present and three men from Harijan Basti attending. Since Harijans do not normally come to village meetings unless summoned, these men were probably called to pay fines for their animals wandering into other people's fields.

The Director, Co-director and Treasurer confer together for a few minutes and then Dadhu presents the first topic; paying dues for animals that have strayed into other villager's fields, eating and trampling their crops. Dadhu reminds everyone the penalty is 10 Rs. for each goat that strayed into a field, 20 Rs. for each cow, and 30 Rs. for each mule. Instead of laying out the facts like a prosecutor, he relates each incident with a sense of humor, telling funny antidotes, such as how several people had tried to get Vinod's bull out of a field and it ended up being a bullfight with the bull chasing people all over the place. It's a tactical maneuver on his part to keep tensions at a minimum. Animals straying into fields is one of the few circumstances in which most Garhwalis, especially the women, will openly fight with their neighbors.

The list of errant animals is exhaustive but Dadhu mentions every episode, detailing whose animal had gone into whose fields on what day, including who saw the incident and who shooed them away. Not surprisingly, Jhagarni Devi was a witness to many of these animal-in-the-field altercations. From her cow's shed she has a bird's eye view of numerous fields and since she works at her cow's shed a minimum of two times a day seven days a week, she spots animals going in and out of people's fields regularly. Remarkably, she's able to identify exactly whose animal it is from a distance, when I, from my deck, a vantage point just above hers, can't even tell that it's an animal.

If the animals are in someone else's fields she hollers out, "So and so's cows are in so and so's fields", starting a chain reaction of hues and cries throughout the village, across the fields and up into the jungle, until the message eventually reaches the owner of the field. The field's owner takes over from there and starts screaming at the animal's owner to get their animals out of her fields or the field's owner comes running to the field's rescue, shooing the animal away herself.

When animals are in Jhagarni Devi's fields, she screams a string of local insults for ten minutes or longer: "Why aren't you watching your mules? They may die!", "Snakes will bite your cows!", "Don't bring your goats home. Throw them off the cliff!" and "Why bring your animals into my fields? Take them down to the cremation plot along the river!"

Animals are rarely left alone to wander, which means the errant animal's owner is invariably nearby, so Jhagarni Devi also addresses them, "Hey widow!" she screams out, even if she can't see the person and even though the person is usually not a widow at all. Alternatively, she'll refer to the animal's caretaker, especially children, as piglets or puppies, derogatory references. If the guilty try to say anything back in their defense, Jhagarni Devi becomes even feistier, retorting, "You will not eat the first day of the next month!"..."Your son will die!"..."This year you will not eat wheat!"

Alluding to the animal or owner's death is a subtle threat that she is putting a curse on either one. This is not taken lightly. Any future calamity, big or small, in the errant animal's owner's family, may be attributed to Jhagarni Devi's words. It would not be unusual if someone were to die in that family, for grieving family members to accuse Jhagarni Devi of being the cause of their loved one's death.

It's as if Jhagarni Devi's name, which means 'fighter', dictated who she'd become. She's a character to say the least, appearing haggard twenty-four hours a day: Her gray-streaked hair is always pulled back in a messy ponytail, as if she has slept on it for several nights in a row, and her saris are invariably sloppily applied, even coming undone. Whenever I bump into her and ask her how she's doing, her answer is always punctuated first with, "Aaaahhhh Baaabaaaaaaa!" and inevitably followed by moans, accentuating her three unrelenting woes: She works all day and night, she's exhausted and none of her daughter-in-laws will live with and take care of her. She then tilts her head back and shakes it while asking, "What can I do, Baaabaaaaaaa?"

In response I suggest to her and her husband, who are both over 70 years old, that they should give up working in the fields and merely tend to their animals. They invariably respond by assuring me they must work the fields in order to feed themselves. I figure differently. By Garhwali standards they're financially secure. Jhagarni Devi's husband receives a retirement pension from the army and he owns rental property in the bazaar. They also receive financial help from their sons; two of whom receive army pensions and now have civilian jobs and a third son who is still in the army. Regardless of what I may think, they continue to work hard every day and state they have no plans to stop laboring in the fields.

Talk of animals straying into the fields ends a half hour after it began. The next issue is the lending of village wedding supplies to people from other villages. Four glasses and a large rug rented for a wedding in Kotla were not returned. The person who borrowed the supplies (who we all know by name but no one says it) has not paid his 2,000 Rs. bill either. One man suggests, "We should not loan out village supplies to anyone other than Chandpur villagers."

Everyone else appears to think this is an extreme solution: "What would small villages that can't afford their own supplies do?"

In the end it's decided the man will be encouraged to pay his wedding supplies rental fee and will also be charged market price for the rug and glasses.

Another old man suggests, "When a person picks up the supplies, they should pay half of the fee. If they can't afford to pay half up front, they shouldn't rent it!"

Everyone nods his or her heads in agreement, although it's not apparent if it becomes an adopted policy.

Jashpal Singh Thakur, JDF's Director, had weeks earlier requested time in this meeting to make further comments about the village meetinghouse, so he's invited up to the front of the room to address everyone. He stands up and has barely turned to face the crowd, when Parvendar jumps to his feet and shouts, "Foreigners should not be allowed to come to our meetings! She's not a member of Chandpur. What? What? Any Muslim, Christian or stranger can come to our meetings? Why? There's no reason. She...She...She comes to our meetings...She shouldn't be allowed! She had me hauled off to jail. What right does she have to have me hauled off to jail? None! She told the sheriff that after I drink I harass Chandpur villagers and torment my family. That's not true! She told the sheriff I poured gas on my wife. It's not true! It's not true!"

Although Parvendar is working himself up into one of his stereotypical frenzies, talking so fast it's difficult for him to keep from tripping over his words, his tirade is one of the most coherent I've ever heard come out of his mouth. Unfortunately, his most lucid complaint is against me. I'm momentarily stunned, but given that I had him hauled off to jail, not surprised at his ire.

Initially no one responds. The awkward silence ends when the Co-Director of the village council, Surendar, retorts, "You need to take your private matters outside Parvendar and not bring them into our meetings."

Parvendar continues his tirade, repeating the same thing again and again but uncharacteristically stopping whenever someone else speaks.

"Why should Madam be kicked out? She doesn't disrupt our meetings. She just watches. She doesn't even talk," defends Lakshu, my loyal neighbor who in the past couple of years has gained confidence to speak out on matters he believes in.

Jashpal asks Parvendar mockingly, "What? Have you suddenly become a Maharaja (great king)? Deciding who can sit in on meetings and who can't? Have you ever watched Parliament? People sit in on those meetings to watch and listen to what is happening." He then adds rhetorically, "Are our meetings so much more important than Parliament that someone can't come to watch?"

Ganesh hollers out his brief opinion, "Madam should be allowed to come."

Jashu elucidates, "Madam lives in our village and is doing good social work in our area. What is she to think when we're talking like this. There's no reason for us not to let her sit in on our meetings."

Balvir Singh stands up and utters his opinion, "She shouldn't be allowed to come to our meetings. She's not a member. It's our village!"

Jashpal goes ballistic. Until now he's figured it's Parvendar's personal animosity against me for having him hauled off to jail that's inspired his current effort to get me kicked out of the village meeting, but when Balvir Singh joins in, it becomes perfectly clear to him what is transpiring. Ever since Parvendar came back from jail, there have been rumors of a budding relationship between him and his former enemy, Balvir Singh; reports that Balvir Singh has been plying Parvendar with alcohol, pumping him and plotting with him against JDF. Now the rumors make complete sense. Parvendar wants me kicked out of the meeting because Balvir Singh goaded him into doing it. Balvir Singh is banking on his assumption that if I'm kicked out, JDF's Director will walk out of the meeting in protest and that's just what Balvir Singh wants to happen. He knows Jashpal is about to expose his and Captain Sahab's long held secret.

Aware of their joint motivation, Jashpal cries out before anyone can stop him, "Balvir Singh has illegally captured village land! He illegally bought land for his school with village money!"

Balvir Singh lunges at Jashpal. Simultaneously several men leap up out of their seats to hold him back. All the while he's screaming at Jashpal, "I'm going to close your foundation down! I'm going to have your foundation investigated and I'm going to close it down!"

Jashpal angrily charges toward Balvir Singh, "Go ahead and investigate! Unlike you, JDF has nothing to hide!"

More men step into the row to hold Jashpal back. A couple of Balvir Singh's fellow clan members of the same age start shouting.

"You're wrong for accusing Balvir Singh."

"He didn't steal the land!"

"You're getting way over your head, Jashpal!"

Young men from both clans yell at Balvir Singh and his men to sit down and be quiet, "It's Jashpal's turn to speak! The Director has given Jashpal permission to speak!"

A dozen or so men move through the crowd, separating the mass of bodies apart with their own bodies, trying to pacify everyone in soft-spoken voices, reminding them, "We can talk about this matter calmly. You can have a turn to speak after Jashpal."

The council Director yells, "Everyone sit down!"

A few of Balvir Singh's clansmen physically lead him and some of his friends back to their seats, forcing them to sit down. Bantering continues back and forth between Balvir Singh, his cronies and Jashpal for several minutes before the group finally quiets down. Tension in the room remains palpable.

My attendance at village meetings is, without any further discussion, deemed a non-issue. Not even Parvendar bothers to bring it up again. Everyone can see the main issue is the village meetinghouse land and the growing hostility between Jashpal and Balvir Singh. The village council Director quickly tries to get the meeting back on course. "Okay, it's time for Jashpal to speak. Let him speak. It's his turn."

Jashpal boldly and blatantly lays out the facts. "Balvir Singh was entrusted during a village meeting six years ago to buy land for the meetinghouse. He convinced Ragvir, who was reluctant to sell his land, that the village needed the strategically located land for the village meetinghouse. When government money arrived to pay Ragvir for the land and start construction of the meetinghouse, Balvir Singh paid for the land. He then had the legal papers drawn up. What Balvir Singh didn't tell anyone was that he divided the land, giving his school two-thirds of the land and the village only one third. This was not in the original deal with Ragvir. His land was not to go to the school nor was Balvir Singh ever given permission to use government money, village money, to buy his school's land. His land registration papers are also suspect. He never registered his papers at the county clerk's office because he knew whoever in Chandpur had to sell, divide or verify their own land would see Chandpur's land records and find out that Balvir Singh had surreptitiously taken part of the village meetinghouse land."

In response to his last statement the room turns into an uproar again. Shouts are deafening, faces red, teeth and fists clenched. Everyone's on his feet, including myself. A couple of old duffers, Parvendar and Balvir Singh are trying to reach Jashpal. Only the latter two are capable of taking a swing at him, but even they don't dare. It doesn't stop them from pressing their bodies against his body though; positioning their faces only inches apart. Jashpal pushes both of them back, but several of the younger men, knowing Jashpal's tendency to punch now and talk later, grab his arms. A few men push and shove, but no one actually slugs anyone. Others shout.

"Settle down!"

"You're going to get it now, Jashpal!"

"Take your seats!"

"It's not true!"

"Yes it is!"

"Jashpal has a right to speak!"

"You've gone too far this time!"

"Let Jashpal speak!"

His arms still held back, Jashpal's mouth is unrelenting, "The land next door to the meeting house, on which they're proposing to build a new room for their school, was purchased with Chandpur village money. Therefore it's village land, not the schools! As I told you all along, they built the meetinghouse with the intention of capturing it for their school in the future."

"Balvir Singh merely borrowed the money!"

"No he didn't! He has never repaid the money he used to buy the land."

"I had incidental expenses before the land was purchased, which I paid for out of my own pocket. I reimbursed myself." Balvir Singh explains angrily.

"You went about it the wrong way. The government check you used to buy your land was meant for the meetinghouse. You can't use government money that way!"

Jashpal's last comment induces Balvir Singh to turn towards me. It's surely an unintentional orientation. He almost certainly intended to turn toward a supporter to vent his anger, but because everyone has jumped into the fray, I'm the only one left standing in the corner. He wraps his two pointer fingers around one another and thrusts them a few inches forward in my direction and then points to Jashpal. Although the gesture means 'tight' friends in America, in Garhwal it means just the opposite, bitter enemies.

About a third of the men are engaged in restraining Jashpal, Balvir Singh or his followers, physically yanking people apart, trying to separate them. Another third is wandering through the crowd, not keen to say or do anything but nonetheless willing to be on hand in case help is needed to control the mob scene. The remaining third slink out the door.

The meek and mild Treasurer, who I'd never expect any action from, is in the middle of the scuffle calmly asking people to quiet down and effectively easing the rowdier crowd out the door in small groups, according to whether they're in Balvir Singh's camp or Jashpal's.

As the group dissipates, the Director pipes up, "The meeting is over!"

He reminds me of a teddy bear, ambling from side to side across the room. His portly shape is bundled in an inordinate amount of clothing: One shirt, two sweaters, a coat, a roughly woven shawl, one pair of long underwear, two-pairs of pants and, covering his gray and balding head, a worn, olive-colored, Nehru cap. His nickname is Gammu, although it just as easily could be 'Pooh'. He has that same child-like wonder and innocence about him.

While he makes his way to the edge of the bed, his grown sons file in behind him. Two sit on the bed next to their father and because of a lack of sitting space the last one to enter the room remains standing. We all ceremoniously greet each other with prayer-shaped hands set at our chins, exclaiming, "Namaskar!"

"How's your wife?" I inquire.

Gammu moans, "Ooonnnhhhh," a sound emanating from the back of his throat or maybe as far down as his stomach. Wherever it came from the message is clear. His wife is still sick and he's feeling the pain.

In case I don't understand, he clarifies, "She's the same."

"What's the name of her illness?" I ask, because 'What's the matter with her?' doesn't translate well.

"Who knows? The doctors don't say a thing."

"Did you ask them what's wrong?"

He ponders the question for a moment before answering, "No...they just give her medicines, but they don't make any difference."

"But didn't the doctors tell you anything, like whether she'll get well or not? Or when?"

"No. We know nothing," his oldest son chimes in.

"Next time you take her to the doctor, you should ask the doctor the name of her illness. If he knows the name, maybe he can tell you something about it. If he doesn't know, maybe he shouldn't be treating her." I tell them what I consider to be common sense, but what I have learned is Garhwalis and I often have a different sense of what is common. I've taken scores of patients to hospitals and not one person has ever asked the doctor the name of their illness, what their course of treatment is, how long the illness will last, what their illness was caused from or which medicines are for what?

What patients do regularly ask is, "Do I take the medicine with hot or cold water or milk?" and "What can I eat?" Both questions stem from traditional treatments, which rely heavily on what a person eats, especially hot or cold foods, since food influences the body's health: Yogurt, buttermilk, rice and halva cool the body and spices, meat, eggs, millet bread, oil, semolina and hot milk heat it up. It's a matter of finding out from the doctor if your body should heat up or cool down to help cure an illness.

Gammu's teenage daughter brings in tea. His wife creeps in slowly behind her. She is so weak she can barely keep her eyes open as she shuffles across the room. Her two sons lift her rotund body up onto the bed. She lies down on the far side, next to the wall, behind her sons. They cover her up with a quilt. Her husband quietly watches. Tears well up in his eyes, as if he's about to cry, but he doesn't.

After a long silence Gammu asks, "Why have you come?"

"A Bakhyin (female Soothsayer) told me to have a kaanthaa (a talisman to ward off evil) made by a Baaman. And propitiously, two weeks ago when you came to Chandpur, you told me if I ever need a Baaman, you would be my Baaman. Can you make a kaanthaa for me?"

"Sure!" He replies and after another long pause inquires, "Why did she say you need a kaanthaa?"

"She told me I have everything and because of my good fortune people are giving me the evil eye."

"Which Soothsayer?"

"The one in Chandpur."

Soothsayers, like Baamans, are conduits to god. Their counsel is highly regarded and sought for a variety of reasons. If a person is experiencing a run of bad luck, is unemployed or barren, he or she will seek a Bakhyaa (male-soothsayer) or Bakhyin's advice on how to change their situation around. If there's conflict with another person, a Bakhyin is sought to find out how to resolve it or, conversely, how to make the other person miserable. If during a god-possession a person is told there is a problem but not how to cure it, the person may ask a Bakhyin what the cure is. If there's been an untimely death in the family, a Bakhyin may be consulted to determine what needs to be done to appease the dead person's spirit in order to make sure the spirit moves on to a better life in the future. If a person is planning to travel or start a new business, he or she will want to know which is the most auspicious day for them to do so. Or if there's a long-term illness, a person will ask a Bakhyin how to cure it—a few months earlier I ran into two of Gammu's son's on their way to the Chandpur Bakhyin's home to ask her how to cure their mother's illness.

All of these questions could be asked of a Baaman too. Which one a person goes to depends on the interplay between what a person's concern is and the level of formality they want to address the matter, albeit the fine line between them is often crossed. Someone would be more likely to go to a Bakhyin regarding a long-term illness, a Baaman about a dead family member's spirit, a Devi/Devta Baaman regarding a god possession, and a Baaman Astrologer regarding a run of bad luck. The difference between them is a Baaman performs formal Hindu rituals. If someone goes to him about a problem, the solution will most likely be an elaborate, traditional and expensive ritual to be held at a later date. A Baaman Astrologer is harder to access because there are fewer of them around and his domain is restricted to interpreting what is written in the stars and how to offset negative celestial influences. His guidance customarily involves telling a person which prayer rituals to do at home and on what days, which stone talismans to wear and on which fingers and he informs the person, for better or for worse, when his or her situation will change. A Devi/Devta Baaman elicits a Devi/Devta in a person to ask the goddess/god about the person's problems (any and all of the aforementioned) and how to cure them. This too is frequently an elaborate puja that involves numerous family members, expenses and a later date.

To seek the advice of a Bakhyaa/Bakhyin is relatively simple and low-key compared to the other options. A person can pop in at any time to speak with a Soothsayer, they're ubiquitous (there are two in Chandpur, one male and one female), they give immediate answers, the initial cost is 10 rupees (22 cents) or a small baggy of rice and the cure will less likely involve expensive elaborate puja. Cures vary widely, but generally include puja ceremonies, restricted food intake, wearing talismans, goat or chicken sacrifice, making amends in relationships and/or tantra-mantra rituals.

Despite their exceptional status, Bakhyins and Bakhyaas are ordinary people. The Chandpur Bakhyin is a thirty-six year old housewife and farmer. She's busy day and night doing the same chores every rural Garhwali woman does. She stumbled onto her sideline job of soliciting advice in the same manner most Soothsayers do; by being regularly possessed by a god and during possession instructing people on how to cure problems in their lives. Although regular possession and giving advice while possessed are typical Garhwali experiences, it is nonetheless at this point where a special indicator leads to the person becoming a Soothsayer. His or her possessions may be so regular that they're deemed abnormal, alluding to the possessions being 'something more'. A god or goddess may tell them during possession that they're a Soothsayer or the person may deduce on their own that they're well suited for the job. His/her guidance may be uncannily accurate or constructive, so that other people notice the person's exceptional ability and either encourage them to be a Bakhyaa/Bakhyin or just start going to them to seek guidance. The Chandpur Bakhyin's reputation for good counsel is what makes her popular.

A Soothsayer's job is not a guaranteed permanent one, however. A soothsayer's gift requires them to maintain purity and do their work sincerely. If not, their ability to divine ceases: "God ordained their ability so if they're not worthy or abuse it, god will take their voice away."

To maintain purity, Bakhyaas and Bakhyins, like everyone regularly possessed by gods and goddesses, pray daily to the god who possesses them; are careful what and where they eat to keep from becoming contaminated, many becoming vegetarians as a result or they completely stop eating food outside their home, including not partaking in village feasts; bathe daily and bathe a second time if they come into contact with anything potentially polluting such as a dead person; and, because Chandpur's Soothsayer is female, she can neither do puja nor provide her soothsayer services to anyone when she's menstruating, in order to keep from polluting others.

Chandpur's Bakhyin divines in the morning before she goes out to work in the fields, during lunch and at the end of the day, so I show up at her doorstep early in the morning to catch her before she leaves. A retired army man from Banekh is already sitting in the bedroom-cum-prayer room waiting for the Bakhyin to finish eating her breakfast downstairs. When I sit down beside him, he jumps into friendly conversation, freely sharing with me why he's come to see the Bakhyin, "I want to cut down a tree, but it's right next to a small temple I built for Narsingh Devta (god). I want to find out if it'll be okay to cut down the tree or whether Narsingh will disapprove."

I reply, "I'm not here to seek specific advice. I will see what the Bakhyin has to tell me." It was a true statement, but I purposely do not reveal my main motivation for coming is curiosity to know what a Bakhyin does and to hear the kind of advice she gives people.

Another man walks in from Thailisain. He glances over at me and with a note of surprise in his voice says, "Madam! Are you here to seek the Bakhyin's advice too?"

Before I have a chance to answer, the retired army man excitedly confirms, "Yes, Madam is here for guidance too!"

The Bakhyin enters and crosses over to the far side of the room where she has an area set aside specifically for her divinations. She sits yoga style on a large grass mat covering the floor and extending out into the middle of the room. A red, wedding shawl with gold fringe stretches overhead, partially covering the ceiling. Pictures of various gods hang on the wall behind her: Lakshmi, the goddess of wealth, with gold coins dripping down through her fingers; Hanuman, the monkey god, holding a scepter; and Kali with a garland of skulls around her neck. There's also a large homemade collage of famous structures from all over the world: The Taj Mahal, the Parthenon, the Kaaba inside the Masjid Al Haram in Mecca and a modern suspension bridge, all interspersed with AUM symbols, swastikas and a lingam (Shiv phallic symbol). In front of her on the mat are two extra-large pie pans, one with rice inside and the other with yellow lentils, and a bronze torte-like pan filled with more rice.

Two Duggada women enter the room and sit down next to me on the wooden bench. One of the women's glass bracelets clink and clatter while she settles into her seat, adjusting her shawl and stowing a large recycled plastic bag on the floor under the bench. The Bakhyin's husband follows them in and squats on the floor along the sidewall, kitty corner to everyone else in the room.

The Bakhyin lights incense and a loosely wrapped stogie rolled in what appears to be tobacco leaves but smells like marijuana. She picks them both up and swirls them around in the air to fan their aromas, purifying the air with the smoke and setting the mood. She then sticks the incense and stogie, butt-side down, into one of the piles of rice to let them continue smoking on their own.

She unties her bun, periodically shaking her head and running her hands through her long, black hair, giving her hair an unkempt, almost wild appearance. Her eyes are purposely averted away from us; sometimes closed, other times staring into space. She begins to rock back and forth.

Eventually the Bakhyin turns her attention to us and asks who will go first. The Banekh man proposes that I should go first because I'm an honored guest in Pauri Garhwal. I suggest he go first since he arrived first and had been waiting the longest. He readily agrees, or at least does not protest. I further add that if he feels his matter is private I will leave the room. He and the Bakhyin break into stifled chortles. Everyone else smiles broadly. The Bakhyin assures me I shouldn't leave and the ex-army man points up toward the sky and rambles, "There's no private business here. It's between the individual and god. That's all. It's all in god's hands. The individual should do something.

They should work, not talk bad about people and so forth. Other than that it's all about god."

The Bakhyin directs the Banekh man to give her his rice. He pulls a small plastic bag filled with a ¼ Kg of rice out of his army jacket and places it on the mat in front of the Bakhyin. She picks up and pours his rice into one of the large pie pans with rice already inside and mixes the two, sifting her hands through the grains, repeatedly. Every so often she lifts handfuls of the rice up to her forehead, resting it there for a brief moment and then lets it run through her fingers back into the pan. When her hand is completely empty, she sifts through the rice again, filtering it through her fingers multiple times before bringing another handful of kernels up to her forehead. This is her particular style. Many Bakhyaas in our area flip rice into the air and catch the grains with a flat hand, counting the number of grains they've caught and looking at the pattern of kernels in order to divine.

The Bakhyin appears agitated now, almost angry: Her eyes grow large and round, her jaw becomes firm, her breathing pronounced. Her swaying body and shaking head become more and more frenzied and stiff to the point where her head jerks every time her gaze shifts from the rice to the Banekh man and back to the rice. Suddenly she begins sputtering, bordering on shouting, cryptic words, "You... No one... Yourself... Think... You... No one... Yourself... Think... Selfish... You... Not family... Not cow... Not water buffalo... No one... Yourself... Think family."

Abruptly stopping, she glowers at the retired army man.

The man stares back, uncertain about her meaning. His blank expression prompts the Bakhyin's husband to interpret for him, "You think about no one but yourself, not your family, not even about your family cow and water buffalo."

The man graciously acknowledges the accusation, "Well, that's true. I'm selfish. But..." He's obviously confused by her train of thought.

He speaks up, "I came here because of a tree near Narsingh's temple. I want to know if it's alright to cut down the tree."

The Bakhyin doesn't appear to be listening. She's already returned to rocking and jerking with even more vigor than before. Her knees bounce excitedly up and down until she's almost hopping off the ground. Concurrently, she sifts through the rice over and over again, flipping it around in her hand, bringing it up to her forehead and letting it fall back into the pan in her stereotypical manner.

Suddenly, she launches into another diatribe, "Tree... You... No one...Yourself... Think... Cut... Tree... No one ... Yourself... Money... Not family... No one... Narsingh... No one... Yourself... Cut tree... Narsingh Devta...Temple... No one... For money... For Yourself!" She slaps both of her hands down on her thighs, producing a loud thunderous clap, and then turns toward the army man and glares at him again.

Her husband explains to the Banekh man that he shouldn't cut down the tree because it would be selfish. He'd only be doing it because he wants money.

The Bakhyin quickly scoops up the equivalent amount of rice the army man gave her earlier and put it in his plastic bag. It's now blessed food that he'll either put in his temple to apply to his forehead with tilak paste, cook and eat or just leave in the temple until one day far in the future it is necessary to clean the temple out. The Banekh man, whose face is expressionless, walks over, places a ten rupee note in one of the Bakhyin's rice filled plates, picks up his baggy and then sits back down to hear what the Bakhyin has to say to the other people present.

The Bakhyin instructs me to give her my rice. I confess I didn't know I was supposed to bring rice and put down a black sweater instead. Two days earlier I'd run into the Bakhyin on a Chandpur trail. She'd asked me if I have an extra sweater at home and said that if I did, I should give it to her because she's having trouble keeping warm on these cold winter days. I told her I'd look and see, so I brought her one of my sweaters as payment for today's services.

The Bakhyin's body, which had been swaying in small continuous circular motions, as if it couldn't remain still, froze for a brief second, her mouth drops open slightly and a blank stare momentary glazes over her eyes, as if she's trying to understand how could I not know that a rice reader reads rice, not sweaters? She quickly regains composure, mumbles "It doesn't matter", and returns to swaying and sifting through her own personal supply of rice, tossing it around and bringing it up to her head. She hurls grains into the air, carelessly scattering them across the mat, working herself into another frenzy, her head swinging back and forth with progressively more vigor, appearing like she's shaking her head 'no' with exaggerated movement.

She speaks in staccato, "You... Work... Boredom ... Tired... Work... Apathy... Evil spells... Boredom... Work... Work ... Evil spells. She stops and stares at me as fiercely as she had the Banekh man.

I turn to her husband, hoping he's going to translate for me as he did for the ex-army man. He obliges, "She says you don't want to work."

I don't know what to say. Pressed by her stark silence and glare, I tell her "I didn't know I don't like to do my work. I do get angry though."

Then her husband clarifies, "You don't like to work because people are putting evil spells on you."

The Bakhyin rocks and sways again. This time she begins playing with the yellow lentils, running her fingers through them numerous times and putting them up to her head, in the same manner she'd previously done with the rice. After a couple of minutes she huffs, "You... Everything... Work... Boredom... Tired... Angry... Evil eye... Jealousy... Evil spells... You... Everything... Mind... Heart... Money...

Everything... Jealousy... Evil eye... Jealousy... Kaanthaa." She abruptly halts and looks at me again with penetrating, transfixed eyes.

Glancing over at her husband for an interpretation, he responds on cue, "You've got everything—a mind, a heart, money. People see this and are envious. They're casting evil spells on you, intentionally and unintentionally."

In her not quite normal voice, but in more coherent sentences, the Bakhyin then advises me, "Have a kaanthaa made by a Baaman and wear it around your neck or on your arm."

Her agitation ceases. She picks up a handful of rice. A perplexed expression flashes across her face as she searches for something to put my rice in. Her husband quickly stands up, goes over to the Thailisain man and, taking his baggy of rice away from him, dumps his rice into the Bakhyin's rice plate and hands the empty bag to his wife. Twisting the bag closed, she hands it to me to take home.

I wonder how the Thailisain man will get his rice home but don't say anything, knowing I would only complicate the situation if I refuse to take his bag. Instead, I put my prayer-shaped hands up to my chin, first turning to the Bakhyin and her husband and then to the other advice-seekers before walking out the door.

A woman climbs up the stairs as I descend them. She's obviously come for a consultation too. It suddenly dawns on me that the constant stream of strangers I see going to and from Harijan Basti have not come to visit friends and relatives as I had always assumed, but to see the Bakhyin.

During my short jaunt home, everyone I meet on the trail asks me where I've been. When I tell them, their eyes light up and smiles spread across their faces, obviously pleased I'm indulging in Garhwali custom. One man even states outright that he's surprised I went to the Bakhyin because it's a practice he knows outsiders think is nonsensical.

I mention to Shakambari Devi that I thought it was odd I was advised to wear a kaanthaa because it seems to me that it's mostly men wear them. She concurs, "Yeah, men are the ones who need them. They're more prone to evil spells, being possessed by ghosts and experiencing strong emotions."

When I mention the same thing to Ramesh, he exclaims, "No, not all! It's generally women who wear kaanthaas. They're the ones who need to be protected from evil the most."

After I arrive home, I realize I'll have to decide whether to do as the Bakhyin advised and have the talisman made or not. It's not a great dilemma. I've jumped into Garhwali culture with both feet on numerous occasions; participating in activities and doing things I don't really hold strong feelings for or against. Besides, 'evil spells' was an unfathomable, even laughable concept back in America, but they are no longer unfathomable or laughable. Intimate anger, blind alliances, heard whispers, unfounded gossip, averted eyes, bitter grimaces and a host of other normal responses arising from misunderstandings and disagreements become potent, tangible forces within the confines of a small village, snowballing and magnifying the darker side of ill-will.

"Do you have a vidhyaa?" Gammu asks.

I reply, "Yes," and pull a one-inch, cylinder-shaped, silver amulet out of my purse.

"And string?"

"Ohhhnnnooo! I forgot." I whine, assuming this means Gammu won't be able to make the talisman today and consequently I'll have to come back on another day. To wait for another propitious day (either Tuesday, Hanuman's day, or Saturday, Shanidev's day) to have the kaanthaa made is not a big deal in and of itself, it's knowing I'll have to hike back up the mountain again to get here that elicited my groan.

"No worry! I have some string," his oldest son offers, while removing a small ball of black string from his shirt pocket. He and one of his brothers are Baamans like their father, learning from him in a lifelong apprenticeship that will end when their father stops working.

"To whom do we pray? Narsingh?" Gammu asks, fully aware Narsingh is many Thakur clan member's family god and no doubt presuming that since I pray with them, Narsingh must be my god too.

Not prepared for his question, my thoughts vacillate for seemingly several minutes before admitting, "I don't know. I don't have a family god. I just know I need to have the kaanthaa made. As far as whom to pray to or not, use your own judgment. I assume you know better than I do if we need to pray to a specific god for the kaanthaa to be effective."

Even though I'm certain he's never heard of someone not having a family god, he doesn't reveal what he's thinking behind a poker face.

His oldest son cuts the thick string, ties the ends and burns them with a match to keep them from unraveling. Gammu takes the string from his son, loops it through the eye of the amulet and ties it on with a knot. Since he's sitting in yoga position with his bare feet exposed, he conveniently wraps one end of the string around his big toe to anchor it in place and, starting at the other end, begins to weave a series of closely spaced knots. When he finishes, he unwraps the string from his toe, flips it over and attaches the other end of the string to his toe. He then begins to weave the same type and number of knots on the other end of the string.

Gammu's son comments on how short the string has become, making it an atypical choker rather than a necklace. Gammu ignores him. Instead he turns to me and gives me a series of instructions for what to do when I get home, "You need to bathe in Ganga water and then light incense. After cleansing yourself and the air, you can tie the kaanthaa on. Be sure to tie it with three knots. For the next 24 hours, don't eat any salty or spicy food, only plain food or food with sugar in it. Do not touch a broom or sweep. If you go outside of your house, be sure not to go beyond your courtyard."

When Gammu finishes weaving the string, he unhooks it from his toe. He fishes a small plastic bag half-filled with tangerine-colored sindhor out of his coat pocket and then takes his wallet out from an interior breast pocket. Inside the wallet's sleeves, where people normally stick business and credit cards, is a wad of paper-thin Birch bark stuck together. While extracting a tiny piece Gammu explains, "This is Bhoj Patra, the bark of a tree found growing only around Badrinath and Gangotri. It's sacred."

Unscrewing the hollow amulet, he stuffs the Birch bark inside. He then drops the amulet, string and all, into the bag of sindhor and, reaching into the baggy with one hand, packs sindhor inside the amulet with his fingers. When no more sindhor can be stuffed around the birch bark, Gammu reseals the talisman and removes it from the plastic bag, not bothering to shake off the extra sacred powder caked on the outside; neither careful not to spill the powder nor concerned as it falls onto his clothes and the floor, staining them a bright orange.

Gammu places the amulet and string in his right hand, intentionally leaving a hole at the top of his fist between his thumb and his pointer finger. He leans his body forward, resting his crooked elbow atop his right knee. With his head hanging down toward the opening in his fist and his mouth hovering just above it, he begins whispering mantras, religious passages intended to put him in contact with god and, in this case, inaudibly whispered to keep from weakening their power. After three or four minutes, without raising his head or taking his mouth away from his hand, Gammu peers over the top of his glasses at me and remarks, "Evil spells have indeed been cast over you," and then returns to whispering more mantras.

I first start hearing rumors of unreported murders two years after I move to Chandpur.

A Chandpur man and a schoolteacher who lives in Chandpur bazaar had gone down to the river to catch fish. They chose the deepest place in the river, where they expected to find the largest fish (8 to 10 inches). Balam Singh could swim, so he undressed down to his underwear and positioned himself in the middle of the river, downstream from the deep pool. The teacher stayed on shore and threw miniature bombs into the water, causing stunned and dead fish to rise to the surface and float downstream with the current. Balam Singh ran back and forth in the water grabbing as many fish as he could, tossing them up onto the shore as fast as he could. The schoolteacher ran around gathering them on shore and placing them in a burlap bag.

Suddenly they noticed something large rising in the water. A second later a bloated body appeared on the surface of the deep pool. Apparently the rocks and ropes holding it down on the bottom of the river had been shaken loose by the multiple bomb blasts. Balam Singh grabbed his clothes and the two men ran back to Chandpur. They proceeded to tell people what they saw but, fearing ghosts, villagers initially hesitated to go down to the river to look at the dead body. A few, however, eventually headed down to the river to see for themselves. By the time they arrived, the body was gone.

A couple of men from Chorik, a village situated on the ridge above the river, upon hearing the bomb blasts, surmised they were coming from the same area where they had hid the body, so they ran down to the river, whisked the body away to the nearby burning ghat and cremated it.

The dead woman was from Chorik. Since her disappearance, her husband's family had been telling fellow Chorik villagers that she ran off. Chorik villagers, however, whispered amongst themselves and to other nearby villagers that the dead woman's mother-in-law and her mother-in-law's brother strangled her to death. Nobody told authorities, not even the dead woman's four brothers, two of who live in the village next door to Chorik and undoubtedly heard the rumor as well.

Another rumor is of a young man who was hung from a tree in Dumka village. He was in love with a girl who had been married off to a man in Dumka. Not long after the wedding, he showed up in Chandpur bazaar late one afternoon and, because his native village was far away, he asked questions in the bazaar about the girl, her new husband and directions to their house. Afterwards, he climbed up the hill to Dumka. The next morning villagers on the way to do their chores found him hanging in a tree outside the village proper. The Patwari declared his hanging to be a suicide. People in Dumka and surrounding villages, however, believe the girl's new husband and his family murdered her old lover. They cite the fact there were no tree branches, ladder or anything else at the scene that would have enabled the young man to climb up into the tree to hang himself.

Then comes a story from Patoti, a village on the other side of the hill from Chandpur. Five Patoti men had gone into the forest behind Patoti to hunt wild boar. They had spread out in various directions when, while separated, one of the hunters shoots and kills one of the other hunters. It's determined to be an accident by authorities because the shooter tells them it's an accident. Thus, prosecution and punishment are deemed unnecessary. Patoti villagers, however, whisper amongst themselves that the shooting was intentional and cite a long-standing, acrimonious dispute between the shooter and the dead man as the reason.

In Kotla a mother-in-law strangled her daughter-in-law while her son was away in the army. In Dulet fellow villagers beat an old woman's son to death. The list goes on.

I don't believe the rumors. How can whole villages and close family members be in on a conspiracy to keep quiet about a murder? Especially about a loved one's murder? Or even if they can all remain silent, how can they not experience animosity or some other emotional fallout from the incident? How can everyone go on with their lives acting as if nothing has happened and remain friends with the perpetrators? How can a sheriff not feel obligated to investigate? It all seems far-fetched to me, until it happens in Chandpur.

On August 22nd, a dozen people gather at Raji Devi and Gurandi Devi's house to watch TV. A new satellite system arrived in our area earlier this year, triggering the few households that could afford it (and that have electricity) to buy one and drawing nightly crowds of up to 20 people into those homes. One of the visitors is 14-year old Raghunath.

Late in the afternoon of the next day, Raji Devi sends a neighbor boy to fetch Raghunath. Raghunath is not at home. He's gone to haul water for an eighty-year old woman and her 50-year old mentally retarded son, both members of his clan. When he finally arrives home around 6:00 pm, he gets the message and heads straight over to Raji Devi's house to find out what she wants. Raji Devi, Gurandi Devi and Shyam (Gurandi Devi's son) tie Raghunath to a chair and begin to beat him with a cricket bat, a hockey stick and a sickle. They accuse him of following Raji Devi's 13-year-old daughter, Geeta, into the outhouse after the television program the night before and raping her.

A woman passing by hears Raghunath screaming, but she thinks either Raji Devi or Gurandi Devi is beating one of her own children so she doesn't interfere. Raghunath eventually falls unconscious. The offenders summon Gurandi Devi's husband, who closes down his ration shop conspicuously early, and a fellow clan member, a woman who is not only a friend but also the areas Jilla Panchayat (District Council Member), to help them figure out what to do with the now unconscious Raghunath.

At dusk, they surreptitiously carry Raghunath's unconscious body along an isolated trail behind their house and dump it alongside the road, ten feet away from the trail. A short time later two men heading home from the bazaar come upon Raghunath and carry him home.

It doesn't take long for Raghunath's father to find out what happened. He knows Raghunath was called over to Raji Devi's house and that he'd gone over there with his friend, Kaliya, so he asks them what happened. Amrendar Singh (Raji Devi and Gurandi Devi's father-in-law, Shyam's grandfather and one of Raghunath's father's best friends, as well as a fellow clan member), Raji Devi, Shyam, Gurandi Devi and Gurandi Devi's husband all downplay the beating as a minor slapping around for Raghunath's egregious behavior of raping 13-year old Geeta. Kaliya, who was innocently caught in the house and witnessed the beating, doesn't say a thing, particularly in view of the skewed story adults around him are telling.

Raghunath is unconscious. His back and stomach are covered with gashes and bruises, his genitals are mutilated and his forehead is split open with brains protruding. Yet, Raghunath's father does not understand the severity of his wounds. Part of the reason for his myopia is it's assumed by everyone that a ghost has possessed

Raghunath because he's unconscious. Thus, Raghunath's father believes it's the ghost possession causing Raghunath's distress and confirming his assumption is Raghunath's out-of-control body, which jerks frequently, especially his arms and legs, and is incontinent. So instead of taking Raghunath to the hospital, his father summons a Soothsayer, who spends the entire night performing a variety of tantra-mantra rituals inside and outside the house to exorcise the ghost.

By morning Raghunath's condition has not changed, prompting his father and several other village men to bring him to the hospital. Amongst them are the perpetrator's father-in-law and friends. During the two-hour car ride, they convince Raghunath's father and the other villagers present not to tell the doctor Raghunath was beaten. Instead they tell the doctor Raghunath's wounds were caused from falling out of a tree and since falling from trees and off steep slopes in search of wood and grass is common and often results in serious head injuries or death, the excuse is accepted at face value. Perhaps it wouldn't have been had the doctor actually examined Raghunath, but he didn't. Upon seeing the fully clothed Raghunath's unconscious state and severe head injury, the doctor explains to Raghunath's father that his condition is serious and the district hospital is not equipped to help him. He refers him to the nearest sophisticated hospital, another six hours car drive away between Rishikesh and Dehra Dun. Raghunath's father asks the doctor to write a referral to a Delhi hospital instead, where he has relatives to stay with and lend support.

Four men drive with Raghunath and his father towards Delhi, an eight-hour car ride away. They get as far as Meerut, a 6-½ hour drive from the hospital, when Raghunath begins making rasping sounds. The men in the car interpret it to mean something is clogging his throat, making it difficult for him to breath. Someone takes out a bottle of water and pours a little into Raghunath's mouth. There's a gurgle and a moment later Raghunath dies.

The men bring Raghunath to a Quack in Meerut to confirm his death and then turn their car around and head back to Chandpur. At home news of Raghunath's death spreads rapidly. People from Chandpur and surrounding villages show up to comfort Raghunath's family. One is a distant relative of the perpetrators from another village. After sharing his condolences, he suggests that no one go to the police, advocating instead for Raghunath's father and the perpetrators to work out a mutual agreement amongst themselves. His particular proposal is for the perpetrators to write and sign a confession to beating Raghunath and make a formal apology to Raghunath's father. In exchange, Raghunath's father will not tell the police about his son's death nor take any other legal action against the perpetrators.

An uncle on Raghunath's mother's side protests. He asserts it's vital to tell the police and to have a postmortem performed. He declares that he wants justice for his dead sister's son (Raghunath's mother died of tuberculosis three years earlier). Neither man is from Chandpur, yet they battle out amongst themselves what should be done about the murder while Chandpur villagers look on, offering little advice and negligible support for either man's ideas. Raghunath's father remains mute throughout the discussion as well. Nevertheless, a compromise is eventually struck. A formal letter will be written by the perpetrators, confessing they had beat Raghunath, and signed by the Chandpur Pradhan and local Patwari and Raghunath's body will be taken for a post-mortem. In exchange, Raghunath's family will not tell the Pauri police about his death nor pursue prosecution of the offenders.

The plan meets with obstacles. The first is the Pradhan refuses to sign the letter, stating he doesn't want to get involved.

Next, two carloads and one truckload of Chandpur men and teens head off to the hospital to have the post-mortem performed on Raghunath's body. Amrendar Singh's car leaves the caravan and stops by the Patwari's office, under the pretense of obtaining his signature.

The Sheriff gets into his car and drives with him and his friends as far as Mausi bazaar, where the Sheriff suddenly disembarks. He goes back home and writes in his daily log that he's on vacation (the day of the beating and the few days thereafter). He does not examine Raghunath's body. He does not record Raghunath's death. He does not come to Chandpur to ask anyone what happened to Raghunath nor to see the crime scene or weapons.

Amrendar Singh meets up with the rest of Chandpur villagers and Raghunath's body at the hospital. He tells them the Patwari refused to sign the letter. Chandpur villagers do not say it to his face, but behind his back they speculate Amrendar Singh paid the Sheriff a hefty bribe not to investigate Raghunath's death, perhaps using the rape allegation to persuade the Sheriff that the beating of Raghunath by his daughter-in-laws and grandson was justified and therefore not worth pursuing.

At the hospital the doctor refuses to do a postmortem. He informs everyone it's absolutely necessary to file a police report first and, because they reveal to the doctor what really happened, he admonishes Raghunath's father for lying to hospital personnel earlier, by telling them Raghunath had fallen out of a tree.

Raghunath's father intends to go to the police to file a report in order to get the postmortem done, but as some insiders tell it, relatives and friends of the perpetrators keep him away from the police station by physically leading him here and there around Pauri, while they forge a new plan. Suddenly, it's decided to burn Raghunath's body. On further discussion, it's decided not to burn Raghunath's body in Chandpur because, as the crowd speculates, "If the police find out about the murder and the body is burned in Chandpur, everyone in Chandpur could be held liable for destroying crucial evidence." So, exactly 24 hours after Raghunath died, a convoy of 30 men and boys secretly cremate Raghunath in Sri Nagar, a city three-hours drive from Chandpur.

The following day a Kangun comes to Chandpur. He's in charge of ten sheriffs in ten districts, although not ours. This Kangun has also been temporarily assigned to do the Niif Tahseldar's job as well, which is to oversee one-third of Pauri District's Kanguns and Patwaris. He has not come on official business though. His daughter-in-law is Raghunath's older sister. He'd heard Raghunath died and has come to give his condolences. When he finds out Raghunath was beaten to death, his body burned without an autopsy and that Raghunath's father isn't going to file a police report, he reprimands Raghunath's father and threatens never to come visit him again. Then he leaves. Despite his open display of anger and being a legal authority in charge of umpteen sheriffs, he does nothing about the murder, not even report it to his colleagues who are responsible for law and order in Chandpur.

Chandpur villagers are saddened and disturbed by Raghunath's death. For a week or two it's as if they are all in shock. They lack vitality. They talk in hushed voices and wear long, ashen faces. There's also an element of fear in the air. Villagers believe that if a person dies a sudden or harsh death, his spirit is disturbed and his process of reincarnation is thrown into limbo. Stuck in a wasteland, the person's ghost returns to his village to haunt and taunt those who live there. As a result, Chandpur villagers are afraid to go out into the dark. Until Raghunath's memory fades, every noise and strange occurrence at night will be attributed to his ghostly presence. When Raghunath's body was dumped alongside the road, the perpetrators stuck his rubber thongs on a nearby woodpile. The thongs are still there because everyone is too afraid to touch them, fearing something bad might happen if they do. The three offenders sleep in their in-laws house because they fear Raghunath's ghost will come back to the house where he was beaten. Gurandi Devi's husband (Raji Devi's husband is away in the army) sleeps in the house where the incident occurred, but only because he has recruited two other village men, Anu and his brother, Dinesh, to sleep with him at night.

Behind closed doors, a few villagers confess their revulsion to the murder: "Something horrible has happened in Chandpur and we've done the wrong thing by not going to the police." Despite these sentiments, however, no one reports Raghunath's murder.

The interplay of cultural tendencies sheds some light on the village's collective silence. For one, there's a deep-seated taboo against speaking openly about someone who's done or is doing something wrong, particularly a fellow villager. Talking behind their back is perfectly okay, but to confront them is just not done (remember the chaos Jashpal, a Delhite, created during the village meeting when he confronted Balvir Singh about buying land for himself with village money). Garhwali's genuinely want to get along with one another and go out of their way not to create conflict. They also have a remarkable ability to forgive a person's transgressions. People are gauging other people's reactions as well and thus far other villagers are not standing up against the perpetrators, which means a person would have to stand up alone and standing up alone is a very scary proposition. People's identity is the group, not the individual self. Village justice has always been in meetings by group consensus, even if only a few outspoken people dominate the decision. Doing anything perceived as being against the group is rare. Fear of reprisal from either the perpetrators or fellow villagers also keeps people from speaking out. People fear being ignored, teased, ostracized or cursed—even if the curse doesn't kill them, the anxiety created from knowing they were cursed could or, at the very least, it could make them sick, essentially fulfilling the curse. Summoning the police is foreign and the legal process alien. Indians, in general, don't like to get involved in matters related to the police anyway. As one Indian explained, "Historically, they have been one of the most corrupt institutions in India, demanding bribes from the guilty and non-guilty alike and the hassles and red tape a witness or victim must endure is often viewed as not worth it." And when a crime is reported and police don't do anything about it, people feel powerless to effect action. Chandpur villagers are fully aware the local Sheriff and the acting Niif Tahseldar know Raghunath was murdered, yet neither have bothered to do anything about it. Last, but not least, Raghunath's father's unwillingness to prosecute the guilty parties is a strong message to fellow villagers not to do anything: "Why should we say something if the Postman [Raghunath's father] doesn't? It's his child. It's up to him to decide what should be done."

Even if nagging thoughts prompt someone to demand criminal justice for Raghunath, to get the police to investigate Raghunath's death and prosecute the guilty would be an uphill battle. First he'll have to motivate the police to be interested in the case. In India, without a family's cooperation, the police have little grounds to pursue this matter, not to mention it appears as though some authorities have already been bribed to be indifferent. If the police take action, there are possible severe consequences for the person or people who speak out. They could even be killed, depending on how the perpetrators' families react and how the sympathies of the village play out. There is little to no evidence to support a claim of murder: Raghunath's body was burned and there are no sophisticated investigative techniques used here to collect DNA or identify murder weapons. The only eyewitness to the beating is Kaliya. Right after Raghunath's beating Kaliya told several Chandpur residents in gory detail what had happened, but their testimony is hearsay and, nowadays, Kaliya is not talking. He's under tremendous pressure to keep quiet. His father, Anu, has been overheard counseling him not to tell people what happened, especially the authorities. The other day I saw him carrying a brand new pair of jeans away from Gurandi Devi's husband's store, specially ordered for him, something his dirt poor family heretofore could not afford to buy him. Since the murder, his father has formed a new alliance with the perpetrator's family and simultaneously come into wads of money. It doesn't take much of an imagination to figure out that the new friendship is based on Anu's son's silence and the perpetrator's gratitude. Besides new money in Anu's pocket, Gurandi Devi's husband helped Anu open a vegetable store next door to his shop— albeit Anu's main business in the dark, unlit room is selling illegal whiskey. Kaliya's mother may also be in on the conspiracy of silence. The other day in the courtyard outside my house she was trying to convince another woman Raghunath had died from a curse, not a beating.

I was not in Chandpur the day of the murder. I return the day after Raghunath's body was burned. Immediately upon arrival people tell me in gory detail about his death and how the village is handling the situation. I'm struck by the realization that all of the rumors of unreported murders have been true: Whole villages can be in complicity to murder. I hope Chandpur villagers will tell authorities, but knowing Garhwali culture, I seriously doubt anyone will. A few people implore our foundation to do something. Most come under the cloak of darkness, saying things like "You must do something. You have the power to do something about a murder. We do not." Others, like Raghunath's great-aunt, begs us in broad daylight in front of her elderly women friends, "You must do something about Raghunath's murder. If nothing else, at least take me to Pauri so I can file a police case myself"—It is something I am more than certain that her men folk will not allow her to do, with or without JDF's help.

I can't do nothing. I like Raji Devi and Gurandi Devi, the perpetrators, and I wonder whether I really have a right to interfere in village justice just because I believe differently, especially since I've already stuck my nose into too many affairs, creating more than one person's share of trouble. But whatever internal conflict I experience or fear of reprisal I envision, it's not enough to keep me from doing something. Within a week of the murder, I write an anonymous letter to the district Superintendent of Police (SP), telling him the details of the murder and giving him the names of all the players.

Two weeks go by and nothing happens. Coincidently, I have to speak to the SP about a different matter, so when we're finished talking I ask him if he received an anonymous letter about a murder in Chandpur. He's taken aback and states that he hadn't. I tell him what is written in the letter. I also propose he not be swayed by the purported rape, "The rumor in Chandpur is that Raghunath and the girl were both fully clothed and that Raghunath didn't have time between watching TV and going home to have had sex or done much of anything else."

The SP explains to me rural Garhwal is not his jurisdiction, but that of the Patwari and Tahseldar. I explain to him, "I know it's not your jurisdiction, but I can't tell the Tahseldar myself. He'll tell the local Patwari and the Patwari may be in cahoots with the perpetrators and, whether he is or not, being Garhwali, he'll definitely tell Chandpur villagers I'm pursuing prosecution of the case, a potential danger for me. Even if it isn't, it could instigate a conflict amongst Chandpur villagers."

The SP promises to talk to the Tahseldar himself and says he won't mention my name.

Two days later the Pauri Police, including the Deputy Superintendent of Police, the Patwari who is still feigning that he'd been on vacation at the time of Raghunath's death and his boss, the Mausi Kangun, show up in Chandpur. They do a cursory investigation.

As they walk around the village talking to people, half of Chandpur's men and boys walk around with them, listening to every word. Needless to say, people are reluctant to talk. By the time the police leave, no one has mentioned the word 'murder' or 'beating', although the police do ascertain that Raghunath died under mysterious circumstances.

I wait another month. No action is taken so I go back to talk to the SP. He justifies police inaction by saying Raghunath's father denied there had been a murder. I inform him that I'm fairly certain Raghunath's father will file a murder case now because circumstances are changing. After the police showed up in Chandpur, those villagers who had been haunted by the incident were bolstered by the police's interest in the case, whispering louder amongst themselves, asserting something must be done to punish the guilty.

The situation inadvertently comes to a head just before a seven-day religious program is to be held in Chandpur. Raghunath's father boldly states he's not going to the event because the perpetrators and their families are going. The man hosting the religious event, Balvir Singh, wants Raghunath's father to come. A fellow clan member and friend not attending an important religious function in honor of his mother and father is disconcerting. Balvir Singh is probably also worried about the repercussions of Raghunath's father's newfound defiance regarding the murder as well. Being a friend, relative and business associate of the perpetrators' father-in-law, Amrendar Singh, Balvir Singh had helped to cover up Raghunath's murder—not to mention the fact there are numerous unreported deaths related to Balvir Singh and his father. Raghunath's father is adamant, however, and even refuses Balvir Singh's offer to have feast food delivered to his home, another serious affront. Since Balvir Singh's family has traditionally been the most powerful family in Chandpur, he thinks if he calls a village meeting, he can persuade other villagers to convince Raghunath's father to forget the murder and attend the program, a seemingly personal decision that can easily be made for a person in a village meeting.

Much to Balvir Singh's chagrin, during the meeting the elderly women of Chandpur join together and not only condemn the murder, they push for the perpetrators and their extended family to be ostracized from the village. Most of the village men waffle on the matter, refusing to commit to either position. The old women, however, stand their ground. In the end, the perpetrators and their families are banned from participating in village functions for two years. After two years their exclusion will be re-evaluated.

Bolstered by the turn of events, Raghunath's father asks fellow villagers attending the meeting to support him in filing a murder case against the perpetrators. The few who speak up agree.

The Superintendent of Police is not impressed with Raghunath's father's change of heart. He tells me the matter is out of his hands anyway. He's written a report about the initial investigation and already forwarded it to the District Magistrate. Being the boss of both the Superintendent of Police and the Tahseldar, the DM is ultimately in charge of all conflicts and legal matters in Pauri Garhwal and the one responsible to decide whether to have a more extensive investigation of Raghunath's murder done or not.

I wait to see what the DM might do. Another month passes. Nothing appears to be happening in the case, so I go to the District Magistrate's office to speak to him in person. He has neither seen the police report nor heard about the murder. Again, I describe what I know of the beating, giving him the names of those involved, including witnesses, and I hint that the local authorities might not be the best people to do the investigation since they know about the murder and have done nothing about it.

Two days after our conversation, the Pauri Tahseldar shows up in Chandpur to investigate. He talks with a few people and then tells all of the major players involved in the case to show up at the Sub-Divisional Magistrate's office (SDM) the following Monday. Raji Devi, Gurandi Devi, Shyam, Geeta, Raghunath's father and Kaliya are interrogated by the SDM. Raghunath's father files a murder case during his interrogation.

December 23rd, a month and a half after the SDM's interrogation and four months to the day after Raghunath was beaten, I go back to the District Magistrate's office and ask him why nothing more has been done about Raghunath's murder since the people were called to the Sub-Divisional Magistrate's office. He grumbles, "Be patient! Filing charges and doing all that other stuff takes time before arrests can be made!"

Mid-January, the Patwari and the Kangun return to Chandpur. They take Kaliya, the teenage witness, to the jail in Mausi. They hunt for the teenage perpetrator, Shyam, to take him to Mausi too, but upon hearing the Patwari and Kangun are looking for him, Shyam runs off and hides in a village five kilometers up the road. The Patwari and Kangun hit Kaliya four or five times during his interrogation, prompting him to confess everything he knows about the case and the beating of Raghunath. The next morning, while Kaliya remains in jail, the Patwari and Kangun come back to Chandpur and catch Shyam, who they haul off to Mausi. They beat him into confessing what happened and why. On the third day they summon Raji Devi to Mausi. As soon as Raji Devi shows up, the trio is taken to a Pauri police station. Kaliya is allowed to go home later in the day. Raji Devi and Shyam are interrogated, beaten and kept in jail.

In the intervening days, the 30 people who'd been present during Raghunath's cremation are summoned to pay a fine or go to jail for destroying evidence. A few days later the Tahseldar unexpectedly shortens the list and directs only eight people, four for the prosecution and four for the defense, to pay the fine and to be responsible for testifying at the trial, regarding the state of Raghunath's body and his cremation.

Although villagers believe the Tahseldar is pursuing the case, they do not think he is innocent. They believe he and the just retired judge have been bribed to go easy on the perpetrators. Shyam was released from jail seven days after his arrest and Raji Devi a week later. A glaring omission in the case is Gurandi Devi's name has been excluded from the police report; subsequently she has never been arrested. Since the Patwari and Kangun are responsible for the report, villagers believe they too have taken bribes to omit Gurandi Devi's name. Villagers maintain a kind of sympathetic, 'that's okay' attitude about it, however, justifying her exclusion with their belief that it would be impossible for the remaining family members to get by if both women are prosecuted: "Who will cook their meals or harvest their crops, if they're both in jail?"

Rumors now circulate in Chandpur and surrounding villages that JDF is pressing police to prosecute Raghunath's murderers. One night in a drunken stupor Balvir Singh blames JDF's Director for the aftermath of the murder and follows his accusation with the statement, "They'll be another incident soon," a reference those present take to mean 'another murder'.

Gurandi Devi's husband now turns his head the other way every time I pass by his shop, as do Gurandi Devi and Raji Devi. Their children, who used to holler out a respectful "Namaste Madam!" in unison with their friends, giggling and waiting with anticipation for my high-pitched, squeaky voice to repeat 'Namaste' back, as fast as I can, as many times as there are children, a game that always elicited peals of laughter, are now banned from talking to me at all. As I pass the perpetrators and a woman relative on the village trail, I hear the relative whisper to an infant she's holding in her arms, intentionally loud enough for me to hear, "Look! There's Madam. Be careful or she'll have you thrown in jail!"

Chandpur villagers anticipate legal prosecution to continue in the form of a long, drawn-out ordeal, tainted with more under-the-table arrangements and perhaps no further punishment for Gurandi Devi, Raji Devi and Shyam, most likely not even a trial. Nonetheless, villagers are satisfied with the punishment the perpetrators have been doled out thus far. Besides being ostracized from village activities, spending time in jail, experiencing the beatings therein and having to pay money to each and every government official who knows their secret, while Raji Devi and Shyam were incarcerated, an article about the case was written by the Tahseldar and published in a local newspaper. A little known detail was revealed. Raji Devi (35 years old) and her nephew, Shyam (17 years old), had been having an ongoing sexual relationship. It is now presumed by villagers that Raghunath had not raped Geeta, but had instead caught Raji Devi and Shyam having sex and was killed to keep him from telling others.

In a scholarly manner, reflecting his 25 years as a teacher and principal, Godiyalji explains, "The current alignment of the Sun, Venus and Mercury is the reason for the recent storms in Garhwal, the excessive snowfall in the Himalaya this year and the earthquake and tsunami that hit Indonesia and India." To support his supposition, he pulls out an astrology book and points to various honeycombed-shaped diagrams and, using numbers from inside the diagrams, makes mathematical calculations, followed by several thunderous declarations, "See this!"..."Look!"..."This is why!"

By day Darshan Chandra Godiyal is a Principal at Bakisain's Intercollege (grades 6 through 12). By night he's an esteemed Astrologer, trained under an apprenticeship with his father, who was also a renowned Astrologer. He's also a highly regarded Baaman, performing puja in primarily large multi-priest ceremonies, in which he's designated the chief priest.

Since the last time I saw him two years ago, his severely thinning, gray hair has either completely fallen out or been shaved bald, giving him a distinguished, handsome appearance. His skin is fair, almost white, and even though his eyes are brown, I always remember them as blue. He's dressed so cosmopolitan in a light blue and frosted-gray plaid dress shirt, dark gray slacks and a newly knitted powder blue sweater vest, he could fit in anywhere in the world. Ironically, he's from an area in Pauri Garhwal considered to be backward. Other Garhwalis refer to these people as "gross talkers" (meaning they use unrefined language), "gross eaters" (eat large amounts of food in one sitting), and "gross dressers" (still dress in traditional clothing, such as blankets). Gross dresser and gross talker definitely do not describe him, however, he may be a 'gross eater'. His physique is much larger and more muscular then the typical slight build of rural Garhwali men.

His village and home are a mere twenty-minute stroll from Bakisain bazaar. Nevertheless, he rents this two-room building in Bakisain bazaar to conduct his astrological consultations and to sleep in when droves of villagers seeking his advice keep him busy late into the night. The rooms are in stark contrast to his impeccable appearance. The ceilings are covered in mildew stains, the walls and floors are crumbling before our eyes and ripe garbage is strewn on the ground outside, mixing with the acrid smell of urine from an open drain running in front of the building, essentially making Godiyalji's place a classic hole-in-the-wall, found in bazaars throughout India. For many foreigners these kinds of conditions are frightfully evident and often overwhelming. After staying in India long enough, however, they are barely noticed. It's a Gestalt trick played on the mind; the appalling fades into the background, becoming mere blemishes, enabling other more subtle aspects of the culture to be highlighted in the foreground.

Godiyalji leans over his desk and, smiling broadly, inquires, "Is there a special reason for your visit today?"

"Well...," I hesitate for a moment trying to figure out how to answer his question. "Yes and no. I knew I'd be passing through Bakisain today, so I thought I'd stop by to say "Namaskar" and have you read my horoscope, but there's no particular reason I want it read."

I pull out my Janm Patra and hand it to him.

Hindu's note the exact time a child is born and within its first month of life, the celestial conditions at the time of birth are written on a scroll of paper called a Janm Patra. Some of the information is displayed in geometric designs and all scrolls are decorated with AUM symbols, lotus flowers and swastikas, added for their auspicious power rather than for aesthetics. The Janm Patra is necessarily read whenever someone begins a new venture, experiences a long-term problem and during matchmaking to determine if a man and woman are compatible, but Garhwalis also take their Janm Patras to Astrologers on numerous occasions throughout their lifetime just to find out where they stand in the world at any given moment.

Upon viewing my Janm Patra, Godiyalji's facial expression changes. It isn't quite a perplexed look, but his perpetually amicable demeanor momentarily loses its smile. He flips the pages back and forth, making loud shuffling noises, his fingertips shouting out what I interpret to be confusion. My Janm Patra's unconventional style (a red, computer-printed booklet made in Jaipur and written in English) seems to have thrown him off, but why? He probably doesn't read English and the format is complicated, but the honeycomb designs, symbols and numbers should all be familiar to him and the last time he read it, he was eerlly accurate.

I delve into conversation to divert his attention, asking simple, extraneous questions from which I hope he will infer that if it's too difficult, a horoscope reading is not essential. "What is my astrological sign? I sometimes see horoscopes listed in the newspaper, but I don't know what my sign is so I'm unable to read what they have to say about me."

"Your zodiac sign is Pisces."

"It's Libra by Western calculations. Why is it different? Do you know?"

Godiyalji readily joins in the mental discourse. "The reason for the discrepancy in horoscope signs is the Hindu calendar is based on the waxing and waning of the moon, as opposed to your calendar, which is based on the sun. Each Hindu month starts and ends with a new moon. There are twelve months and about 30 days per month like in your calendar, but the Hindu New Year starts in March and each month starts roughly halfway through one of your calendar months and ends halfway through the next."

Another question that no one seems to be able to explain fully to me, at least in a way that I can understand, pops into my mind, "Why is Molmas necessary?"

"Molmas occurs about every three years, whenever there are two dark phases of the moon in a single month. From the first disappearance of the moon until the second disappearance, it's extremely unlucky for a new husband to see his wife's face. For this reason, women married during the year preceding Molmas return to their native villages to stay for the entire month in order that their husbands won't see their faces."

I nod my head repeatedly, already aware of everything he told me, and then narrow my question to exactly what I want to know, "But why is Molmas unlucky?"

"It's an inauspicious time period," he restates as the conclusive fact.

"Yeah, but why is it unlucky?"

"Because it's an inauspicious time period."

Since everyone I've asked has given me the exact same answer, I finally, reluctantly, concede that maybe there is no answer beyond the obvious.

Godiyalji adds, "There's another period called Jyeshtha, the same name as the Hindu month in which it falls [the last half of May and early part of June]. It too is an inauspicious time period for a new bride's husband's family, but this time it's bad luck for the groom's older brothers to see their sister-in-law's face, so every new bride with an older brother-in-law goes home to stay in her native village during the month of Jyeshtha."

Just then a man breezes in through the door. He sits down next to Godiyalji and, after glancing over at me, shoves his Janm Patra into Godiyalji's hand, before embarking on a series of frantic explanations and questions.

Taking turns is neither an Indian motto nor the way things are done. What would be an orderly line in America is often a huddled mass of bodies in India, with everyone jostling to be the first person to get their business done. Someone whose just joined the line is just as likely to be served as the person who has been standing in line for an hour because the new arrival, with no qualms whatsoever, will squeeze his arm, leg or whole body through the crowd in order to toss his papers up on the counter before anyone else. There's no whining to the person sitting at the counter about the injustice, as he too barges to the front of lines. Often the only way to get one's business done is to join the muddled mass with wild abandon, forget any manners your mother taught you, push and shove whenever a strategic gap presents itself and remind yourself over and over again this is the perfect opportunity to foster patience.

While Godiyalji proceeds with the stranger's reading, I scrutinize my surroundings.

Furniture in the front room consists of a large heavy desk made of pine, behind which Godiyalji is sitting, and five reasonably intact wooden chairs. In the back room is a wooden cot with a woven fiber mattress, a gas stove and an odd assortment of pots and pans set on the floor. On the far wall hangs a colorful poster of Saraswati, the goddess of learning and consequently a favored goddess of teachers and principals, and hanging nearby are two large portraits: One is of Nehru, the first Prime Minister of India, and the other is of a barely recognizable Mahatma Gandhi. The perpetually emaciated, balding man who wears a loin cloth, carries a cane and sports John Lennon-like gold rim eyeglasses is pleasingly plump, has a full head of black hair, merely peppered with gray, and is wearing a black Nehru cap and matching vest with a Nehru collar.

"Shani Dev is over you," Godiyalji tells the man. "This situation will last three more years." The stranger nods his head, seemingly already aware of this fact.

The news captures my attention. Hindus wait with anticipation to know if Shani Dev (the god Saturn) is in their horoscope or not. It's a fairly likely scenario, since he enters everyone's horoscope three times during their lifetime, lasting 7 ½ years each time, but his presence can be disastrous, essentially prohibiting a person from opening a new business, going on a trip, moving or starting any other new venture and necessitating elaborate pujas and adorning oneself in talismans to mitigate his negative influence. These negative powers came from a curse from Shani Dev's wife. He was a devotee of Krishna and prayed to him day in and day out, keeping his eyes three-fourths of the way closed in meditative trance when, according to his wife, he should have been doing other things. One day she became so fed up with Shani Dev's inattention to her and other household matters, she plied him with alcohol and cursed him. Now, whenever he opens his eyes, fire emanates from them, scorching whomever he gazes upon.

Godiyalji returns to reading the man's Janm Patra, which entails a series of mathematical calculations. He counts on his fingers, using his thumb as a pointer, counting the tips and three joints of each of his four fingers, giving him a potential counting base of 16 on each hand, 20 if he counts on his thumb as some people do.

"He's in his own house right now, so he won't cause you any major problems." Godiyalji assures the man.

The stranger gives an audible sigh of relief.

I butt in, "I'm puzzled. I thought if Shani Dev is over you, it's always bad news?"

Godiyalji clarifies, "Shani is not a good sign, but if Shani is accompanied by the right celestial bodies, his presence can be okay."

Like many astrology-savvy Hindus, the stranger understands exactly what Godiyalji means. He enthusiastically elucidates, "When Shani Dev's in his own house, he's not going to tear down the walls! He'll look after his house, not destroy it!" He then flashes me a big grin, apparently delighted by his clever use of analogy or my engagement in his reading.

"Your Shani Dev was not good for your mother and father either."

"They're both dead now."

"Hmmm. They didn't have an opportunity to see how you've progressed in life.

The stranger confirms Godiyalji's assessment. "Yeah, before, my life wasn't going anywhere when my parents were alive and now that my life is moving forward, that I'm in an okay position, both of them are dead."

"Even though Shani Dev's position isn't in a terribly bad place, you should never take advantage of Shani Dev, even if he's in the right company. You should have 2 snake idols made, one from silver and the other from iron."

"Hold on! Do you have a piece of paper?" The stranger asks.

Godiyalji pulls out an obsolete date book, opens it to a blank page and places it on the table in front of the stranger.

The stranger grabs a pen lying on the desk and repeats what Godiyalji has just told him, "I should have 1 silver and 1 iron snake idol made?"

"Yeah, you know the kind. The small, almost shapeless size will do."

Godiyalji pauses to give the man ample time to write and then resumes, "Place the silver idol in a Shiv temple. And put the iron one in a river."

"Which river?"

"Any river will do. Get at least a 1/4th Kg of wood coal and place the iron snake in between the coals, then place the whole lot into the river at the same time."

"You should also fast on 21 consecutive Saturdays."

"Onnnhhhhh," the stranger groans. "I don't know if I can fast. I'm always going here and there and eating whenever and whatever."

Ignoring the stranger's comment, Godiyalji continues, "Fast from the time you wake up until the sun goes down. In the evening you can eat khichari [rice and lentils cooked together] without salt and laddu [a yellow, golf ball-shaped sweet made from a cereal grain and sugar]."

Godiyalji watches the stranger write feverishly. When he finishes, he advises, "Every Saturday morning that you fast, go to the bathroom. After urinating and doing a bowel movement, rub your body with any kind of oil that has a sweet scent and then bathe. You should also give some mustard oil to a poor person. If you don't have anyone to give it to, then pour the oil under a Peepal tree. You should also feed a cow some laddu each time you fast."

"These actions will help to keep you from running into any problems. If you can't fast, your wife can fast for you. It's the same thing."

"Rahu and Mangal Graha (Mars) are working together in your horoscope. Whatever good deeds you do, you will not reap benefit from it right now, but you must continue doing good deeds. It keeps negative forces in check and you will benefit from it in the future."

The stranger speaks up, "I have a question for you? Why don't I benefit from my bus business? Every month all of the money I earn from my bus is eaten up maintaining the bus."

"Because Shani Dev is over you and Shani Dev doesn't like iron. Your bus is made of iron. Anything you do related to iron will be unsuccessful. You can never have an iron business in your name. Change the name."

"It's in my daughter's name." The man asserts and digs into his bag, pulls out his daughter's horoscope and hands it to Godiyalji.

After taking a brief look at the daughter's Janm Patra, Godiyalji observes, "She's Aries. Aries doesn't like iron either."

"Paint your bus brown…uh…er…the shade of Nehru's coat," he says, pointing to the picture on the wall. "That is a compatible color for Aries."

The stranger writes down everything Godiyalji has just told him, pausing for a brief moment to describe a place in the back of his bus that would be perfect to paint brown, adding, "I can't afford to paint the whole bus brown, nor would it be aesthetically pleasing to paint a bus all brown."

"Venus is in a good place for you right now. You've taken numerous turns and made numerous transitions in your life and with this current placement of Venus you will benefit from these transitions."

Godiyalji turns toward me and repeats exactly what he'd just said to the stranger. I'm not sure if he's trying to include me in on the conversation or whether he's checking to see if I understand, so I play off the stranger's use of analogy and offer an interpretation, "The road this man has traveled on looks like the roads in Pauri Garhwal; long and twisting and turning at every fold in the mountain, seemingly going no where, but now that Venus is in the picture, the road is finally going to take him where he wants to go. He's going to arrive at his destination."

Both men burst out laughing, delighted I understood and probably even more so that I used a local analogy.

"Jupiter is in the 5th house, which is your enemy's house. This is not good. Are you ill with high blood pressure? Arthritis? Uric acid? Have you had a heart attack?"

I butt in again, "What does it mean to be in your enemy's house?

The stranger answers, "Those people you think are your friends aren't really your friends at all."

Godiyalji concurs and warns the stranger of future consequences, "You need to watch out for these people and try not to antagonize them. They will attack you."

"Yeah, I know what you mean," the stranger retorts without elaborating.

"For this reason, when you had your first daughter, and your first should be a daughter because a boy would have caused you harm, you benefited in life. Your life has improved since your daughter's birth, right?"

"Yes that's true!" The stranger agrees, seemingly surprised Godiyalji already knew. "Since my daughter was born my life has turned around little by little."

"Whatever progress you've achieved so far in your life is from the good luck of your mother, your father and your ancestors. For this reason you should do pind-dan in Haridwar."

"Last year I did pind-dan in Badrinath at Brahma Kapal [a slab of stone along the Alakananda river marking the place where Brahma's fifth head landed when Bhaironath cut it off]. The Pandit there told me anyone who does pind-dan for his ancestors at Badrinath should never have pind-dan done anywhere else. It's counterproductive."

"You've already done it in Badrinath? Even so, do it again.

"This time have one silver idol made for your father and one for your mother or you can buy them ready-made. During puja in Haridwar, place them in the Ganga. Afterwards go to Badrinath and have the pind ceremony redone."

After several minutes of insignificant chitchat, it's apparent the stranger's reading is over. He gets up and says, "Namaskar," offers prayer-shaped hands to Godiyalji and slips a 10-rupee note into Godiyalji's hand.

Godiyalji burbles, "It's not necessary," while slipping the money into his pocket.

The stranger offers prayer-shaped hands to me, smiling warmly. I watch him walk away, wondering what of Godiyalji's advice he'll follow. I'm sure he'll follow some of it although not necessarily expediently, especially since he's in a reasonably good astrological situation. Nevertheless, I'm certain he will not take his reading or Godiyalji's advice lightly. The Vedic planets are gods and their placement in the sky and the resulting influence on a person's life is fact, not fortune-telling.

Just as the stranger walks out the door, two more men show up. They're friends of Godiyalji's, stopping by merely to visit. One man is the local Patwari. He's limping around on a severely twisted leg. When I ask, he tells me that he fell down some stairs the day before yesterday and now his leg is stuck, turned outward at a 90-degree angle. When I impress upon him he should go to a doctor to get it reset, he responds casually, "Yeah, I should probably go get it x-rayed."

His lack of expressed pain is striking. It has to be extremely painful, yet with incredible fortitude he not only doesn't complain, he smiles cheerfully and chats amicably. He informs me that Godiyalji, during an astrological reading two weeks earlier, had foreseen the accident and had even given him a series of puja rituals to do to try to prevent the accident from happening. The Patwari ends by saying, "I intended to do them. I just didn't realize how soon the accident would happen. Had I done them right away, this wouldn't have happened."

Godiyalji turns to my Janm Patra and begins to read my horoscope. "This year is not a good year for you. Before August 2004 your bad luck started and will continue until January 2006. Rahu has moved into your astrological space."

Rahu is dreaded. Along with Ketu, he causes lunar and solar eclipses and is the force which influences the orientation of celestial bodies, an often harmful power bestowed on him after a run-in with the gods. Shiv and several minor gods and demons had churned the ocean to extract an elixir of eternal life called amrit. After it was extracted the gods lined up to take a sip of immortality. Hidden in line was a demon. Surya Dev, the Sun god, spotted the demon and told Lord Vishnu, preserver of the world. Vishnu presumed evil would be impossible to vanquish if the demon and his future generations became immortal from the potion, so he snuck up behind the demon and cut off his head. The lower part became Ketu and the upper part became Rahu. Rahu pointed out to Vishnu the unfair and sneaky way in which he'd chopped his head off. Vishnu concurred that it was not fair play, but claimed it was impossible to put Rahu's head back on his body so to compensate for his actions, he blessed Rahu with supreme power to manipulate people's horoscope.

"Because of Rahu, you need to take care of your health. This is very important. Are you sick?"

"Yes. Last June I was diagnosed with Hashimotos disease and I have other medical problems that have started in the last two years. I take medicine for all of them.

"Have Rahu puja done to try to lessen his negative influence."

"What is Rahu puja?"

"A Baaman will do puja, which includes reciting Rahu's name 18,000 times in your honor. Maybe he'll write it too. It takes about a week to complete."

"Chandra Dev (Moon god) is not in your favor either. Don't take any risks."

The Patwari who hadn't listened to Godiyalji's advice a week earlier, chimed in with a concerned voice, "Yes, you should not take any unnecessary risks!"

Godiyalji counsels, "Wear gomeed."

"What's gomeed?"

"A stone. Hmmm. What's its name in English?" He ponders aloud and glances over at the other two men. They shake their heads indicating they too don't know.

"Never mind, I'll look it up in my dictionary when I get home." I inform him and although he didn't say to wear it as a ring, I knew that's what he meant so I ask, "In what metal do I need to have it set? And on which hand and finger should I wear it?"

"Silver. Wear it on your right hand, middle finger.

"What's the ring for?"

"To help offset the negative effects of Rahu. When celestial bodies are arranged like this there's not much you can do…but this may help."

"Mercury is also not positioned well right now. From this you will lose money."

He reviews my Janm Patra for a few more minutes and states frankly, "Pisces is not in a good position for you either."

The Patwari shakes his head dejectedly and states, "It's all in the stars. It's just the way it is."

Godiyalji adds, "You should do suryanamaskar. Everyday you must bathe. Afterward fill a copper container with water…."

"Hold on, I'm going to have to write this all down too." I grab his date book and the pen and begin to write.

"Just as the sun rises in the morning, face the sun. Pour the water like this." He demonstrates by stretching his arms out, raising them slightly upward and cupping his hands together, pretending they're a vessel pouring water towards the sun.

"Pour slowly. The water should fall into a bronze plate. After you've poured the water, you need to circle the plate seven times, while holding your hands in prayer hand-shape. Remember the Sun god and repeat 'AUM Surya Namo' (sacred sound of the universe, Sun god, 'Glory to thee'). Throw red tilak and rice toward the sun as well, but right above the bronze plate in order that most of it lands in the plate. Sit down and, with prayer-shaped hands, recite this mantra several times:

> "Glory to the Supreme Being, honorable Raghunath Vasudev, honorable Hari, make distant my every problem, Oh Govind to you again and again my regards, accept my honorable regards."

It's now apparent it was not confusion Godiyalji experienced when I first handed him my Janm Patra, but concern about the foreboding astrological news he was about to impart. I thank him, take back my Janm Patra and head home, fully intending to follow his advice, not so much because of an abiding belief in Astrology or Hinduism, as for a growing respect for Garhwalis and ritual.

I go to Haridwar, buy a chunk of Zircon and have it set in a ring. I ask a local Baaman, Nandaram, to perform Rahu puja for me, which he insists be done in mid-July because it's an auspicious time period—not to mention he wants to do it in concert with a huge seven-day, seven priest, village-wide puja to be held at the same time in Chandpur. During the ceremony, however, Nandaram is busy from sun up until way past sun down; reciting Sanskrit prayers for hours at a time every day, meticulously constructing one sacred altar after another, orchestrating elaborate preparations for puja, conducting a multitude of rites. He appears so haggard the entire seven-days, I don't have the heart to remind him to recite Rahu's name for me 18,000 times. I decide to skip Rahu puja for now and do puja to Surya Dev. I buy the requisite copper water jug and bronze plate and set them on the desk next to my bed to remind myself when I wake up each morning to do suryanamaskar. I've managed to pull them out a couple of times, once during an eclipse of the sun, which is a particularly auspicious day to pray to Surya Dev. Otherwise, they spend most of their time collecting dust.

Instead, I take my cue from fellow villagers and seek favor from a god closer to home. There are twenty-two Devi/Devtas living in Chandpur: Bhaironath, Narsingh, Kachyaa, Nanda Devi, Ghandiyaal, Krishna, Heet, Nag, Bhima, Yudhishtira, Arjun, Binsar, Uphrain, Rama, Sita, Lakshman, Sahadeva, Nakula, Kali, Chandi Devi, Shiv and Parvati. Cement or rock temples have been constructed in their honor or entire rooms of houses set aside for them to live in and for the devout to pray. The exceptions are rather than a temple for Kali, there's a grassy knoll across the river where goats are sacrificed in her honor; related gods share temples such as Nanda Devi and her brothers; and, along the river winding through Chandpur, there are seven small, naturally-occurring caves, all dedicated to various incarnations of Narsingh Devta, an avatar of Vishnu.

Besides tradition, Narsingh Devta's appeal is he answers personal prayers and protects the devout, as illustrated in the story of Prahlada:

Prahlada was to be the fourth son of King Hiranyakashipu and his wife, Kyadou. King Hiranyakashipu was a pious king who fervently worshipped Brahma, creator of the world. Brahma noticed and, impressed by the King's devotion to prayer and austerities in his name, offered to grant him a boon. The King requested a wish that he could not be killed by man or animal; neither by day nor by night; neither inside nor outside a house. Brahma granted him his wish.

Eventually Hiranyakashipu's immortality made him believe he too was god, arrogance that caused him to lose his humanity. He began forcing people to worship him, becoming so audacious, he even ousted minor gods from their heavenly abodes. These gods complained to Vishnu, preserver of the universe. Vishnu, knowing the conditions of Brahma's boon, contemplated what to do.

Meanwhile, Kyadou was pregnant. While Prahlada was in her womb, Yamaraj, the god of death, came to take Kyadou away. Narada, a great sage, stopped Yamaraj and asked him what he's doing. Yamaraj explained that he's taking Kyadou away before her son is born because if he doesn't, when the boy is born he'll grow up to be evil like his father. Narada persuaded Yamaraj to give Kyadou to him and told him that after Prahlada is born, he will send Kyadou back to him. Yamaraj agreed.

Narada brought Kyadou back to his ashram and taught her about god. She repeated Narayana's name with fervor, "Narayana, Narayana, Narayana,

Narayana, Narayana." Prahlada heard his mother's faithful and unremitting prayers to Narayana from the womb and was thus born a devout disciple of Narayana's. His mother was sent to Yamaraj as promised and Prahlada was sent to live with his father.

Prahlada prayed to god day in and day out, year after year. Hiranyakashipu strongly disapproved, becoming increasingly angry, demanding Prahlada worship his father as the true god. When Prahlada turned five, he was sent to study with Shukaracharya, a guru to demons. Prahlada and his brothers studied daily. But whenever Hiranyakashipu drilled Prahlada on what he had learned, he'd recite his studies correctly, but afterward he would repeat the name of god like his mother used to do, "Narayana, Narayana, Narayana, Narayana, Narayana."

At first, Hiranyakashipu scolded Prahlada's guru, blaming him for not teaching his son proper respect. However, as the years went by, he grew angrier with Prahlada. His son's love of god and continual recitation of god's name made him so mad that one day he told the guru to beat sense into his son. The guru tied Prahlada up, but Prahlada began to recite the name of god and miraculously his ropes loosened and he went free.

Eventually Hiranyakashipu became so fed up with Prahlada's love of god that he decided he wanted Prahlada dead, so he had him thrown off a mountain. Prahlada, reciting the name of god as he fell, landed unscathed. Hiranyakashipu then had his sister, who had a boon against being burned by fire, to take his son into a fire and hold him there until he burned to death. While in the fire, Prahlada repeated the name of god and is even reported to have been laughing as the flames engulfed them. His aunt turned to ashes and he again survived unscathed.

Hiranyakashipu finally decided to take care of the matter himself. He tied Prahlada to a pillar and, just before hacking him to pieces with his sword, taunted Prahlada, "Where is your god now?"

Prahlada answered confidently, "Everywhere."

Hiranyakashipu replied sarcastically, "Is he in this pillar too?"

Prahlada assured him that he was.

An angry Hiranyakashipu struck the pillar with his sword, breaking it open to show Prahlada that god was not inside. Out jumped Narsingh Devta. He had the body of a man and the head and hands of a lion. Narsingh Devta seized Hiranyakashipu and took him to the threshold of a nearby door. At the precise moment of dusk, he ripped Hiranyakashipu apart with his claws.

Rising at the crack of dawn, I bathe and refrain from eating, drinking only tea, and fill recycled whiskey bottles with fresh cow's milk and kerosene oil and pack matches, incense and a piece of cotton into a recycled plastic bag. Just as the sunlight falls on the mountaintop above Chandpur, I make my way along the main trail through the fields, far away and out of sight from the village proper, eventually winding my way downward, skirting the edge of one field after another on unrefined paths, until I reach the river. I wade across and bushwhack my way up the next hill until I reach a twelve-foot long, narrow path that hangs along the cliff, ten feet below the bluff, twenty feet above the riverbed. I flip off my thongs and carefully traverse the precarious trail, which accommodates only one foot at a time and slants toward the river.

At the mouth of the cave, I perch on a 2-½ foot square piece of turf, sharing it with a scraggly tree sprouting sideways from the crag. I remove a flat rock leaning up against the hill, revealing a 1 ½-foot square cavern behind it. Inside are a worn iron trident and a brass oil-burning diya, both roughly hewn, suggesting they were made generations ago, in even more simpler times. Also inside the cave are a box of matches, incense and kerosene left behind by the last worshipper for others to use, as well as a recently installed clay diya, which I assume was placed there because the antique one is too shallow to hold much oil.

I take everything out and begin pulling encroaching weeds from inside and outside of the cave and sweep debris away with my hands. After brushing off the trident and diya, I wash them with milk, blithely splashing the leftover milk around the cave like a child splashes water in a bathtub, fully aware that in any other context I'd be seen as a nut, a religious fanatic or, at the very least, out of place, but imbued with a Garhwall sense of the world, it seems natural, even right.

Returning the trident, I prop it against a rock jutting out from the back wall and pour oil into the clay diya. I fashion a wick out of cotton, lay it in the oil and then set the diya on the cave floor before lighting it. Taking short gummy incense out of a box, I rub it between my hands, shape it into a cone and flatten the fat end in order for the incense to stand up on it's own. I light it, hold it in my right hand and deliberately bring my left hand fingers over to my right elbow and rest them there, while I move the incense around in clockwise circles. Smoke wafts inside the cave and out, filling the air with the sweet smell of rosewood. After a few minutes, I set it in the cave, pull out a handful of incense sticks, light them and prop them up inside, against a wall. A continuous cloud of smoke streams out of the cave. I place my hands above the incense, scooping smoke into my face and up over my head. Once the incense burns a fourth of the way down, I shake a pinch of ash off, dip the middle finger of my right hand into it and apply it onto my forehead, between my eyebrows. Dipping my finger into the ash again and again, I apply tilak to the trident, the diya and on the walls inside and outside the cave. In a final homage to Narsingh Devta, I clasp my hands together in prayer-shape and bring them up in front of a bowed head, before sliding the rock back in front of the temple.

Prologue

When people ask me how I wound up in Pauri Garhwal, I'm reminded of an old woman with a crinkled face and a twinkle in her eyes. I'd bumped into her one day while strolling through the countryside. After chatting for a few minutes, she'd stated more than asked, "You're from a place far away from here, aren't you?" And upon confirming her assumption with a nod of my head, she had taken her coarse, work worn hand and rubbed it fondly down my hair and across my cheek, twice, while offering an explanation, "You must have lived here in another life time and now you've come home."

www.ingramcontent.com/pod-product-compliance
Lightning Source LLC
Chambersburg PA
CBHW032031150426
43194CB00006B/239